CAREERS IN CRIME

CAREERS IN CRIME

AN APPLICANT'S GUIDE

Michael Weinberg

Andrews McMeel
Publishing, LLC
Kansas City

08 09 10 11 12 RR2 10 9 8 7 6 5 4 3 2 1

ISBN-13: 978-0-7407-5708-2
ISBN-10: 0-7407-5708-3

Library of Congress Control Number: 2005933798

www.andrewsmcmeel.com

ATTENTION: SCHOOLS AND BUSINESSES
Andrews McMeel books are available at quantity discounts with bulk purchase for educational, business, or sales promotional use. For information, please write to: Special Sales Department, Andrews McMeel Publishing, LLC, 4520 Main Street, Kansas City, Missouri 64111.

CONTENTS

$3.⁰⁰

HOW WE RATE

THE CAREERS IN CRIME 50

We are often told that the ideal job is the one we'd do for free. So how do we find that fabled job? Sadly, there is no magic formula for matching worker to workplace. The happy alternative worker balances complex economic, physical, and psychological factors to sustain a harmonious, independent life. Suppose you get that overdue promotion to Hit Man (page 88). The hours are good, the perks are generous, and there's plenty of room for advancement. Yet, if you are unaccustomed to strict deadlines, frequent law enforcement interactions, and severe sentencing risk, you may be miserable. To be successful in his or her chosen profession, the career-minded criminal must factor in his or her temperament, abilities, legal history, and ethical orientation to meaningfully assess real-world opportunities.

THE FACTORS

Ignorance is a crime that never pays. If you really want to bulletproof your career choices, get to know your options and yourself. *Careers in Crime* offers the most actionable collection of information on criminal occupations ever assembled. In addition to eyewitness profiles of fifty major American criminal careers, we score and rank each job according to:

1. **COMPENSATION AND REWARDS**
2. **ENFORCEMENT AND PENALTIES**
3. **STRESSES AND HAZARDS**
4. **WORK ENVIRONMENT**

THE FORMULA

Ranking careers is a pretty subjective business. We've done our best to identify the essential building blocks of job satisfaction and to combine them in intuitive, meaningful ways. Each ranking component incorporates two subfactors that receive letter grades ranging from A to F. These letter grades correspond to numerical scores. Some factors weigh more heavily than others. An A in Earnings, for example, adds 60 points to a job's overall numerical merit. The same grade in the related Perks category counts for just 20 points. Sectional scores are combined to calculate an occupation's overall score and numerical ranking—with the ideal job theoretically earning a score of 260 points and ranking number one among all criminal careers.

I. COMPENSATION AND REWARDS POINTS

a. Earnings	60
b. Perks	20

II. ENFORCEMENT AND PENALTIES

a. Frequency of Arrests	40
b. Severity of Sentencing	40

III. STRESSES AND HAZARDS

a. Dangers	40
b. Pressures and Demands	20

IV. WORK ENVIRONMENT

a. Hours	20
b. Comfort	20

TOTAL   **260**

HOW THE CAREERS RATE

Rank	Career	Earnings	Perks	Arrests	Sentencing	Dangers	Pressures	Hours	Comfort	Score	Avg.
1	Drug Counterfeiter	A-	C	B+	A-	B+	B+	B-	C+	210	B+
2	Cigarette Smuggler	A	C	B+	B-	B+	B+	C+	C+	205	B
3	Organ Broker	B+	C+	A	B	B-	B	B	B	204	B
4	Identity Thief	A	B+	B	C-	B+	B	B+	C+	201	B
5	Telemarketing Scammer	A-	B	B+	C-	A-	B-	A-	B-	199	B
6	Rustler	B+	C	B+	B+	B-	B+	C+	C	194	B
7	Baby Broker	B+	B-	B-	C	B+	B+	B	B+	193	B
8	Forger	B+	C+	B+	C	B	B	B+	B-	192	B
9	Paperhanger	B	B+	A	B	C+	C	C+	B-	191	B
10	Currency Counterfeiter	A-	B	C	C+	B	B-	B+	B	188	B
11	Fence	B+	B+	B	C	B	C	B	B-	186	B
12	Art Thief	B+	B	A	B-	C	C-	B	C	185	B
13	Spammer	B+	C	B-	B-	B+	C	C-	B+	182	B
14	Industrial Spy	B	B	B	C+	B	C	C+	B	181	B-
15	Poacher	B	B-	B+	A-	C	C	C+	C	180	B-

16	Shoplifter	B-	B+	C+	B	B+	C	C+	B-	179	B-
17	Pickpocket	B	B	B	B	C+	B-	C	C	177	B-
18	Bookie	B	B+	A-	B	C	C-	C	C	176	B-
19	Auto Thief	B-	B+	A	C-	B-	B-	B-	C	174	B-
20	Snitch	B+	B+	B+	B+	D	D	C+	C	173	B-
21	Crooked Cop	B+	B	B	B-	C-	C-	C+	B-	171	B-
22	Burglar	B	B	B+	B-	C-	C+	C+	C	170	B-
23	Money Launderer	B+	B+	C+	C-	B-	C	C	B	169	B-
24	Scalper	B	C-	B	B	C	B-	C+	C	168	B-
25	Protected Witness	B-	B+	B	B	C+	D+	D+	C	164	B-
26	Jewel Thief	A-	B	C+	C-	C+	C	C	C	163	C+
27	Human Smuggler	B+	C	C+	B-	C	B-	C	C-	162	C+
28	Pimp	B	B+	B-	C	C	C-	C	B	161	C+
29	Marijuana Cultivator	A	B-	C-	D	B-	C+	B-	C	160	C+
30	Blackmailer	C-	A-	B+	B-	C-	C-	B+	B	158	C+
31	Outlaw Biker	A-	B+	C-	C-	C-	C	B	B-	157	C+
32	ATM Attacker	B	C-	B	D	C	B-	B	B	156	C+
33	Slave Trader	A-	B	C+	D+	C	C	C	C-	155	C+
34	Pirate	B+	B+	C+	C-	C-	C	C+	C-	154	C+
35	Loan Shark	B	B+	C	C-	C	C	B	C	153	C+
36	Firearms Trafficker	C+	D+	B+	C	C-	B	C+	C	150	C+
37	Safecracker	B	B	B	D	C	C-	B-	C-	149	C
38	Arsonist	B-	D	A-	C-	C-	C	B-	D	140	C
39	Hit Man	B-	B	C	D	C-	C+	B	C	137	C
40	Crack Dealer	B	B	D+	C-	C-	C	C+	C-	136	C
41	Mugger	C-	B+	B+	C-	D+	C	C	C	135	C
42	Carjacker	C	B	A-	D	D	C-	B	C	134	C
43	Pirate Radio Operator	D-	B	C-	B-	B+	C+	C	C-	130	C
44	Meth Lab Operator	B	B	C	D+	D	C+	C-	D	129	C
45	Prostitute	C+	C-	C+	B	D	D	D	D	123	C
46	Gangbanger	C+	B+	C-	C-	D	C-	C-	C	121	C
47	Bank Robber	C-	D	C-	C-	C	D	B	C+	113	C-
48	Mercenary	C+	C	B	D+	D-	D	D	D	111	C-
49	Kidnapper	B+	D	F	D	C-	C-	C-	C	108	C-
50	Prison Wife	F+	B	B	B-	F	D	D	D	92	D+

HAVE GUN, WILL TRAVEL
Jobs with killer travel opportunities

Travel Rank	Career	Overall Ranking
1	Mercenary	48
2	Money Launderer	23
3	Human Smuggler	27
4	Slave Trader	33
5	Pirate	34
6	Organ Broker	3
7	Cigarette Smuggler	2
8	Firearms Trafficker	36
9	Industrial Spy	14
10	Hit Man	39

THE HOOKUP
Looking for a little . . . uh . . . companionship? Try these frisky careers

Dating Rank	Career	Overall Ranking
1	Pimp	28
2	Prostitute	45
3	Prison Wife	50
4	Slave Trader	33
5	Human Smuggler	27
6	Outlaw Biker	31
7	Meth Lab Operator	44
8	Gangbanger	46
9	Jewel Thief	26
10	Shoplifter	16

ARSONIST

RANK: 38 out of 50   **AVERAGE GRADE:** C

DUTIES: Arsonists, a.k.a. *torches*, intentionally set fire to commercial, residential, and institutional structures, as well as to vehicles, forests, farmlands, watercraft, and other assorted combustibles. About one-quarter of all activity in the arson sector is attributed to profit seekers. Money-motivated business or property owners commit or commission acts of arson to secure fraudulent insurance settlements, dispose of unprofitable inventories, illegally eject objectionable occupants, demolish protected structures, dissolve contracts, or discharge onerous obligations. Although pyromaniacs loom large in the popular imagination, such lighter-loving characters actually account for only about 1/10 of 1 percent of arson arrests. Nihilistic juveniles are implicated in 42.1 percent of domestic flare-ups. Adult revenge-seekers are credited with 14 percent of arson fires, and 7 percent are set to cover other crimes (including suicide, which accounts for one-third of all fiery fatalities in Japan).

In most cases, arson professionals strive to maximize incendiary devastation, while conveying the look and feel of acciden-tally induced combustion (and allowing ample time for easy exits). Expert torches are meticulous in their selections of site-appropriate points of origin, accelerants, fuels, and ignition systems. Amateurs, on the other hand, often start accelerant-aided fires near furnaces, electrical outlets, fireplaces, or heat-producing appliances. Arson investigators know that accidental fires typically start above floor level and travel upward. Clumsily set fires usually burn down to floor level or below.

MAN'S BEST FRIEND CAN BE AN ARSONIST'S WORST ENEMY
K-9 patrol pet Rosie learns to detect liquid accelerants at a Bureau of Alcohol, Tobacco, Firearms and Explosives training school.
Source: Santa Clara, California, Fire Department

In one recent study, three out of four for-profit flambé artistes employed delayed-ignition devices. Many pros favor multiple points of ignition that they connect through flammable *trailers*. On the downside, trailers carry a substantially higher risk of evidentiary persistence and periodically cause the accidental immolation of inexperienced handlers.

COMPENSATION AND REWARDS   *EARNINGS:* **B-**   *PERKS:* **D**

Annual revenues for the entire U.S. insurance fraud sector are estimated at $96.2 billion. Although payouts to arson beneficiaries are closely held trade secrets, the 66,308 suspicious fires in 2002 alone caused $1.9 billion in direct structural damage.

Individual compensation varies remarkably. Many arson assignments are undertaken on a handshake basis by associates of insolvent individuals. A Pittsburgh furniture storeowner, on the other hand, introduced too much formality into his contractual arrangements when he itemized a $10,000 payment to his arsonist on his federal tax return. However, when intelligently arranged, fires commissioned by midtier business owners can bring spectacular returns. A single blaze at the Texas office/warehouse of a national computer sales company netted $4.5 million in insurance reimbursement.

INDUSTRY FLAMEOUT?
Arson rates keep falling

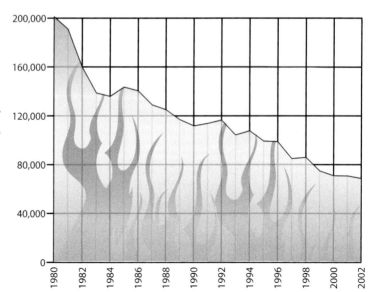

Source: U.S. Bureau of Alcohol, Tobacco, Firearms, and Explosives

Catching fire is easy; catching firebugs is singularly difficult. Eighty-five percent of arsons are unsolved, half of all suspects are never prosecuted, and about one-third of those prosecuted are exonerated. Altogether, a scant 2 percent of set fires lead to convictions. Career arsonists are even more difficult to cool down. The nation's sixteen urban arson task forces devote 82 percent of their investigative man hours to pursuing the elusive incendiary elite. The unlucky convicted few, however, face average sentences of ninety-plus months. Don McAuliffe, an Ohio judge who torched his house for a $235,000 insurance payout in 2004, got a taste of his own medicine when he was sentenced to seventeen years.

ENFORCEMENT HEATS UP
Arrests are on the rise

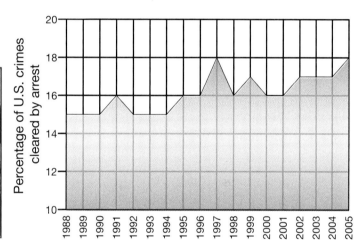

Percentage of U.S. crimes cleared by arrest (1988–2005)

Source: FBI

STRESSES AND HAZARDS

DANGERS: **C-** *PRESSURES:* **C**

Arsonists typically endeavor to minimize human occupancy during their high-octane escapades; however, accidents *do* frequently happen. In 2002, 630 civilians perished in an estimated 68,800 intentionally set structural fires, and 100 people died in ignited vehicles. Twelve responding firefighters also were killed during this period, qualifying the responsible offenders for felony murder charges. Self-injury is also a constant concern, as are "misfires" resulting in underwhelming damage to property or incomplete incineration of evidence.

Attention to detail is indispensable. In 2001, for instance, a Pennsylvania restaurateur faked an oven fire at his failing establishment, claiming losses of over $150,000. *His* goose was cooked when the state police noticed a still-frozen roast in the oven in question.

WORK ENVIRONMENT

HOURS: **B-** *COMFORT:* **D**

Arsonists typically toil on nights, weekends, and holidays to avoid prying eyes and potential casualties. Although year-round opportunities abound, incendiary assignments tend to cluster from summer to late autumn.

Structural fires account for 41.3 percent of all work activity, 60.7 percent of buildings burned are residences, and 71.0 percent of those residences are single-family units. Mobile properties (primarily autos) are targeted in 33.1 percent of incendiary incidents.

Although many arsonists work in pairs, opportunities for coed commingling are rare, as 84.8 percent of arson arrestees are male.

ART THIEF

DUTIES: Art thieves improperly acquire fine art objects from the premises or persons of their lawful possessors. Although elaborate, *Pink Panther*–style museum heists are synonymous with art theft in the collective imagination, thefts from museums actually account for only about 12 percent of all objects stolen worldwide. A whopping 54 percent of the world's purloined art is plucked from domestic dwellings, which seldom have armed security and are frequently left obligingly unattended. Art thieves often pose as workmen to enter and *case* residential targets. In an inspired variant on this ploy, a twenty-six-year-old German call girl used her erotic wiles to penetrate the home of a libidinous Los Angeles art lover, whom she later screwed in a far less pleasant manner. Other common work sites for art thieves include galleries (12 percent of items stolen) and churches (10 percent). Although warehouses and storage spaces are patronized in only 2 percent of all art thefts, they are involved in a disproportionate number of lucrative attacks. In one recent incident, $1.5 million in paintings and sculptures was stolen from a St. Louis art storage warehouse.

TOO HOT TO HANDLE

These masterpieces were stolen from the Swedish National Museum in 2000. They are worth an estimated $45 million. The cash-strapped thieves who acquired them were nabbed in 2005, after offering the Rembrandt to an FBI agent for a paltry $100,000.

Source: U.S. Bureau of Immigration and Customs Enforcement

Rembrandt's Self Portrait

Renoir's Young Parisian

The new millennium has witnessed some exceedingly violent performances in the arena of institutional art theft. The machine gun–assisted removals of Munch's *The Scream* and *Madonna* (from Oslo, Norway's Munch Museum in 2004) and of masterworks by Rembrandt and Renoir (from Sweden's National Museum in 2000) are particularly notable.

The majority of institutional interceptions, however, are perpetrated with monotonous stealth. Many heists are carried out by obscure academic moonlighters who mis-appropriate minor works through deletion, alteration, or forgery of records. Take the case of Anthony Melnikasow, a retired art history professor from Ohio State University, who purloined a few spare pages from a fourteenth-century illuminated manuscript while working in the Vatican library. Other *inside jobs* are more active, such as the brazen theft of a $250,000 Salvador Dali painting from New York's Rikers Island jail by four corrections officers, who used a fire drill for cover.

PICTURES PLUS
Inside the $8 billion market in pre-owned cultural riches

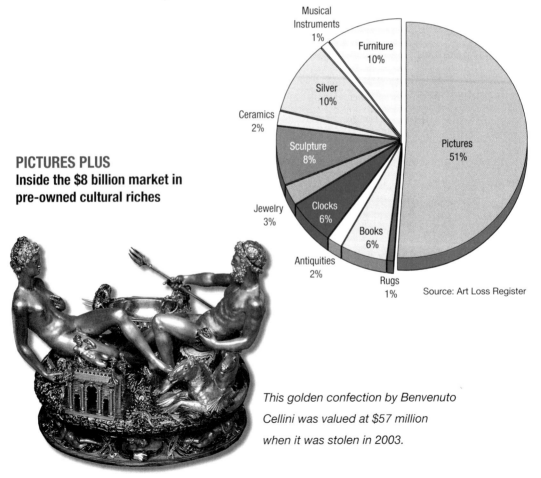

Musical Instruments 1%
Furniture 10%
Silver 10%
Ceramics 2%
Sculpture 8%
Pictures 51%
Jewelry 3%
Clocks 6%
Books 6%
Antiquities 2%
Rugs 1%
Source: Art Loss Register

This golden confection by Benvenuto Cellini was valued at $57 million when it was stolen in 2003.

Reports of stolen art have more than tripled since the late 1970s, with the annual value of goods lifted estimated at more than $8 billion. According to Interpol, art theft has quietly become the fourth-highest-yielding international criminal activity, after drug trafficking, money laundering, and illegal arms trading. Increasingly, art pros are working in concert with distinguished distributors of narcotics, crime dollars, and weapons. Big-ticket art is an ideal proxy for cash in illicit transnational trade. Most items are easily concealable, and customs agents are unlikely to recognize their true value even if they

SCREAMING TO BE STOLEN?

Versions of Munch's The Scream *have been stolen* twice *in recent years.*

are discovered or declared. The ubiquity of gray and black art markets ensures that stolen items can be discreetly acquired, traded, or liquidated—usually on an entirely cash basis.

Some nouveau riche drug dealers are also bedazzled by the "instant class" conveyed on them by purloined treasures. Like other passionate, ethically challenged collectors before them, they are willing to buy and hold art that is too hot for distribution through standard illicit channels. Pablo Escobar, the legendary boss of Colombia's Medellin drug cartel, was notoriously partial to stolen works by his countryman Fernando Botero. In 1996, San Salvador police intercepted an undocumented Picasso he had tendered in trade for a drug shipment.

COMPENSATION AND REWARDS   EARNINGS: **B+**   PERKS: **D**

In 1990, two falsely mustachioed males relieved Boston's Isabella Stewart Gardner Museum of more than $300 million in Postimpressionist masterworks—the single largest art extraction ever executed. The still-unidentified interlopers claimed to be policemen responding to a commotion within the compound. The spoils of that legendary looting were dwarfed by a series of obscure thefts from regional museums by Stephane Breitwieser, a thirty-one-year-old French waiter.

Starting in 1995, he liberated 172 artifacts worth more than $1.4 billion, only to see them all destroyed by his panicked mother after he was jailed for the theft of a rare bugle. Although these cases are exceptional, earning opportunities abound for strategically positioned part-timers. In 2003, for instance, a security guard at the Georgia O'Keeffe Museum leveraged his insider access to stage a phony robbery and spirit away a $500,000 O'Keeffe painting he admired.

ENFORCEMENT AND PENALTIES   ARRESTS: **A**   SENTENCING: **B-**

In the wake of the Boston's blockbuster Isabella Stewart Gardner Museum heist, a red-faced Senator Ted Kennedy rushed through the Theft of Major Artwork statute, mandating jail stays of up to ten years for theft of iconic art older than a century. The law also extends the statute of limitations to twenty years. The diversity of national property laws is a continued boon to well-traveled thieves, with many nations still subscribing to a "don't ask, don't tell" judicial posture. Generally, midtier stolen works can be relocated and resold long before warning is spread through the under-regulated labyrinth of international markets.

Overall recovery rates for stolen fine art hover between 5 percent and 10 percent. Almost 51 percent of all recovered art is identified through auction catalogs. Auction giants such as Sotheby's and Christie's conduct *provenance* (background) checks on major items, but U.S. law does not mandate that thefts be reported or provide a standardized mechanism for making such reports. The *Art Loss Register*, a database of more than 100,000 stolen items, has been instrumental in the recovery of over 1,000 items worth more than $100 million since 1991. Interpol maintains an additional *Stolen Works of Art*

CD-ROM, which catalogs 26,000 notable thefts. Worrisomely, the FBI recently chartered an elite, eight-agent art crime unit that has already recovered nearly $100 million in fraudulent or filched art in fewer than four years.

STRESSES AND HAZARDS

DANGERS: C PRESSURES: C-

In addition to engaging in occasional gunplay, advanced institutional theft workers frequently employ high-powered vehicles in rapid, high-risk getaways. The team behind the $31 million raid on Sweden's National Museum (2000) tested new waters, employing a speedboat in the final stage of their bullet-strewn getaway. The boisterous thieves who looted $325,000 in memorabilia from Las Vegas's Elvis-A-Rama Museum (2004) also made dangerously innovative use of a vehicle— plowing a stolen tow truck through the museum's back door. Aspirants should note that the power tools, torches, cutting, and battering instruments associated with this field pose significant risks if proper safety regimens are ignored or abridged. Psychological challenges include split-second time pressures, frequent betrayal by apprehended associates, and illiquidity of resale markets.

WORK ENVIRONMENT

HOURS: B COMFORT: C

Art thieves work primarily indoors, in temperature- and humidity-controlled environments. Institutional and commercial thefts are usually undertaken in low-light, nighttime conditions, whereas the majority of residential assignments take place in daylight.

Most art thieves work alone and enjoy considerable autonomy and flexibility of work schedule. However, the increasing clout of organized crime is bringing a new focus on teamwork and hierarchical work roles.

Some assignments may call for prolonged physical toil in untenable positions. A 2002 attack on Paraguay's National Fine Arts Museum mandated two months' incessant digging to complete a twenty-five-meter art access tunnel.

ATM ATTACKER

RANK: 32 out of 50 **AVERAGE GRADE:** C+

DUTIES: ATM Attackers attain funds from automated teller machines via interception of account numbers and PINs, electronic or mechanical tampering, forcible theft from machine users, or physical removal and penetration of devices. ATM fraud and theft are swelling by as much as 85 percent a year in many Western countries. In 2004, Gartner Group scandalized the U.S. banking community with its contention that domestic ATM losses had already risen to $2.75 billion, affecting 3 million Americans.

Although armed robberies at ATM locations and brute-force machine removals remain ever popular, the richest gains in this field are achieved through more sophisticated means. Today's most advanced practitioners actually acquire and deploy *their own* ATMs to harvest card data and

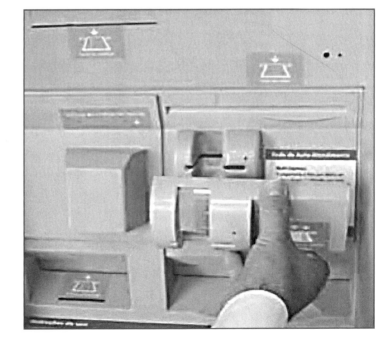

ONE LITTLE IMPROVEMENT . . .
False-front skimmers are cost-effective and convincing!
Source: *Identity Theft: Trends, Techniques, and Responses,* U.S. Department of Justice

hijack consumer accounts. In 2001, a single ATM ring purchased more than fifty machines, positioning them in stores in New York, California, and Florida. They successfully linked the devices to the nation's electronic banking backbone and—to forestall suspicion—actually dispensed cash. The gang duplicated the cards that passed through its machines and subsequently used them to withdraw cash from legitimate ATMs. More than 21,000 accounts at 1,400 banks were compromised, for total gains of at least $3.75 million. Less ambitious Trojan horse ATM schemes have achieved wondrous results without the complications of actually dispensing cash or connecting to banking networks.

Trapping is a popular technique for obtaining genuine cards. In this gambit, a freelance ATM technician inserts a slim mechanical device known as a *Lebanese loop* into the throat of a card reader, preventing the card from being returned at the end of a transaction. When the card user shows distress, the nearby technician suggests that the soon-to-be-victim reenter the PIN—which the helpful technician inconspicuously observes and memorizes. After the hapless cash-craver leaves the area, the ATM attacker uses a fishing hook to retrieve the abandoned card.

Skimming is the most common method of illegally obtaining card data. *Skimmers* are magnetic capture devices temporarily positioned over or in proximity to an ATM's factory-provided card reader. Most are smaller than a deck of cards, and can capture and retain information from more than two hundred cards, including balances and verification codes.

Skimmed or trapped cards are useless without accompanying PIN data. *Shoulder surfing* is the most basic PIN acquisition technique—involving visual observation of

SURF'S UP!
Shoulder surfers keep a watchful eye on America's personal finances.

customers' fingers. Cautious surfers employ binoculars or telescopic camera lenses. Sophisticates conceal miniature, wireless video cameras on or near compromised ATMs. Thin *PIN pad overlays* capture and store finger data for eventual criminal retrieval. Electronic *PIN interception* techniques exploit terminal and network vulnerabilities to capture and record encrypted or raw user data as it is transmitted to a central computer.

Some ATM exploits succeed without account *or* PIN data. *False presenter* schemes use fake enclosure fronts, adhesive tape, or motorized transports to simulate errors in dispensing cash. When the customer leaves empty-handed, the ATM robber returns to "unstick" the cash. *Transaction reversal* scams are designed to fool central computers into believing that cash has not been dispensed when actually it has.

 COMPENSATION AND REWARDS **EARNINGS: B PERKS: C-**

ATM robbers earn a national average of $900 per intercepted account. Though potential gains per card are tempered by daily withdrawal limits and other low-level security practices, volume is key in this endeavor. In December 2003, three speedy New Yorkers were charged with withdrawing $225,000 in a single day, using information skimmed from three hundred cardholders at a Manhattan candy-store ATM.

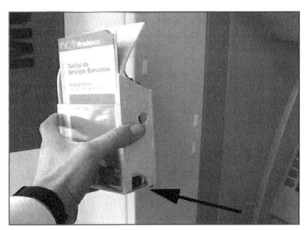

SERVICE WITH A SMILE
A fake info dispenser hides a miniature camera.
Source: *Identity Theft: Trends, Techniques, and Responses,*
U.S. Department of Justice

 ENFORCEMENT AND PENALTIES **ARRESTS: B SENTENCING: D**

Applicable laws and penalties vary with techniques employed and dollars liberated in this lucrative, cross-disciplinary occupation. Potential charges include grand larceny, wire fraud, identity fraud, credit card fraud, conspiracy to commit fraud, and armed robbery. Interstate rings may even qualify for prestigious RICO prosecutions. Nationally, however, clearance rates for ATM-related fraud are quite low, and work prospects remain rosy. Although preventative technologies such as strong encryption of card data, bank-specific magnetic code strips, and computer-assisted remote monitoring have been available for many years, nearly 50 percent of U.S. banks continue to shun such new-fangled foolishness.

STRESSES AND HAZARDS

DANGERS: C   PRESSURES: B-

New technologies can minimize personal exposure during the card- and information-gathering phases of this activity, but physical redemption of these slyly gotten gains can involve discomfiting levels of "face time." Some of our era's most accomplished and prolific card harvesters have been thwarted by video or human security in the thorny "home stretch." At the other end of the scale, aspiring amateurs may be moved to ill-considered action by the proliferation of alluringly unattended cash stations. Take, for instance, the Pittsburgh snowplow driver who used his eight-ton truck to plow away an outdoor ATM.

WORK ENVIRONMENT

HOURS: B   COMFORT: B

Sixty percent of forcible robberies of ATM customers occur between seven P.M. and four A.M., though this period accounts for only 11 percent of daily transaction volume.

Perpetrators of this entry-level ATM activity usually are lone males under twenty-five years of age. They typically position themselves within fifty feet of a visually obstructed ATM and wait for victims to approach. Fifty-one percent of ATM robberies occur after cash withdrawal; in most other cases, a weapon is brandished to encourage the customer to complete a substantial withdrawal.

AUTO THIEF

RANK: 19 out of 50 **AVERAGE GRADE:** B-

DUTIES: Auto Thieves take unauthorized possession of motor vehicles through stealth, mechanical manipulation, deception, or force. Confiscation techniques vary considerably with the expertise, tool sets, and preferences of individual practitioners. The security features, location, and model of the target vehicle are also key decision criteria. Passenger cars account for 78.3 percent of all vehicles usurped, though trucks and buses account for 16.5 percent. Motorcycles and specialty craft make up a mere 5.2 percent of the overall auto theft market.

More than 50 percent of vehicles stolen are left obligingly unlocked, and 25 percent to 30 percent actually have keys in the ignition. Entry through glass breakage (usually a passenger-side window) is quite popular among novices. Other techniques necessitate greater experience and finesse. *Air wedges* empower thieves to gently pry doors open, creating gaps large enough to insert hooked tools and manually disengage lock buttons or latches. *Slim Jims* are inserted in the narrow window channels of doors to grasp and disengage internal locking elements. Alternatively, advanced workers occasionally use *jiggler keys* or lock picks to defeat conventional locks. Once inside the auto, auto thieves generally can defeat steering wheel locks such as The Club in less than a minute with the proper know-how. Brake-pedal locks also can be speedily defeated with specialty tools.

Professional auto thieves seldom are deterred by alarms. Typically, they can

OLD RELIABLE
It's tough to beat these low-tech standbys.

Jiggler keys

Air wedge

Wedge

Slim Jim

cut a single wire and silence an alarm in seconds. Newcomers sometimes will bump an alarmed car repeatedly, until its owner is shamed into disabling its noise-polluting alarm. In 90 percent of forced entries, thieves *hot-wire* the compromised vehicle, bypassing its ignition lock and providing power directly to its starter motor. First-generation electronic immobilizing devices—designed to automatically withhold power from the starter—were relatively simple to locate and disable. Second-generation solenoid immobilizers, however, have proven very difficult to defeat.

As electronic countermeasures increase in popularity and sophistication, auto thieves have shown proportionally increased interest in obtaining copies or originals of legitimate keys. Popular acquisition techniques include treasure hunts for *Hide-A-Key* spares, theft, bribery of valets, and forgery of ownership creden-

tials to support replacement requests from auto dealers. Alternatively, well-equipped thieves may employ tow or flatbed trucks to remove vehicles without the fuss of starting them. In 3 percent of thefts, control of a vehicle is forcibly seized from its operator (see Carjacker for a full exploration of this challenging subspecialty).

In 1970, 75 percent of vehicles snatched were commandeered for joy rides—the opportunistic short-range transport of amateur thieves. Today, at least 70 percent of stolen cars are intended for resale—in whole or in part(s). A large percentage of professionally diverted vehicles is transported to *chop shops,* where *strippers* rapidly factor them into their constituent parts. Many parts actually appreciate as they age and become rare. Chop shop operators can usually recoup two to four times a vehicle's used Kelly Blue Book value by "parting it out."

STILL SLUGGISH
The underperforming auto theft industry needs a tune-up
Sources: U.S. Department of Justice, *Uniform Crime Reports*

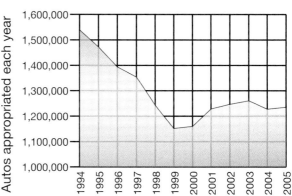

The annual take from stolen airbags alone exceeds $50 million.

Approximately 225,000 vehicles each year are returned to the domestic market with falsified titles and VIN (vehicle identification number) plates cloned from legitimately registered vehicles of the same year, make, and model. In the spirit of free trade, more than 200,000 other autos are exported to Eastern Europe, Southeast Asia, the Middle East, Africa, the Caribbean, and South America, where luxury cars can be sold for four times their North American market value.

COMPENSATION AND REWARDS — EARNINGS: **B-** PERKS: **B+**

HOT RIDES
Top 10 theft cars of 2005

Rank	Year, Make, Model
1	2001 BMW M Roadster
2	1998 Acura Integra
3	2004 Mercury Marauder
4	1999 Acura Integra
5	1995 Acura Integra
6	2002 Audi S4
7	1996 Acura Integra
8	1997 Acura Integra
9	2001 Acura Integra
10	1998 Jaguar XJR

Source: CCC Information Services Inc.

With an annual societal cost of almost $8.6 billion, auto theft is now America's number-one property crime! In fact, this criminal industry outstrips all others except perennial favorite drug trafficking. A motor vehicle is stolen every twenty-six seconds in the United States, with an average value per incident of $6,797. With over 1.2 million thefts annually, American auto thieves are credited with inflating the average family's insurance bill by more than $200 per year.

Although opportunities for solo practitioners still abound, a large percentage of the auto theft workforce is now employed by rings with ties to Asian gangs, outlaw motorcycle clubs, and the Russian and Italian mobs. One of the largest independent operations (operating under the cover of a Brooklyn front business, Astra Motor Cars Inc.) netted nearly $20 million for its eleven principals before being exposed.

Per-vehicle compensation for hired thieves ranges from a few hundred dollars for drug-addicted *smash-and-grabbers* to several thousand for specialists targeting in-demand luxury vehicles. Additional job benefits include extensive travel opportunities and substantial discounts on auto-related items.

ENFORCEMENT AND PENALTIES   *ARRESTS:* **A** *SENTENCING:* **C-**

If you are averse to risking your long-term liberty, this job could be for you. Overall, only 13.1 percent of auto thefts in 2004 were cleared by arrests. Rural police, however, cleared 32 percent of their cases, so farm living might not be your healthiest option in this occupation.

Although 62 percent of *all* stolen vehicles are recovered, almost 95 percent of cars equipped with radio tracking devices such as LoJack are eventually found. Other new technologies could have similar impacts on recovery rates. DataDots (microdots that bind to car parts), VIN etchings (unique identifiers inscribed into windows and windshields), and parts-level labeling each present significant new challenges.

Thieves with managerial ambitions are cautioned that operating a chop shop is a federal crime under the *Anti-Car Theft Act* of 1992, carrying possible jail terms up to twenty years.

MOTOR CITY Top 10 U.S. areas for auto thieves in 2005	Rank	Metropolitan Area	Vehicles Stolen	Thefts per 10,000 Residents
	1	Modesto, California	7,071	1,419
	2	Las Vegas/Paradise, Nevada	22,465	1,361
	3	Stockton, California	7,586	1,167
	4	Phoenix/Mesa/Scottsdale, Arizona	41,000	1,103
	5	Visalia/Porterville, California	4,257	1,060
	6	Seattle/Tacoma/Bellevue, Washington	33,494	1,057
	7	Sacramento, California	20,268	1,005
	8	San Diego, California	28,845	984
	9	Fresno, California	8,478	978
	10	Yakima, Washington	2,212	965

Source: National Insurance Crime Bureau

DON'T TAKE THE BAIT!
This unlucky auto thief ingested methamphetamine, then stole a self-locking, video-equipped police bait car. He tried fourteen times to fire his gun to escape, but it was jammed.
Source: www.baitcar.com (maintained by British Columbia's Integrated Municipal Provincial Auto Crime Team)

Professional thieves are prepared for a host of technical challenges, but Universal Electronics' Auto Taser represents a new category of risk and difficulty. The device delivers a 50,000-volt charge to uninvited drivers. (South African carjackers face the even more daunting prospect of encountering The Blaster, a pedal-triggered dual flamethrower.) As with any vehicle-centered occupation, accidents and mechanical failures are always worries, as are injuries from hastily shattered auto glass.

As auto theft organizations mature and grow, independent-minded workers may have difficulties adapting to increasingly bureaucratized work cultures.

WORK ENVIRONMENT

HOURS: B- COMFORT: C

Auto thieves favor crowded outdoor work sites where masses of cars linger for extended periods, such as shopping centers, sporting events, and movie complexes. Cars in lots are four times more likely to be targeted than those street-parked near a driver's home or workplace—and two hundred times more likely to be stolen than are cars in the owner's garage.

Nearly 60 percent of those arrested for auto theft are under twenty-one years of age. Established rings recruit young males to insulate their senior membership from perilous field work, so vehicle theft can open an exciting gateway into a life of organized crime.

Work schedules are quite flexible in this field, but Friday and Saturday are major workdays, accounting for one-third of vehicle thefts. Assignments are split fairly evenly between night-shifters (44.5 percent) and daytimers (55.5 percent).

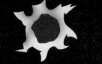

BABY BROKER

RANK: 7 out of 50   **AVERAGE GRADE:** B

DUTIES: Baby Brokers arrange, facilitate, and profit from gray- and black-market private adoptions. They co-opt, deceive, and coerce birth parents, guardians, adoption officials, hospital workers, and clergypersons into selling, trading, or otherwise corruptly conveying newborns and tots. In the forties, America's wealthy and childless turned to high-society broker-kidnapper Georgia Tann, She vended more than five thousand taken toddlers to such old-time luminaries as Joan Crawford, June Allyson, and Dick Powell. Today, most baby brokers employ or partner with street-savvy foreign surrogates to locate, negotiate for, obtain, and export marketable child-stock in underdeveloped donor nations. In 1992, there were 6,536 adoptions of foreign juveniles by American families. A decade later, with more than 500,000 U.S. households seeking to buy pre-owned bundles of joy, the importation

FACTORY FRESH
Visas issued to orphans in 2004

Visas	Country		Visas	Country
7,044	China		202	Belarus
5,865	Russia		196	Philippines
3,264	Guatemala		110	Bulgaria
1,716	South Korea		102	Poland
826	Kazakhstan		89	Mexico
723	Ukraine		86	Liberia
406	India		73	Nepal
356	Haiti		71	Nigeria
289	Ethiopia		69	Thailand

Source: U.S. Bureau of Immigration and Customs Enforcement

of alien children had more than tripled. American parents now account for two-thirds of *all* international adoptions.

In Romania, freshly minted moppets can be snapped up for as little as $700. With salaries there averaging less than $1,000 per year, the temptation to monetize infant overstock can be too great for many pauper-parents. "Buy me a new house and she's yours," a Romanian mother told a reporter for ABC's *20/20* in 2001. In some "family businesses," children are nurtured as a renewable cash crop. One couple-cum-baby-factory claimed to have sowed, reared, and sold a dozen fruits of their own loins. Domestic brokers charge $20,000 to $60,000 to deliver a healthy, handsome Romanian "Cadillac Baby" to American end-parents. They often work through corruptible adoption foundations to legitimize and obscure outright purchases of young persons.

The U.S. State Department is so leery of adoptions inked in some export-oriented areas that they require the donor-mothers to give blood evidence of maternity and reavow their informed consent in open court. To avoid such stringent infant import controls, some brokers instead ship pregnant mothers. Broker-lawyer Janice Doezie leveraged her skills in visa fraud and human smuggling to bring ripening Hungarian mothers-to-be directly to the California market. Corrupt officials can also be invaluable. Lauryn Galindo, a Hawaiian broker, "facilitated" hundreds of Cambodian adoptions between 1994 and 1997. Under a 2004 plea bargain agreement, she admitted to paying out roughly $3,500 per child to a chain of bureaucratic coconspirators. Galindo, who collected $10,500 to $11,500 per adoption, tendered an estimated $2.45 million in career bribes. The disenfranchised Cambodian parents, on the other hand, collected stipends of as little as $30 per child.

 COMPENSATION AND REWARDS — *EARNINGS:* **B+** *PERKS:* **B-**

Stork-starved U.S. couples spend an estimated $1.4 billion a year on private adoptions (kosher and crooked). Per-patrimony pricing and profit margins vary greatly, but the small packages generally deliver outsize returns in this discipline.

In 2005, for instance, a Vietnamese government newspaper had harsh words for a former California schoolteacher it said had facilitated at least two hundred illegal adoptions, with profits of over $10,000 per infant. French and U.S.

resellers, it is estimated, generated profits of $27 million in six years, on sales of 7,700 Vietnamese youngsters. Free-market foundlings typically fetch $5,000 to $30,000, but Russian tots are rumored to have been reparented for up to $150,000 per placement. When they run short of adoptees, some brokers supplement their revenues by overbooking their clients, or soliciting advance payments for imaginary wares. Pennsylvania's Child Haven agency, for instance, accepted consignments from fifty pregnant teenagers, then extracted $500,000 in downpayments from twice hat many hopeful couples.

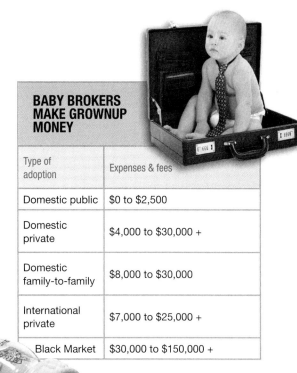

BABY BROKERS MAKE GROWNUP MONEY

Type of adoption	Expenses & fees
Domestic public	$0 to $2,500
Domestic private	$4,000 to $30,000 +
Domestic family-to-family	$8,000 to $30,000
International private	$7,000 to $25,000 +
Black Market	$30,000 to $150,000 +

ENFORCEMENT AND PENALTIES   ARRESTS: B-   SENTENCING: C

Punishments for interdicted intermediaries vary substantially. Hawaii's Lauryn Galindo was convicted of conspiracy to commit visa fraud, conspiracy to launder money, and structuring of financial transactions for purchasing Cambodian babies and systematically misrepresenting them as orphans. She received a modest 18 months in prison, 3 years of supervised release, and 300 hours of community service. She was also compelled to surrender her $1.4 million home and her late-model Jaguar. Janice Doezie's case illustrates the other end of the punitive spectrum. Doezie faced 70 years in federal prison for illegally importing pregnant Hungarians, but plea-bargained her way down to 15 years of federal time (still ten times Galindo's sentence).

STRESSES AND HAZARDS — DANGERS: B+ PRESSURES: B+

Most brokers walk a fine line between gray- and black-market practices. Often, they rely on dubious legal constructs or interpretations that may not bear the long-standing test of time. A single well-chronicled unpleasantness sends ripples through the entire illicit adoption industry. In 2003, for instance, a mentally unstable Illinois woman was convicted of the involuntary manslaughter of her underdocumented Russian ward.

Although Americans have adopted more than forty-three thousand Russian-born children since 1991, the future of the Russo-American baby trade is now in grave doubt. Civil liabilities are also a climbing concern. In 2004, a California court ordered attorney David Leavitt to pay $8 million for conspiring to help a woman give up her child for adoption in contravention to the father's wishes.

WORK ENVIRONMENT — HOURS: B COMFORT: B+

Many brokers conduct illegal or questionable business under the cover of well-appointed, putatively legitimate adoption agencies, legal practices, medical clinics, or social service bureaus. The Internet has had transformative effects on legitimate and black-market adoptions alike. It empowers brokers to cheaply advertise their wares and services, and to deliver targeted offers to a galaxy of gullible donors-in-waiting. In 1999, a short-lived eBay offering set the starting bid for an unborn boy at $155,000. Public outrage over Internet adoptions peaked in 2000, after a Seattle-based Web broker vended the same set of six-month-old twin girls to two different couples (one from Wales and the other from California).

BANK ROBBER

RANK: 47 out of 50 **AVERAGE GRADE:** C-

DUTIES: Bank Robbers utilize force, violence, or intimidation to obtain property or monies in the custody or possession of banks, credit unions, or savings and loans. Typically, a lone robber presents an on-duty teller with a demand to surrender readily accessible funds or else suffer immediately violent consequences. In 37.7 percent of bank robberies, the demand is tendered orally. Written notes are employed in 35 percent of heists. Communication is achieved silently via brandished firearms in 19.9 percent of forced banking transactions. Overall, firearms are present—brandished or concealed—in about 32 percent of all robberies. The favored firearm is a handgun.

Takeovers are an advanced robbery variant in which one or more robbers overtly convey extortionate threats to all patrons and personnel present at a targeted institution. Takeovers are often initiated by advanced aggressors to afford unfettered access to bank vaults. Gains from these violent and difficult assignments average at least five times the take from typical, semi-covert "note jobs." In 2004, takeovers accounted for fewer than 5 percent of all robberies, down from 10 percent in 2003.

Overall, bank robberies declined from 8,528 in 2001 to 7,469 in 2004. California leads the nation with over 1,300, more than twice its closest rival, Florida, and more than the entire Northeastern region. Los Angeles alone had 537 robberies in 2004. Although bank work accounts for just 2.4 percent of all robbery in the United States, a bank robbery occurs every fifty-two minutes.

SAY CHEESE
Dressing for your big close-up!
Sources: Bank surveillance tapes

Good *Better* *Best*

Professional bank robbers are dedicated specialists who typically conduct extensive due diligence on potential targets, keep abreast of new security devices and practices, and carefully plan entry and egress of the work sites. The FBI, which investigates 85 percent of all bank robberies, credits professionals with 20 percent of all such activity. The amateurs who perpetrate the remaining 80 percent, by contrast, act spontaneously in response to short-term personal needs. "Most bank robbers either have a $1,000-a-day heroin habit," says retired FBI bank robbery specialist Bill Rehder, "or are going through a divorce or lost a job."

Carl Gugasian, the "Friday Night Bank Robber," provides the ultimate role model for aspiring professionals. Over thirty years, he robbed fifty to seventy banks without detection or apprehension, amassing career earnings of at least $2 million. Gugasian was a Special Forces veteran with a third-degree black belt and a master's degree from the University of Pennsylvania. His preparation rituals included memorization of complex topographical maps, three-day surveillance sessions from concealed, wooded locales, and application of scent-deflecting chemicals to evade pursuing police dogs.

The rising popularity of bank branches inside grocery and drug outlets has ushered in a new era of soft targets for both seasoned and aspiring bank robbers. In Chicago, for example, such branches constitute just 6 percent of all area banks yet account for about 25 percent of bank jobs. Although retail establishments often make significant investments in electronic surveillance and security personnel to combat shoplifting, such measures are ill-suited to the challenges presented by a properly trained bank robber. Effective, banking-specific deterrents are available but can be prohibitively costly to deploy in small, in-store branches. Basic electronic entrance-control units run from $30,000 to $40,000 per branch. Bulletproof "bandit barriers," which create defensive perimeters around teller stations, reduce the probability of robbery by 75 percent but cost about $1,000 per linear foot.

Dye packs, conversely, are inexpensive deterrents that can take the sheen off an otherwise successful caper. The devices, used in over 75 percent of U.S. banks, are intended to render the fruits of a robbery useless by permanently staining stolen money bright red. They consist of a stack of real bills that conceals a thin bag of dye and a tiny radio receiver. When the dye pack passes through the bank door, a radio trigger signal is sent. Ten seconds or so later, when the robber believes he or she is safely away from the crime scene, the package explodes, releasing 400-degree Fahrenheit red smoke, red dye, and/or tear gas. To date, dye packs have been responsible for losses to bank robbers of nearly $20 million and resulted in almost 2,500 apprehensions.

Although the combined *take* from all U.S. bank robberies averages $70 million to $100 million annually, the per-job gains average less than $8,000. Adding insult to economic injury, roughly 20 percent of all funds seized are recaptured by law enforcement, yielding an effective average gain of just $6,400 per job. Criminologists and sociologists have theorized that the elite social status and self-esteem derived from a bank robbery are actually more important to many perpetrators than are the occupation's meager financial benefits. While takeover robberies do yield a much richer average of $25,000 per successful attack, they typically involve higher risks of apprehension and injury, and

require a financial split with at least one accomplice. Overall, however, bank robbers are a solitary group, with 79.9 percent of all robberies involving solo efforts.

Although modest gains are the rule in this business, there have been some very rewarding exceptions. In 1981, three robbers wearing Ronald Reagan masks withdrew a cool $3 million from the First National Bank depository in Tucson, Arizona. That group, allegedly masterminded by one David Grandstaff, is thought to have amassed lifetime earnings of more than $10 million. Grandstaff was eventually brought to trial, but questionable strong-arm tactics by FBI investigators led to a surprise acquittal.

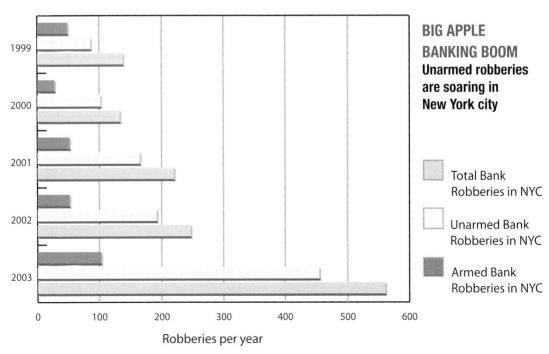

BIG APPLE BANKING BOOM
Unarmed robberies are soaring in New York city

- Total Bank Robberies in NYC
- Unarmed Bank Robberies in NYC
- Armed Bank Robberies in NYC

Robberies per year

The generic crime of robbery has a typical clearance rate of less than 25 percent, yet the clearance rate for bank robbery currently averages around 60 percent. Of all major criminals, only murderers (caught 62.4 percent of the time) face bleaker prospects of success. Although average apprehension and conviction rates have been falling in recent years, current statistics on this industry are skewed by a large number of unsolved cases by a small cadre of highly successful serial robbers. Sentences for these criminals average a moderate five to seven years, but penalties for exceptionally violent individuals can be much harsher. In February 2004,

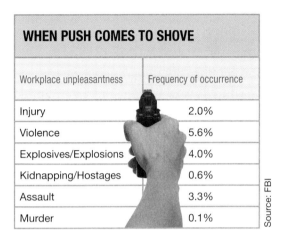

WHEN PUSH COMES TO SHOVE

Workplace unpleasantness	Frequency of occurrence
Injury	2.0%
Violence	5.6%
Explosives/Explosions	4.0%
Kidnapping/Hostages	0.6%
Assault	3.3%
Murder	0.1%

Source: FBI

for instance, Jeffrey Charles was sentenced to 33.5 years for robbing a Tucson, Arizona, bank while wearing a long, black wig and brandishing a hand grenade.

STRESSES AND HAZARDS   *DANGERS:* **C**   *PRESSURES:* **D**

Although firearms are present in nearly one-third of all bank robberies, actual violence occurs in only 5.6 percent of incidents, and injuries occur in only 2 percent. Fatalities are extremely rare. In 2004 there were only twenty deaths nationwide, with perpetrators accounting for the lion's share (thirteen).

Newcomers to this field should exercise caution when implying the possession of a nonexistent or nonfunctional weapon. In July 2005, a Worthington, Ohio, man was shot to death after inadvisably parking his getaway vehicle next to an unmarked SWAT van. Moments earlier he had indicated to tellers at the bank he robbed that he had a gun. No weapon was found in his possession.

Maintaining a judicious veil of anonymity can also be challenging for novices. Frederick McDowell of Fort Worth, Texas, presented his robbery demands on the back of his résumé, obscuring his name with a taped piece of black paper. Sadly, the police were expert in forensic tape removal and apprehended him.

Most bank robberies occur between nine and eleven A.M., so night owls need not apply! Historically, Friday has been the payday for much of the United States, mandating large deliveries of cash to branch banks. Thus, this is the most popular workday for bank robbers, followed in popularity by Monday and Tuesday. Although 93.85 percent of all bank robberies take place on weekdays, the extended hours offered by many grocery-based bank branches may buck this long-term trend.

Although 95 percent of bank robbers are male, female practitioners such as "Miss Piggy" and "Large Marge" (each tipping the scales at over three hundred pounds) have achieved sizable notoriety. An exceptionally attractive former bank teller garnered national attention for her positive physical attributes when she was dubbed the "Miss America Bandit" by the FBI. Although aspirants to this field typically strive to project an aura of machismo, a three-man takeover team who dressed as a biker, a cop, and a hard-hatted construction worker were obviously emulating the homoerotic antics of seventies fad phenomenon the Village People.

This is a youth-oriented occupation, with 42 percent of bank robbers falling between the ages of eighteen and twenty-nine. With the proper attitude, however, intrepid robbers can forge ahead into their twilight years. J. L. Hunter Rountree, for instance, robbed the First American Bank of Abilene, Texas. At age ninety, he led police on a chase at ninety miles per hour.

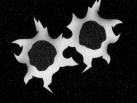

BLACKMAILER

RANK: 30 out of 50   **AVERAGE GRADE:** C+

DUTIES: Blackmailers obtain money, property, and other items of tangible and intangible value by threatening individuals, organizations, or groups with criminal prosecution or the diminution of reputation or social standing. They gather or fabricate damaging or discomfiting details about their intended targets, then exact compensation to forgo the conveyance of said suppressibles to interested third parties (e.g., friends, family associates, police, or the general public). Technically, blackmail is defined as "a threat to disclose a violation of United States law," and disclosures of unsavory-but-legal information are classed as "extortionate threats." Blackmailers set fee schedules, tender demands—in person or through intermediaries—and establish parameters for the delivery of their payoffs.

Despite blackmailers' frequent adoption of aliases and their attempts to communicate anonymously, the delivery of demands can result in troublesome trails of evidence. In 2002, Grammy award–winning producer Michael Morales sought to secure a $280,000 "consulting fee" from Texas gubernatorial candidate Tony Sanchez. Morales claimed to be in possession of some allegedly unsavory details of the politician's past. He faxed and phoned-in a series of vaguely menacing messages to the candidate's office, using the clever alias "Wendel Smith." San Antonio police promptly traced the faxes and the phone card used in the attempts to Morales, after Sanchez declined to suppress the supposedly damning disclosures. The careless Morales ultimately was sentenced to two years' federal penmanship.

Sexual indiscretions and peccadilloes have been the traditional bread and butter of career blackmailers. In 1961, 90 percent of all British blackmail prosecutions involved threats to out homosexuals. Recent scholarship suggests that J. Edgar Hoover, himself, was the victim of a national blackmail ring operating out of a New York gay bar. In 1969, Ed Murphy—owner of the Stonewall Inn—allegedly escaped the attentions of Interpol and the NYPD by threatening to publicize incriminating photos of the iconic supercop.

CELEBRITY SLAM

CAMERON DIAZ—In 1992, the nineteen-year-old Diaz posed for a series of bondage-themed, topless photos for photographer John Rutter. Eleven years later, on the eve of the release of *Charlie's Angels: Full Throttle*, Rutter requested $3.5 million to suppress the purportedly damaging evidence of the pert star's youthful romp. Unfortunately, Diaz's "people" rebuffed his demands and engaged criminal authorities. The signature on the model release for the photo session proved to be a crude forgery, and Rutter was sentenced to four years in prison for forgery, perjury, and attempted grand theft in 2005.

RENÉ ANGELIL—After amassing nearly $1 million in Las Vegas gambling debts, Korean native Yun Kyeong Kwon Sung demanded $13 million to forgo rape charges against René Angelil, husband to pop diva Celine Dion. Angelil paid Sung $2 million to settle her original allegation that he'd fondled her in 2000.

BILL COSBY—In the largest blackmail attempt on record, Autumn Jackson attempted to extort $40 million from comedian Bill Cosby, who she claims is her father. Jackson, who can be heard on audiotape dropping her demands to a bargain $25 million, was convicted in 1997 of extortion, conspiracy, and crossing state lines to commit a crime. Although Cosby admitted having had an extramarital affair with Jackson's mother, Jackson refused to cooperate with paternity tests. Cosby maintains that Jackson is not a "Cosby kid."

LANCE ARMSTRONG—In April 2005, Mike Anderson, a former personal assistant to the six-time Tour de France winner, allegedly demanded $500,000 to scuttle a breach of contract lawsuit in which he charged that Armstrong had used illegal performance-enhancing drugs. "He should have worn a ski mask," Armstrong's attorney said of Anderson's "settlement" demand. Armstrong refused the demand and countersued. A French sports daily, *L'Equipe*, later claimed that samples of Armstrong's urine from 1999 tested positive for the endurance-enhancing hormone EPO when retested in 2004.

Although the National Coalition of Anti-Violence Programs reports a 33 percent drop in 2004 attempts to blackmail lesbian, gay, and transgender Americans, opportunities for creative practitioners still abound in these areas. In May 2004, for instance, a Chicago man was arrested for demanding a series of wire transfers from a married man whom he had induced to share nude photos in an Internet gay chat room. Later that same month, a Chicago woman was arrested for an innovative heterosexual blackmail gambit: the former Seattle prostitute and sheriff's informant set up an unlicensed massage parlor where she videotaped liaisons with her intended blackmailees, then collected their used condoms for ironclad DNA evidence. In-the-know extortionists often allege to be victims of sexual harassment or wrongful termination, and threaten to pursue these allegations in open civil proceedings. Some U.S. courts have held that threats to file lawsuits—even those made in bad faith—can never constitute extortion. Recently, hackers have been stretching traditional definitions of blackmail by accessing vast collections of customer data from financial institutions (credit card numbers, PINs, etc.) and demanding large payments to suppress the compromised information. In 2004, thirty banks around the world admitted to such electronic blackmail victimization.

COMPENSATION AND REWARDS   *EARNINGS:* **C-**   *PERKS:* **A-**

Although the multimillion-dollar demands of the highest-profile blackmailers are tantalizing, available data suggest that most workers in this field accept much smaller stipends. The median per-incident property loss in 2002 cases was less than $1,000. In addition to cash gains, however, blackmailers enjoy a gamut of perks and benefits, including work promotions and preferred assignments, insulation from criminal prosecution, and sexual favors.

WHY BURN BRIDGES?
Save a copy for a rainy day!

ENFORCEMENT AND PENALTIES   *ARRESTS:* **B+**   *SENTENCING:* **B-**

Blackmail is a largely underreported activity that is seldom prosecuted in the absence of other criminal deeds. Although the median sentence for felony blackmail is 2.5 years, individual punishments vary with the amount of compensation demanded. Blackmailers convicted of demanding $90,000 or more face median sentences of more than 5 years. Defendants with no prior convictions receive median sentences of nearly 4 years, whereas those with two to four prior felonies receive median sentences of about 6 years. By comparison, the median sentence for extortionists, who make their livings through threats of violence, is 8 years.

STRESSES AND HAZARDS   *DANGERS:* **C-**   *PRESSURES:* **C-**

Casual practitioners of this craft are primarily reactive and must wait for information and work opportunities to find them, contributing to disempowering feelings of financial insecurity. More significantly, blackmailers face physical, financial, and professional retribution from would-be victims. Although there were no known murders of U.S. blackmailers in the last few years, 2005 witnessed homicides of sex-related blackmailers in Iraq, China, and Australia. Despite the elevated climate of threat, blackmail arrestees are very rarely armed.

WORK ENVIRONMENT   *HOURS:* **B+**   *COMFORT:* **B**

Most blackmailers are self-taught moonlighters who take up this time-effective sideline as a rewarding adjunct to their primary criminal or conventional careers. Although 79 percent of blackmail arrestees are male, assignments involving sexual entrapment provide better than average opportunities for opposite- and same-sex relations.

Although advanced blackmailers employ a variety of photographic, video, audio, and computer equipment to assist in evidence gathering and client communications, common blackmailing chores can be completed from rudimentary home offices.

BOOKIE

RANK: 18 out of 50   **AVERAGE GRADE:** B-

DUTIES: Bookies accept, process, and underwrite bets on amateur and professional sporting events. Bookmakers must maintain client anonymity while providing accessible, reliable points of contact for repeat bettors. They employ specialized language to signify wager parameters, and utilize code names and electronic countersurveillance techniques to protect the identities of customers, associates, and in-house personnel.

Bookies earn profits through a per-wager commission known as *vigorish* (from the French *vignes*, "vine" or "vineyard") or *the juice*. The conventional vig is 10 percent, with an additional risk premium of 5 percent imposed for college basketball. Ultimately, the bookie pays out 92.5 to 95.5 cents of each dollar wagered (see Figuring the Vig), representing an outstanding consumer value, compared with the 72.5 cents paid out at the track or the approximately 35-cent yield of state-run lotteries.

The total action a book agrees to cover in a given week is his *handle*. Bookies weigh complex statistical measures of event conditions, historical performance, and bettor expectations against their personal instincts and experience, to create a point spread or game odds—*the line*. Sophisticated bookmakers crosscheck their judgments against lines set by Vegas casinos and Internet books, monitor breaking weather and news, and teleconference with tipsters, colleagues, and deputies in the field.

FIGURING THE VIG

Suppose two bettors wager $100 each on opposite outcomes to a sporting event. The bookie adds his 10 percent vig and collects a total of $220. The winning bettor is paid $210—his $110, plus $100 in profit. This leaves the bookmaker with a $10 gross profit, or 4.55 percent of the $220 risked.

In traditional bookmaking, the goal is to create a line that balances the handle so that winning bets exactly offset losing ones. If a bookie can't balance his handle, he may elect to *lay off* some of his *action* or *sheet* with a specialized bookie (known as an *out*), who takes a 5 percent commission. In recent years, unbalanced handles have become common among sophisticated practitioners. Risk-friendly bookies assume asymmetrical handles to mirror the judgments of elite professional gamblers, leverage the statistical advantage of the vig, or exploit systemic arbitrage or *scalping* opportunities.

Small bookmakers rely heavily on personal trust to minimize bettor defaults, police tip-offs, employee competition, and theft. Typically, high-level employees are drawn from a pool of close relatives or long-time business associates. Client familiarity, proximity, and shared background can also greatly enhance trust. A recent study by the University of North Carolina at Chapel Hill found that 66 percent of bettors studied lived within two miles of their small-scale bookmaker, and 80 percent of them lived in neighborhoods ethnically and economically similar to that of the bookmaker. Physical coercion of bettors is rare, but annoyance calls to spouses and intimates of deadbeat bettors are commonplace. When a customer does default, the employee responsible for recruiting him or her is usually held liable for the debt.

KNOW THY CUSTOMER

- More than a quarter of all adult Americans gamble at a casino each year.
- Suicide rates for compulsive gamblers are 200 times higher than the national average, and 150 times higher for their spouses.
- A major depressive disorder is likely to occur in 76 percent of pathological gamblers.
- Problem drinkers are twenty-three times more likely to have a gambling problem than are persons without a drinking problem.

Offshore Internet sports books are rapidly emerging as major challengers to local practitioners and Nevada-based, licensed bookmakers. In 1995, there were fewer than two dozen Web-based bookmakers. In 2005, Americans placed an estimated $2.3 billion to $4.2 billion in illegal wagers through nearly 2,500 Internet sites. A 2006 federal law prohibiting U.S.-based banks, credit card companies, and Internet payment systems from tendering payments to gambling sites could slow the online gravy train.

Although the prevalence of Mafia influence in contemporary bookmaking is subject to debate, the FBI has recognized illegal gambling as the single largest source of revenue for organized crime, amounting to at least $10 billion a year. Book-making provides financing for a range of critical activities, including wholesale drug purchases, bribery, loan sharking, and leveraged acquisitions of "straight" front businesses.

COMPENSATION AND REWARDS   *EARNINGS:* **B**   *PERKS:* **B+**

Pay scales and formulas vary significantly, according to the work roles. Wire room phone workers, called *writers* or *clerks*, usually receive weekly salaries of $200 to $500. Collectors (a.k.a. *bag-men* or *runners*), who transfer payments to and from bettors, receive comparable wages, despite the additional dangers associated with their positions. *Sheetholders* recruit or refer bettors. They are responsible for monitoring their bettors, and may also assume some of the duties of the Bag-Man or Runner. Sheetholders receive weekly commissions, based on the cumu-lative losses of the bettors on their sheets, averaging more than $1,500.

Seasoned bookies sit at the top of the pay pyramid. Though the largest urban operations have estimated handles in excess of $200 million per year, superbookies accept high degrees of risk for profit margins as small as 1 percent. Independent owner-operators of midsize establishments occupy the sweet spot, with annual profits commonly exceeding $1 million. Common perks include complimentary tickets to sporting events, and out-of-town travel.

BIG BOOK, NARROW MARGINS	
Bet volume	$11,459,310
Number of bets	10,252
Net revenue	$129,632
Percentage hold	1.31%
Sheetholder commissions	$99,189
Delinquent debt payment	$11,486
Salaries to writers and collectors	$2,520
Rent	$3,100
Line service subscriptions	$200
Utilities	$497
Total costs	$116,992
Profit	$12,640
Estimated annualized profit	$210,000

This ledger provides rare insight into the economics of a high-volume "superbookie." It represents three weeks' worth of transactions for a New York–based operation with 75 sheetholders, 22 subsheetholders, and more than 300 active bettors.

Source: Nassau County Police Department

Enforcement expenditures and conviction rates in this field should continue their historic thirty-year decline, as manpower, funding, and equipment are diverted to the nation's wars on drugs and terrorism. Overall, felony convictions for bookmaking have fallen by 75 percent since 1970, while revenues have steadily risen. Infrequent raids, moderate assets seizures, and overnight jail stays are the norm in this field, but there are notable recent exceptions. In January 2001, New York police jailed eleven members of the Califano Operation, seized $90,000 in assets, and filed a $3.8 million civil lawsuit against its bosses and managers. The organization, which had an estimated annual handle of more than $30 million, had employed call-forwarding, prepaid cell phones, and redundant wire rooms to avoid detection.

STRESSES AND HAZARDS

DANGERS: **C** PRESSURES: **C-**

Carpal tunnel syndrome and accidental injuries are rare. Theft- and competition-related violence, however, remain serious concerns. Insolvency is also a common worry. Several established Boston bookies, for example, were forced into default following the New England Patriots' long-shot victory in the 2002 Super Bowl.

Entrepreneurial lone wolves who compete in traditional "family" markets could also be subject to the *crack out*. In this scenario, a consultant with specialized skills in intimidation and physical violence is subcontracted to place a series of large bets with an independent operator, occasionally employing innocuous intermediaries known as *beards* to

HOW THE BETTING PIE GETS SLICED

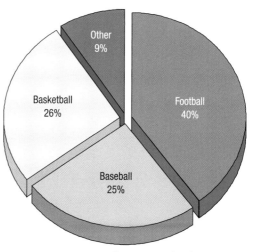

Source: www.rivercitycasino.com

conceal the true extent of his bets. The following week, he collects on his winning bets but forcibly refuses to make good on any losses. An independent who has deep enough cash reserves to avoid immediate insolvency can expect a prompt sales call from a dignitary from the local crime family, eager to offer the mark their expensive (but nonrefusable) protective and collection services to indemnify him or her against catastrophic loss of capital or life.

WORK ENVIRONMENT

HOURS: **C**   *COMFORT:* **C**

The bookie's primary workplace is the *wire room*, an inbound call center designed for inconspicuousness, accessibility, and privacy. Bookmakers relocate frequently, and nonessential investments in these temporary quarters are rare. Wire rooms are usually spartan, crowded, and noisy. Most provide service from eleven A.M. to eight P.M. (with an afternoon break), and operate every day of the year. After hours, bookies often visit sports bars, poolrooms, and athletic venues to acquire and entertain customers. Although established practitioners enjoy a great deal of autonomy, entry-level workers may chafe at the regimented and repetitive nature of their duties.

TIME-HONORED SHORTHAND WAGER DENOMINATIONS	
Code Term	Amount of Bet
Dollar, or buck	$100
Fifty cents	$50
Nickel	$500
X (multiplication sign)	$5 (20 X = $100)

BURGLAR

DUTIES: Burglars enter dwellings, outbuildings, or residential grounds without the awareness or assent of their occupants—usually with the intent of committing theft. Sixty-four percent of burglaries involve forcible entry; 12 percent occur through an unlocked door. Other preferred points of entry include basement windows, garage doors, and sliding doors. In situations mandating forcible ingress, most burglars employ pry bars and screwdrivers—others simply break a window or kick in a door. Although real-world applications of lock picks, battering rams, electronic door scanners, and other specialized tools are quite rare, a New Jersey–based burglary ring, dubbed the "James Bond Gang," utilized a BMW complete with secret compartments, a road-slickening oil-jet system, and blinding halogen headlamps to discourage would-be pursuers.

Burglars typically select their targets on the basis of convenience, occupancy, visibility, security, and potential rewards. Most burglaries take place within three miles of the practitioner's home, although older professionals travel much farther to locate choice prospects. Burglars scrupulously avoid entering occupied premises, often ringing doorbells as

GETTING YOUR FOOT IN THE DOOR
Most popular means of unauthorized entry
Source: *US Department of Justice*

2% Second story

6% Unlocked entrances and storage areas

23% Back door

9% Garage

4% Basement

34% Front door

a final preentry double check. Single-parent, one-person, and pet-less homes are reliably vacant targets of choice. Although burglars strongly favor houses with significant cover, poor lighting, or secluded surroundings, the presence of an electronic security system is the key determinant in target selection. Homes without security systems are 2.7 times more likely to be visited.

Although professional burglars devote substantial effort and energies to site assessment and surveillance, they spend an average of under a minute entering a job site, and only eight to twelve minutes on the job. Americans tend to concentrate their valuables where they sleep, so burglars typically visit the master bedroom first. In 2003, the average residential burglary yielded $1,626 in stolen goods. The most frequently purloined items in the United States are cash, jewelry, electronic equipment, silver, and guns.

The majority of burglaries are committed in multiunit dwellings by unskilled juveniles or drug-addled amateurs in need of immediate gratification. Sixty-three percent of burglars arrested in 2003 were under the age of twenty-five. Beginners average minimal gains, burglarize nearby dwellings (frequently of acquaintances), and are easily deterred by dogs, alarms, or locks. They generally vend their goods to pawnshops, taxi drivers, bar patrons, and gas station staff.

Roughly 45 percent of residential burglaries involve two or more cooperating offenders. Juvenile practitioners are substantially more likely to work with a partner, and commonly undertake two or more burglary attempts per week. Professional burglars usually offend in concert with professional fences (see Fence, page 69). On average, pros are older than novices, executing fewer burglaries with much larger yields. They are considerably more mobile and are more likely to engage targets with visible evidence of security systems.

COMPENSATION AND REWARDS   EARNINGS: B   PERKS: B

U.S.-based burglars initiated an estimated 2,153,464 work assignments in 2003, representing a 0.1 percent increase over fiscal 2002. After thirty years of steady decline—with victimization rates per thousand households falling from

over 110 to less than 30—the moribund burglary industry is showing tentative signs of a comeback. With an estimated $3.5 billion in annual costs, burglary is the second-most-common serious crime in the nation (narrowly trailing larceny-theft), accounting for 18 percent of all serious American crimes. A burglary is committed every fifteen seconds, with up to 50 percent of attempted entries going unreported by obliging victims.

Although heroin and cocaine addicts receive only pennies on the dollar for stolen items vended on the street or bartered for drugs, professional burglars are well compensated and frequently enjoy long careers. A seven-man ring from New York's Nassau County is estimated to have fenced $5 million in property over fifteen years. The so-called Codwise Gang from Queens, New York, amassed an estimated $1.5 million in cash and jewels in just two years.

ENFORCEMENT AND PENALTIES   *ARRESTS:* **B+** *SENTENCING:* **B-**

The solution rate for U.S. burglary cases remains comfortingly low, averaging a mere 14 percent. Sixty-five percent of investigations fail to yield any actionable leads. In 2002, state prosecutors secured a scant 79,300 felony burglary convictions, with a median sentence length of twenty-four months. Generally speaking, the greater the gain is from a given burglary, the less likely it is to be solved. Rural law enforcement agencies marginally outconvict their urban and suburban counterparts, but incarceration risks in this field are generally quite low. Burglars are dedicated to their chosen craft. Once convicted, they lead all property offenders in recidivism and rearrest.

A JOB WITH SOME LEGS
Burglaries hold steady while other property crimes decline

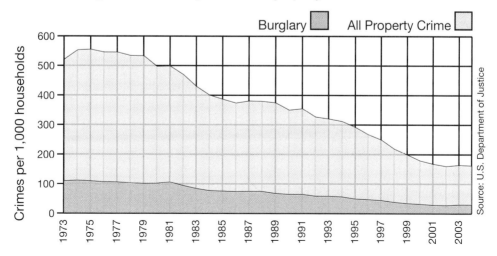

Source: U.S. Department of Justice

Law-abiding Americans brandish firearms to defend against criminals almost 2.5 million times a year. Though eleven out of twelve weapon-wielders merely fire a warning shot, a 1989 survey revealed that 78 percent of gun owners state they would shoot a burglar if they felt gravely threatened. Academic interviews with burglars confirm that they are substantially more afraid of injury from victims than of harm or arrest from police. Burglars also face substantial risks of self-injury from

"I DON'T DO WINDOWS!"
Even old hands get nervous around broken glass.

falls, cuts, and vehicular misadventures during getaways. Stresses from seasonal downturns and the possibility of betrayal by distribution partners, co-offenders, or customers are also endemic to this ever-popular occupation.

Source: istockphoto.com

WORK ENVIRONMENT

HOURS: **C+** COMFORT: **C**

Burglars enjoy enviable flexibility in scheduling, but plum assignments do cluster around times when homes are likely to be unoccupied (weekdays from ten to eleven A.M. and one to three P.M.) Almost 60 percent of today's burglaries occur in daytime, compared with only 16 percent in 1965. Burglary activity is hottest in August and coolest in February, but regional weather variations and micromigration patterns are much more significant than changes in season.

Sadly, this occupation offers limited prospects for collegial concourse with the opposite sex, as 87 percent of U.S. arrestees are male.

CARJACKER

DUTIES: Carjackers commandeer occupied motor vehicles from their drivers and/or passengers by force or threat of force. To secure control of target vehicles, carjackers customarily strike, shoot, stab, or pummel drivers, pull or push them from the driver's seat, or simply order them to vacate their mobile premises. Carjackers employ weapons in 74 percent of all assignments. Firearms are used in 45 percent of attacks, knives in 11 percent, and assorted other weapons in 18 percent. Occasionally, carjackers are less than vigilant in ensuring that they have fully separated former occupants from their vehicles. In several such cases, drivers who became entangled in their seat belts or the front grille were subsequently dragged to their deaths. In other well-publicized cases, carjackers have unintentionally sped away with onboard infants and pets. Occasionally, carjackers opt to remain in the company of a vehicle's occupants for purposes of kidnapping, sexual assault, or subsequent robbery.

Carjacking is not a new crime, but its stock soared in the go-go 1980s, after a series of high-profile attacks inspired copycats across the country. Today, carjackers play a vital role in the auto-theft industry, staging more than thirty-four thousand attempted vehicle appropriations annually. As alarms and other antitheft devices continue to improve, carjacking presents an increasingly attractive—if primitive—alternative to traditional means of theft.

Roughly 44 percent of carjackings take place in open areas on the street or near public transportation stops. Twenty-four percent occur as the owner is entering or exiting a vehicle in a parking lot, in a garage, or near a commercial facility. Regardless of locale, carjacking is a difficult, often dangerous undertaking, and 55 percent of all attempts end in failure and frustration. To maximize the chances of a gainful and safe automotive transfer, carjackers have evolved a variety of time-tested gambits:

THE JACKER'S PLAYBOOK
Your guide to the tactics of the takedown

GOOD SAMARITAN—One or more carjackers simulate an apparent accident. When the intended vehicular victim pauses to assist, the attack is staged.

RUSE—The carjacker pulls behind the target and honks, waves, or flashes his or her lights to call attention to a fictitious problem with the target car. When the victim pulls over, trouble ensues.

BUMP—The carjacker bumps the target vehicle from behind. When the victim exits to survey the situation and exchange insurance, the carjacker makes his or her full intentions clear.

ROUND ROBIN—The carjacker jumps from his own vehicle, yanks open the unlocked driver's door of an adjacent target vehicle, and forces the driver out the passenger door. This technique allows for a quick escape but carries significant risk of observation and/or pursuit by nearby drivers.

CORNERING—After identifying an appropriate target vehicle, the carjacker follows covertly, hoping the vehicle will eventually stop in a confined space. As the target car comes to a stop in a driveway or parking slip, the carjacker pulls behind and blocks the victim's avenue of escape.

Ninety-three percent of carjackings take place in urban or suburban settings. Proximity to freeway entrances is viewed as particularly auspicious for quick escape, while intersections with major stoplights are favored by exceptionally adrenaline-driven practitioners. The demographics of target selection are enlightening: unaccompanied drivers are targeted in 90 percent of carjacking attempts; men are victimized more often than women, blacks more than whites, and Hispanics more than non-Hispanics.

BEHIND THE DRIVER'S SEAT
The vital statistics

M.O.	
Male	93%
Firearm used	45%
Knife used	11%
Other weapon used	18%
More than one assailant	56%
Victims	
Resisted carjacker	67%
Injured	24%
Hospitalized	1%

Source: National Crime Victimization Study (1996–2003)

COMPENSATION AND REWARDS   EARNINGS: C   PERKS: B

With approximately thirty-four thousand work actions per year, carjackers account for less than 3 percent of the thriving $8.6 billion U.S. auto theft sector. Still, this amounts to more than $243 million worth of vehicles violated, cars with an average Blue Book value of $6,797. Unfortunately, carjackers tend to be extremely short-term thinkers with ever-pressing addictions to drugs, gambling, and other street vices. Their minimal time-horizons, limited criminal networking skills, and cash-intensive streetlife styles may preclude them from maximizing the monetary fruits of their brutish labor. In a recent St. Louis survey, twenty-eight canvassed carjackers reported per-car profits ranging from a regrettable $200 to a very respectable $5,000—with an average take-home of

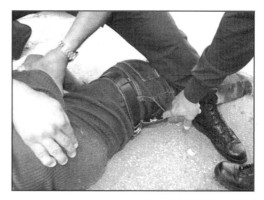

TIME FOR A CAREER CHANGE?
Florida police detain an on-duty carjacker.
Source: Florida Highway Patrol

$1,750. The most enterprising survey respondents stripped the vehicles themselves, vending sought-after parts to the public on street corners or to chop shops at premium peer-to-peer pricing. After-market rims and *phat beats* (expensive stereos) particularly were praised for their potential.

ENFORCEMENT AND PENALTIES   ARRESTS: A-   SENTENCING: D

Although 98 percent of carjackings completed and 58 percent of thwarted boardings are reported to police, in many areas clearance rates for auto attacks average less than 10 percent. Federal law prescribes a fifteen-year minimum sentence for all cases in which a stolen car is moved across state lines. A minimum twenty-five-year sentence is assessed for carjackings resulting in serious injury, and the death penalty may be applied for mortal mishaps. First-time carjacking convicts who forgo the use of firearms can expect median sentences of about five years. If a gun is brandished but not fired, the median sentence increases to about eight years. If a gun is fired with minor injury, the ante jumps to approximately ten years. A serious injury will cost a carjacker sixteen years.

FIREARMS DRAMATICALLY IMPROVE A CARJACKER'S COMPLETION PERCENTAGE

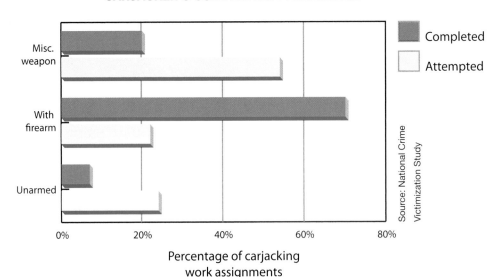

Percentage of carjacking work assignments

Source: National Crime Victimization Study

STRESSES AND HAZARDS   *DANGERS:* **D**   *PRESSURES:* **C-**

Carjackings usually pit a highly motivated, drug-fueled attacker directly against an aghast or enraged motorist. Such primeval confrontations are, at best, stressful and uncertain. In two-thirds of carjacking attempts victims mount some form of resistance. A full 24 percent of victims threaten, attack, chase, or attempt to apprehend their attacker. Roughly one-third offer nonconfrontational resistance by fleeing, crying for help, or seeking the assistance of others. About 32 percent of completed carjackings end in injury to the motorist; about 17 percent of thwarted attempts end in such harm. Gunshot and knife wounds, internal injuries, broken bones, and other major traumas occur in 9 percent of jackings. Although statistics on vehicular injuries are not methodically kept for workers in this field, anecdotal evidence suggests that they are highly prevalent.

Almost 70 percent of carjackings take place under the veil of darkness. Despite the popularity of night work, only 42 percent of nocturnal attacks succeed, whereas 50 percent of daytime attempts end fruitfully.

Aggressive males are responsible for 93 percent of carjacking activity; coed groups perform 3 percent of this work. Groups of two or more cooperating criminals stage about 56 percent of all jacking attempts, while lone women complete about 3 percent. Juveniles make up about 25 percent of the carjacking workforce.

CIGARETTE SMUGGLER

RANK: 2 out of 50 **AVERAGE GRADE:** B

DUTIES: Cigarette Smugglers transport genuine or counterfeit name-brand carcinogens across national or state boundaries for the purpose of illegal wholesale or retail distribution. The United States leads the tobacco-tending world, with domestic production of over 500 billion cigarettes in 2003. Up to 6 percent of all cigarettes vended in the United States have been smuggled at some stage of their life cycle. Most commonly, smugglers procure legitimate cigarettes from low-tax states such as Virginia ($0.20 state excise tax per pack) and North Carolina ($.05), and truck them to high-tax markets such as Maryland ($1.00), New York ($1.50), or New Jersey ($2.45). The "diverted" smokables are then vended to distributors, retailers, or end customers at generous discounts.

Mom-and-pop, *over-the-road* operations purchase and *flip* fewer than one hundred cartons at a clip. They tend to buy from out-of-state big-boxers and sell through flea markets and other informal outlets. Major smuggling operations frequently collude with corrupt wholesalers, undiscriminating chain retailers, and "connected" vending machine operators to facilitate large-scale acquisition and distribution. Top-tier smoke smugglers have cultivated specialized expertise in counterfeiting tax stamps and altering interstate distribution reports and other paper-based audit controls.

THE SNIFF TEST
A customs inspector checks questionable combustibles.
Source: U.S. Immigration and Customs Enforcement

Huge volumes of tax-exempt tobacco product are exported to other countries and U.S. possessions from bonded warehouses. Underpaid underlings at these strategic locales (usually sited near airports, seaports, or international borders) have proven to be indispensable partners for alternative entrepreneurs in search of large reserves of divertible tobacco. Other advanced smugglers actually import counterfeit "squares" from China, Malaysia, Korea, Russia, Latvia, Mexico, Brazil, Paraguay, Uruguay, or the Philippines.

"Big Tobacco" has often been accused of exaggerating smuggling to justify inflated prices. The world's second-largest tobacco company took a much more proactive posture . . . by actually encouraging the practice. Internal memos from British American Tobacco (parent to Brown & Williamson) reveal that company executives actually set inventory and price levels for a global network of smugglers, in an effort to increase their share of the burgeoning tax-free market. For decades, corporate reps coordinated with local black-market distributors—offering them structured sales incentives including tickets to Wimbledon.

The boundless opportunities in this burgeoning field have also caught the attention of enterprising terrorists. The U.S. Bureau of Alcohol, Tobacco, Firearms, and Explosives (ATF) initiated eight tobacco trafficking investigations with substantiated links to Hamas, Hezbollah, and al Qaeda between 2002 and 2003. The first major nico-terrorist case was tried in North Carolina in 2002. A federal jury convicted Mohamad Hammoud of funneling profits from the felonious sale of at least $7.9 million in North Carolina cigarettes to Hezbollah fund-raisers. He was sentenced to 155 years in prison.

 COMPENSATION AND REWARDS   *EARNINGS:* **A**   *PERKS:* **C**

U.S. participation in the multibillion-dollar contraband market has arched steeply since 2002. A carton of cigarettes purchased in Virginia for $25 can be sold in New York City (where the state and city taxes total $3 per pack) for about $75. This represents a best-case profit of $50 per carton. A single truckload can hold 48,000 cartons, with a potential profit of $2,400,000. Cartons of Asian-rolled counterfeits can be imported for as little as $3, promising even greater prospective rewards. In 2004, Jorge Abraham of Sunland Park, New Mexico, was convicted of single-handedly orchestrating the smuggling of 107 million cigarettes with an estimated street value of $37.5 million. He was sentenced to sixty months' prison time and ordered to pay $4.8 million in restitution.

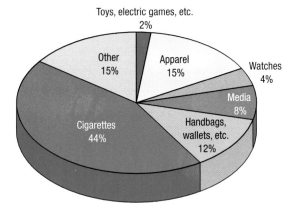

#1 IN THE STREETS
U.S. counterfeit goods seized in 2005

Toys, electric games, etc. 2%
Other 15%
Apparel 15%
Watches 4%
Media 8%
Cigarettes 44%
Handbags, wallets, etc. 12%

Source: U.S. Customs and Border Protection

ENFORCEMENT AND PENALTIES   *ARRESTS:* **B+**   *SENTENCING:* **B-**

"Extinguishing" the nation's illegal cigarette trade is the combined responsibility of the ATF, U.S. Immigration and Customs Enforcement, and the U.S. Border Patrol. Their joint investigations are cumbersome and complex, typically taking twelve to twenty-four months to complete. With nearly three hundred ongoing inquiries, the investigative capacities of these agencies already have been severely stretched. A pending bill, known as the Prevent All Cigarette Trafficking Act, would reduce the numerical threshold for felony cigarette smuggling from sixty thousand cigarettes to ten thousand, extend the ATF's authority over federal cigarette laws, and allow the bureau to use proceeds of undercover stings to fund investigative outlays.

STRESSES AND HAZARDS

DANGERS: **B+** PRESSURES: **B+**

Anyone contemplating a career in tobacco distribution should acquaint him- or herself with the proven dangers of ingesting primary and secondhand tobacco smoke. Auto-based smugglers are cautioned that asset forfeiture provisions could result in the seizure of vehicles employed for work assignments. Chronically anxious individuals may fail to thrive in an environment where stings, moles, and searches are facts of everyday life.

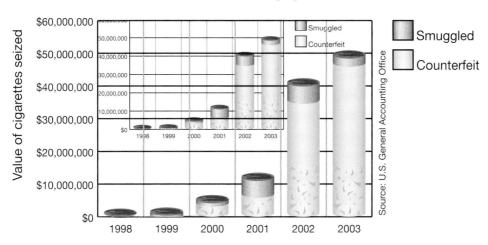

UP IN SMOKE
Seizures are surging

Value of cigarettes seized — 1998, 1999, 2000, 2001, 2002, 2003

Source: U.S. General Accounting Office

Legend: Smuggled, Counterfeit

WORK ENVIRONMENT

HOURS: **C+** COMFORT: **C+**

Over-the-road operators make frequent resupply runs, which can become tiring or tedious if the distribution point is far from the supply state. They often attend all-weather markets and interface extensively with end-consumers of illicitly carted "cancer sticks." Storefront-based sellers blend zero-tariff tobacco sales with their customary indoor duties. Advanced smugglers manage extensive workforces and liaison with far-flung warehousing, shipping, wholesale, and retail partners. Though effective smugglers delegate extensively, they travel ceaselessly to circumvent unsupervised slippage from their all-cash operations.

CRACK DEALER

DUTIES: Crack Dealers vend a solid, smokable form of cocaine, America's favorite narcotic stimulant. Most crack is refined domestically—by retailers or secondary cocaine wholesalers—through a simple stovetop *cooking* process. The resulting single-dose *rocks*—weighing 0.1 to 0.5 grams—are packaged in vials, glassine bags, or film canisters. Under ideal conditions one gram of high-grade *coke* yields 0.89 grams of quality crack.

The vast majority of world coca production is centered in the Andean *snowbelt*: Colombia, Bolivia, and Peru. While Colombian cartels and their Mexican smuggling affiliates dominate U.S. cocaine wholesaling, African-American and Hispanic youth gangs oversee most street-level retailing in major metropolitan markets. Haitian, Jamaican, Puerto Rican, Cuban, Mexican, Middle Eastern, Dominican, and Pacific Islander

syndicates are also significant urban players, whereas local independents provide service for rural crack enthusiasts.

In primary markets such as Manhattan and Chicago, more than 75 percent of all crack sales take place in outdoor, open-air markets, and almost 90 percent of all indoor sales take place in residences. Overall, *crackheads* are an impulsive, impatient lot, who shop very near home—on

CRACK MARKET ROUND UP

Per ounce pricing	National range	$500–$1,500
	Miami	550–850
	New York City	1,000–1,500
	Chicago	500–1,000
	Los Angeles	500–1,200
Per rock pricing	National range	$5–$100
	Miami	10–20
	New York City	7–10
	Chicago	10
	Los Angeles	20–40

Source: Drug Enforcement Administration

a 24/7/365 basis. Typical urban consumers make several purchases a week, from a pool of fourteen to twenty-five loosely known dealers. Between 7 percent and 10 percent frequent abandoned buildings for their resupply needs. Static outdoor markets are generally situated in economically enervated neighborhoods, near major transport hubs or arterial routes.

Though crack addicts are infamously insensitive to attention from law enforcement, street dealers leverage high-value local accomplices to minimize their personal exposure. *Lookouts* signal activity by police or rival belligerents via mobile electronics, hand signals, or verbal warnings. *Holders* conceal all or part of a dealer's drug *stash* between transactions. *Steerers* and *touts* make initial qualifying contacts with potential customers, and *middlemen* buffer the physical transfer of money and drugs. Most street vendors maintain limited daily inventories, owing to insufficient credit for large advance purchases, and fear of arrest with quantities triggering statutory minimum sentences. If demand is especially brisk, however, they may renew their on-hand supplies several times a day.

 COMPENSATION AND REWARDS   *EARNINGS:* **B**   *PERKS:* **B**

Per-rock prices range from $2 to $50, with most 0.1 to 0.2 gram rocks retailing for $10 to $20. Retail pricing for powdered cocaine (with a typical purity of 56 percent) averages about $80 per gram.

Estimates of overall domestic cocaine revenues vary so wildly that any single index should be treated with suspicion. The Office of National Drug Control pegs user expenditures at $36 billion per year.

THE MAN ON THE STREET
Corner dealers are the backbone of the crack workforce

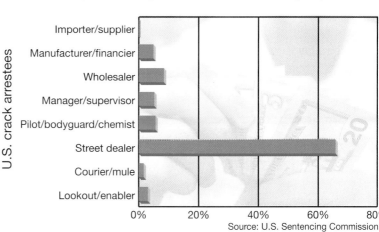

Primary work roles of U.S. crack arrestees

- Importer/supplier
- Manufacturer/financier
- Wholesaler
- Manager/supervisor
- Pilot/bodyguard/chemist
- Street dealer
- Courier/mule
- Lookout/enabler

0% 20% 40% 60% 80%

Source: U.S. Sentencing Commission

Individual compensation is another closely guarded trade secret. Many street dealers are, themselves, inveterate crack aficionados who deal part time to defray their "habitual" expenses. An academic study of D.C. cracksters found that part-time addict-sellers had median profits of just $721 per month, while their full-time counterparts netted $2,000 per month. The windfalls in this field go to managers and supervisors (composing roughly 6 percent of the crack workforce) and high-level importers, suppliers, organizers, leaders, and wholesalers (15 percent).

ENFORCEMENT AND PENALTIES   ARRESTS: **A-**   SENTENCING: **C-**

All forms of cocaine produce identical physiological and psychotropic effects. However, since 1986, possession of just five grams of crack has triggered a five-year minimum penalty, whereas five hundred grams of powdered cocaine are required to trigger the same statutory minimum. Defendants convicted of trafficking less than twenty-five grams of powder average 13.6 months jail time; their crack-loving cousins, on the other hand, average 64.8 months.

In fiscal 2003, federal agencies seized 245,499 pounds of cocaine-based confections. National antidrug expenditures now exceed $12 billion per year.

STRESSES AND HAZARDS   DANGERS: **D+**   PRESSURES: **C-**

PEACE!
Gunplay is rarer among today's young crack workers

Weapon on person 16%
Weapon deployed 2%
Weapon nearby 8%
No weapon 74%

Source: U.S. Sentencing Commission

A large percentage of crack merchants make the age-old error of getting high on their own supplies. Risks include elevated temperature, heart rate, and blood pressure, tremors, vertigo, paranoia, and sudden death. Although the use of weapons in crack transactions has declined tremendously, about 25 percent of crack-related arrests still feature small arms, and about 3 percent involve one or more violent deaths. Robberies by customers, rivals, and opportunistic bandits have declined, but disturbing anecdotal evidence suggests that robberies and shakedowns by corrupt law enforcers (see Crooked Cop, page 54) are on the upslope.

WORK ENVIRONMENT

HOURS: C+   COMFORT: C-

At their all-weather outdoor posts, intrepid dealers brave the full gamut of temperature extremes, contending with street noise, car emissions, litter, and vermin. Only 40 percent of street-level arrestees are believed to sell crack daily, so part-timers actually account for the bulk of sales activity.

Apprehended retail dealers average about fifteen sales per day. Almost 95 percent are U.S. citizens (compared with 64 percent for powder cocaine), 94 percent are male, and 85 percent are black. Today's average dealer is twenty-nine years old. In 1995, 14 percent of crack offenses involved minors; by 2000, youth participation had fallen to 4.2 percent.

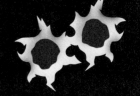

CROOKED COP

RANK: 2 out of 50   **AVERAGE GRADE:** B-

DUTIES: Crooked Cops abuse their prerogatives as peace officers for personal gain and professional vainglory. Traditional police corruption involves mutually beneficial collusion between officers and offenders. Under *the fix*, corrupted cops tender onetime assistance in undermining individual criminal indictments or investigations. Officers *on the take* provide longer-term informational, protective, and advocacy services to illicit tradesmen and organizations. Occasionally, their service offerings extend to the commission of major crimes on behalf of criminal clientele. Throughout the 1980s, Brooklyn crooked cops Louis Eppolito and Stephen Caracappa collected Mafia stipends of up to $4,000 a month for services that included kidnapping, murder, money laundering, and daily intelligence briefings. After retirement, Mr. Eppolito pursued opportunities in method acting, portraying wiseguys, drug dealers, and thugs in nearly a dozen movies, including *Goodfellas*.

The dynamics of police misconduct changed dramatically with the rise of the cocaine economy. In 1974, the NYPD's Knapp Commission reported that the dominant mode of corruption involved bribes collected for overlooking ongoing illegal activities, such as bookmaking. By 1995, 57 percent of all police corruption convictions involved active commission of drug-related crimes. Popular extracurricular activities among today's crooked cops include theft of money and merchandise from drug dealers,

NOTHING BOOSTS A CRIMINAL CAREER LIKE A BADGE!
Source: Los Angeles Police Department

SILENCE IS GOLDEN
Police attitudes toward abuse of authority

Attitude	Strongly agree	Agree	Disagree	Strongly disagree
"The code of silence is an essential part of the mutual trust necessary to good policing."	1.2%	15.7%	65.6%	17.5%
"Whistle-blowing is not worth it."	3.1%	21.8%	63.5%	11.7%
"An officer who reports another officer's misconduct is likely to be given the cold shoulder by his or her fellow officers."	11.0%	56.4%	30.9%	1.8%
"It is not unusual for a police officer to turn a blind eye to improper conduct by other officers."	1.8%	50.6%	43.3%	4.4%
"Police officers always report serious criminal violations involving abuse of authority by fellow officers."	2.8%	36.2%	58.5%	2.5%

Source: National Institute of Justice, *Police Attitudes Toward Abuse of Authority*

sales of stolen drugs, framing of rival dealers, protection of favored drug operations, and submission of false crime reports.

Like their unsullied counterparts, crooked cops rely heavily on teamwork. Most drug-related police corruption cases involve from nine to thirty officers working together in structures reminiscent of traditional street *crews*. A 1994 report by the Mollen Crime Commission documents a national pattern of "small, loyal, flexible, fast moving and often hard-hitting" groups of entrepreneurial, rogue enforcers. Their productivity can be impressive. In 1994, an FBI sting resulted in the conviction

of twenty-seven members of an elite Los Angeles antinarcotics unit for skimming confiscated drug monies. One convicted L.A. County sheriff's deputy testified that the group netted $60 million over a two-year period.

Los Angeles set the gold standard for U.S. police corruption with the 1998 arrest of Rafael Perez, a decorated member of the Rampart police division's CRASH (Community Resources Against Street Hoodlums) antigang unit. When Perez was "made" for removing six pounds of cocaine evidence from the LAPD property room, he agreed to give testimony that would eventually implicate nearly seventy brother officers in theft, drug dealing, extortion, murder, false testimony, and bank robbery. David Mack, one of Perez's former partners, eventually was convicted of stealing $722,000 from an L.A. branch of the Bank of America. Mack—an associate of the Piru Blood gang—was also a suspect in the 1997 murder of East Coast rap star Biggie Smalls, a.k.a. the Notorious B.I.G. Over 3,200 arrests by Rampart officers were tainted by the scandal, and settlement costs for roughly 140 civil suits could ultimately exceed $125 million.

COMPENSATION AND REWARDS   *EARNINGS:* **B+**   *PERKS:* **B**

Crooked cops participate in a broad spectrum of misdeeds at a variety of pay grades. Borderline-corrupt activities like planting or augmenting evidence (*flaking* or *padding*, respectively) may be undertaken gratis for career advancement, or out of professional zeal. Officers who accept gifts or small bribes for fixing parking tickets and other minor offenses—*grass feeders*—typically supplement their annual salaries by less than a few thousand dollars.

At the high end of the market, potential gains can be impressive. Rene De La Cova, a DEA supervisor who took custody of Panamanian strongman Manuel A. Noriega in 1989, single-handedly stole $760,000 in laundered drug profits. Veteran immigration officer Richard Lawrence Pineda took home $350,000 in bribes for allowing twenty-five illegal immigrants and 3,550 pounds of marijuana to pass through his inspection lane at the San Ysidro Port of Entry over a twelve-month period.

THE RISE OF THE NINETIES "DRUG COP"
Renowned gangbanger/cop David Mack faces the music after stealing $720,000

Fiscal year	FBI corruption cases opened	Percentage drug-related
1993	186	33
1994	185	46
1995	210	37
1996	183	46
1997	190	48

Source: FBI

ENFORCEMENT AND PENALTIES — ARRESTS: **B**   SENTENCING: **B-**

The Civil Rights Division of the U.S. Department of Justice (DOJ) has been responsible for the federal prosecution of police misconduct since its inception in 1957. This division is responsible for both criminal damnation and civil litigation against crooked cops and complicit departments. Although the DOJ employs 9,168 attorneys, only twenty full-timers currently are assigned to criminal misconduct cases. Despite the apparent strength of many cases brought by the Criminal Division, juries are often sympathetic toward officers and suspicious of their alleged victims, so conviction rates are leniently low. The leaders of a notorious group of rogue Oakland, California, cops known as "the Riders" went free in September 2005, after a yearlong trial that prosecutors had promised would be open-and-shut. Still, the number of law enforcement officers in prison increased more than fivefold between 1994 and 1998—from 107 to 548.

STRESSES AND HAZARDS — DANGERS: **C-**   PRESSURES: **C-**

Although the police "code of silence" is legendary, the targets of recent high-profile investigations have shown disquieting predispositions to "rat out" fellow officers in exchange for plea bargains. Outside moles can also be a serious concern. Robbing major gangs and narcotics retailers is hazardous duty, and crooked cops must be on guard against retaliatory attacks and territorial challenges. Officer-on-officer violence is also quite common.

Disgraced cops can be their own worst enemies. In 2000, a Georgia sheriff avoided arrest for conspiracy to cultivate more than one thousand pounds of cannabis by shooting himself.

Corrupt cops work double duty, inter-mixing unsanctioned duties with official ones, or undertaking after-hours moon-lighting shifts. Most enter law enforce-ment with the intention of serving so-ciety but are eventually desensitized by widespread "shortcuts" in investigative procedure and ultimately tempted into overtly criminal acts. Others choose en-forcement careers at the behest of crimi-nal organizations to which they owe pre-vious allegiance. For instance, 53 percent of gangbangers (see Gangbanger, page 81) surveyed by the National Gang Crime Research Center report that their gang has active members working as moles within the criminal justice system.

CURRENCY COUNTERFEITER

RANK: 10 out of 50   **AVERAGE GRADE:** B

DUTIES: Currency counterfeiters craft realistic facsimiles of United States legal tender or alter existing notes to increase their apparent face value—with the ultimate aim of circulating their negotiable work products. Counterfeiting is a time-honored American occupation whose popularity predates the formation of our Union. Our thrifty forefathers indiscriminately counterfeited Native Americans' wampum, ultimately destabilizing their bead-based economy. By the time of the Civil War, one-third of all circulating U.S. currency was counterfeit. In 1865, Abraham Lincoln created the Secret Service to combat the mounting funny-money menace. In 2003, the Secret Service was rolled into the Department of Homeland Security in supposed recognition of the singular import of securing the national money supply.

Traditionally, counterfeiters have been highly trained professionals who cultivated arcane skills in engraving, stencil-making, and photolithography through work in legitimate print shops or via apprenticeship with established practitioners. The tools of

Security thread — Color-shifting ink

Watermark

CAN YOU PASS THE TREASURY CHALLENGE?

the *pen-and-ink men's* trade—plates, presses, and process cameras—were cumbersome and capital-intensive. Today, desktop counterfeiters can mint passable *P-notes* (short for "printer notes") with an investment of less than $1,000 and rudimentary training in graphic software. The ubiquitous availability of inexpensive, high-quality scanners, inkjet printers, and color copiers has revolutionized American counterfeiting. In 1990, less than 1 percent of all *queer* passed in the United States was produced with the assistance of computers. By 2004 that figure had swelled to 46 percent.

Nearly anyone, it seems, can access the technology and information needed to enter this exciting field. In 2002, four students from the tiny town of Tallapoosa, Georgia, were nabbed for desktop publishing more than two hundred negotiable notes in their high school drafting class. Since then, counterfeit currency has been popping up at school lunchrooms across America. In the late 1990s, Envisions Corporation ran an ad proudly proclaiming: "No other scanner can scan a hundred bucks and capture the hidden detail as well as ours." Many dabblers, first-timers, and technophobes forgo computers in favor of no-fuss color copiers.

Though plain paper stock may suffice for defeating change machines, papers with significant rag content are used to lend a more realistic "money feel." A mixture of

THE FUZZ FACTOR
The mustachioed mugs of the Secret Service's most wanted counterfeiters

Funny money hall of famer			
Birth Name	Omar Horacio Cabral	Tghassan Nadem Al Moutragi	Jimmy Campodomico
a.k.a.	Acosta, Nestor Ricardo	Matragi, Matrajie	Campodomico, Jimmy Fernando
Height	5'10"	5'8"	5'9"
D.O.B.	5/21/1955	7/21/44	1/07/58

Source: U.S. Secret Service

hot water, tea, and food coloring can be used to cultivate a green, weathered tone. For the ultimate in realism, perfectionists employ the "washing" technique: bleaching genuine dollar bills in a conventional washing machine, blowing the bills dry, then printing bogus denominations on the genuine paper.

The cruder *paste-up* or *raising* technique involves grafting new numerals onto the corners of a genuine bill to increase its apparent denomination. Typically, ones are upgraded to twenties. Overall, the twenty is the most commonly domestically duplicated note, whereas hundreds are most popular abroad.

As small-scale P-note attacks by opportunistic amateurs have become the industry norm, the Secret Service's esti-mated domestic seizure rate has fallen from 70 percent in 1995 to less than 20 percent in 2004. The U.S. seized approximately $10.7 million in counterfeit currency in 2003, but the Secret Service estimates at least $37 million was successfully passed. Worldwide, counterfeiters are thought to have printed at least $180 million in bogus money in 2003. More than $31 million was seized in Colombia alone.

Some *governments* are suspected of sponsoring the large-scale manufacture of high-quality dollar counterfeits. A virtually undetectable species of hundred-dollar bills bearing the series number C-14342 (dubbed the "superdollar") is believed to be printed in the North Korean city of Pyeongseong, on the same sort of intaglio press employed by the U.S. Treasury.

COMPENSATION AND REWARDS   *EARNINGS:* **A-**   *PERKS:* **B**

Entering the rewarding field of counterfeiting is like having a license to print your own money! Take Brooklyn's tight-knit Taftsious family. After running *up* several thousand dollars in gambling debts, fifty-three-year-old Bardul Taftsious enlisted his tech-savvy son to run *off* over $1.2 million in hundred-dollar bills on a printer the pair purchased for $9,000. Taftsious's wife, daughter, and eighty-year-old mother were also allegedly enlisted for a family gambling/

COUNTERFEITING IS LIKE HAVING A LICENSE TO PRINT YOUR OWN MONEY!
Source: U.S. Secret Service

distribution junket to Atlantic City.

In another impressive achievement by a New York family, a Uzbekistan national and his two sons passed $9.5 million in bogus bills over six years. The three operated a Queens, New York, video store.

In one of the largest known copier-based cases, Ricky Scott Nelson and five other Philadelphia men used a plain-Jane office machine to run off at least $800,000 in phony hundreds. So, though you may just be looking for a little extra lunch money now, the sky's the limit in *your* counterfeiting future.

ENFORCEMENT AND PENALTIES   *ARRESTS:* **C**   *SENTENCING:* **C+**

Counterfeiting is a full-fledged federal offense carrying sentences up to fifteen years and fines up to $5,000. The conviction rate for apprehended offenders is almost 99 percent. Roughly 17 percent of P-note seizures involve juveniles. Youths without previous criminal experience usually receive probation and are forced to make restitution and surrender their computer equipment.

Currently there are no mandatory minimum sentencing restrictions in place for this occupation, so many veteran criminals (particularly drug dealers) view it as a lower-risk alternative to their former trades. Although the ranks of the Secret Service have swelled to more than 6,100 and the agency has launched electronic crime task forces in twelve states and seventeen foreign nations, seizure rates continue their steady decline.

STRESSES AND HAZARDS   *DANGERS:* **B**   *PRESSURES:* **B-**

The U.S. Treasury has established a long-term goal of introducing new currency designs every seven years, so career counterfeiters should resign themselves to periodic retooling and retraining. Although anticounterfeiting currency features such as microprinted security threads, color-shifting inks, and watermarks are well-known challenges, the rapid evolution of exotic detection techniques may be stressful to those passing product in the field. Advances in "printer forensics" techniques, which can track documents back to their printers of origin, are particularly worrisome. In general, though, overconfidence may be the counterfeiter's greatest enemy.

Though most passers of counterfeit coinage select low-scrutiny distribution points (such as nightclubs or yard sales) and prepare elaborate cover stories in case of detection, others rely far too heavily on the gullibility of their victims. The poster person for this is Alice Pike, who attempted to purchase $1,650 worth of goods from her local Wal-Mart with a million-dollar bill. The Treasury Department has never minted a note of this grand denomination, and Wal-Mart did not have enough change on hand, so her deception was quickly detected.

WORK ENVIRONMENT

HOURS: B+   COMFORT: B

Desktop-based operations are highly portable and can be situated in a variety of hospitable locales. Top professionals still favor large commercial presses, which can present substantial noise hazards and may involve a range of noxious chemicals.

Although this is a year-round occupation, counterfeiting activity spikes during the holiday season as dabblers run off a few bills to pay for gifts and professionals target overworked, distracted tellers. Counterfeiters can produce large inventories of paper in very limited work hours, but industry best-practices suggest a much more substantial time commitment to achieve judicious, widely dispersed distribution.

Opportunities for on-the-job dating are quite rare, as the vast majority of counterfeiters are male.

DRUG COUNTERFEITER

RANK: 1 out of 50   **AVERAGE GRADE:** B+

DUTIES: Drug counterfeiters knowingly mislabel curative compounds to conceal their source, chemical composition, dosage, or date of manufacture. Counterfeiters package, market, distribute, and occasionally manufacture branded and generic products. Their offerings include look-alikes with insufficient or imaginary active ingredients, drugs banned or unrecognized by the FDA, medications with injurious or inert ingredients, generic drugs sold as their branded equivalents, and out-of-date goods.

In 2003, the World Health Organization estimated global sales of phony pharmaceuticals at over $35 billion. In the same year, the FDA initiated fifty-eight counterfeit drug investigations in the United States—a nearly tenfold increase over the year 2000. In Nigeria and Pakistan, counterfeit drugs are thought to account for 40 percent to 50 percent of the entire market. Although the prevalence of counterfeit drugs in the United States is believed to be less than 1 percent of the total supply, Internet-based drug sales and relentless price increases for branded drugs are fueling an unprecedented boom in the U.S. counterfeit sector.

Ninety percent of U.S. pharmaceutical distribution is administered by three super-suppliers. The remaining 10 percent of the pie is split among a shadowy network of sixteen thousand secondary wholesalers, who buy up odd lots and excess inventories for resale at sharp discounts. A single drug may pass through a dozen wholesalers in half a dozen states before reaching an actual patient. Although a

YOU CAN'T ALWAYS FAKE IT IN THE BEDROOM
Bogus Viagra can look frighteningly real!
Source: U.S. Immigration and Customs Enforcement

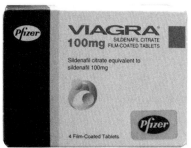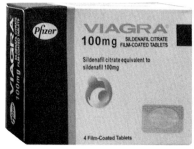

PHARMACEUTICAL FOCUS

VIAGRA AND CIALIS—MyRxForLess, a fraudulent Internet pharmacy run by a San Diego couple, claimed its prescriptions were filled in association with a reputable Mexican pharmacy. Instead, they employed a variety of street characters to purchase questionable concoctions in Mexico and drop-ship them to stateside customers. They also commissioned monthly shipments of fake Viagra and Cialis from a San Diego entrepreneur with his own makeshift laboratory. According to the U.S. Attorney's Office, MyRxForLess sold up to $2.5 million worth of suspect products over two years. The court recovered just $150,000 from the couple, and sentenced the husband to two years' custody and the wife to six months.

LIPITOR—Domingo Gonzalez of Hialeah, Florida, admitted to selling more than 4 million counterfeit tablets of the anticholesterol drug Lipitor between December 2002 and March 2003. Gonzalez and coconspirators bought genuine Lipitor intended for South American distribution and illegally diverted it into the United States. Buoyed by import profits, the group shipped chemicals and equipment to Costa Rica and Honduras to manufacture home-brewed Lipitor. A Kansas City distributor eventually paid $12.8 million for the tablets, claiming ignorance of their phony pedigree.

BOTOX—Toxin Research International (TRI) advertised its version of botulinum toxin as a cheaper alternative to Botox. The firm offered its unapproved "Botox equivalent" for less than $300 a dose, versus $560 for FDA-approved Botox. TRI allegedly purchased the concoction for $9.67 per five-dose vial. Two hundred and nineteen doctors purchased the cut-rate wrinkle cure. One of those doctors and three patients were subsequently hospitalized with botulism, a potentially fatal condition that paralyzes muscles. All four survived but suffered serious complications. The FDA ordered TRI to stop distribution and indicted the company's key officers.

CONTRACEPTIVE PATCHES—The FDA and Johnson & Johnson recently warned the public that an Internet pharmacy operated by American Style Products of New Delhi, India, was vending counterfeit contraceptive patches that contain no active ingredients. The counterfeits were promoted as Ortho Evra transdermal patches, which are FDA approved for birth control.

1988 law requires wholesalers to maintain a "paper pedigree" of a drug's journey from manufacturer to end-dispenser, lobbying groups convinced the FDA that enforcement of this rule would be ineffective and prohibitively costly. Thus, the conventional U.S. distribution system provides a plethora of virtually untraceable opportunities for enterprising wholesalers to introduce high-profit counterfeit items.

The most concentrated form of the anemia drug Epogen (epoetin alfa) retails for $495 a vial. In 2002, a Florida-based group of counterfeiters reaped an estimated $28 million profit from a shipment of eleven thousand boxes of counterfeit Epogen and Procrit (another epoetin alfa product), consisting almost entirely of Miami tap water. Florida, in fact, leads the nation in drug counterfeiting, with fifty wholesalers under criminal investigation in 2005 and over $15 million in seizures of bogus drugs.

SUSCEPTIBLE SUBSTANCES

Ambien®	Crixivan®	Diflucan®
Epogen®	Gamimune®	Immune globulin
Lipitor®	Neupogen®	Procrit®
Retrovir®	Serostim®	Trizivir®
Venoglobulin®	Viagra®	Zocor®

Source: FDA

In addition to broad-based opportunities in conventional wholesaling, the Internet has matured into an extraordinarily efficient channel for advertising and distributing substandard substances directly to retail customers. Pfizer and Microsoft recently brought joint suit against two international Viagra-counterfeiting rings that drove swarms of customers to shady offshore pharmacy sites by sending hundreds of millions of spam messages to users of Microsoft's Hotmail e-mail service. Operation Cyber Chase, a recent DEA crackdown on Internet-based sales of controlled substances, netted twenty arrests in five states, Costa Rica, and India. The DEA alleges that two Indian nationals masterminded an international operation that vended 2.5 million doses of Indian-manufactured steroids, narcotics, and amphetamines per month to Web-based American customers. In a recent spot check of "generic" Viagra and Lipitor available on the Internet, the FDA concluded that not a single pill met U.S. manufacturing standards. On average, the "generic" medicines included only 65 percent and 81 percent, respectively, of the active ingredients listed on their labels. Internet-vended so-called Ambien equivalents, on the other hand, were often as much as twice as strong as their labels indicated.

EARNINGS: A-   PERKS: C

Potential gains in this emerging occupation can be enormous. David Srulevitch, convicted of manufacturing 700,000 counterfeit Viagra tablets at an improvised lab in Azusa, California, shared $5.8 million in revenues with his Chinese code-fendant. Another Californian, Mark Kolowich of San Diego, convicted of manufacturing unauthorized "generic" Viagra, Levitra, and Cialis, admitted to illicit sales of almost $7 million between 1999 and 2004.

The secondary pharmaceutical wholesale market is a $126 billion behemoth, presenting outstanding opportunities for ethically flexible individuals and organizations. Jemco, a Florida-based purveyor of adulterated Epogen, had annual sales of nearly $55 million. After the scrap-

UNDER A MICROSCOPE
The FDA takes an unhealthy interest in drug counterfeiting

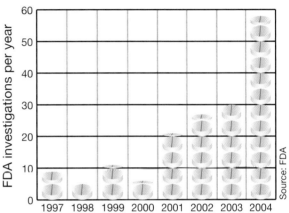

Source: FDA

py company's Florida wholesale license was revoked, Jemco promptly resumed operation in Yadkinville, North Carolina, under a new name, Medi-Plus International.

ENFORCEMENT AND PENALTIES   *ARRESTS:* **B+**   *SENTENCING:* **A-**

In most cases, counterfeit drug infractions are treated as misdemeanor violations of intellectual property and truth-in-labeling statutes. Forty-nine percent of the arrests made in 2003 for counterfeit, stolen, or di-

verted drugs occurred at the point of sale. The 361 arrests made in 2003 represented a fourfold increase over 2002. The total value of seized drugs rose to $192 million averaging nearly $3 million per seizure.

STRESSES AND HAZARDS

DANGERS: **B+**   PRESSURES: **B+**

The well-publicized successes of early entrants in this field have attracted the attention of ruthless, seasoned competitors. "This is where the dollars are," says FDA Commissioner Mark McClellan. "This is where organized crime is being attracted." In addition to increasingly hard-boiled competition, drug counterfeiters face worrisome new legislative challenges. The Counterfeit Drug Enforcement Act of 2005, sponsored by Congressman Steven Israel (D–New York), would increase maximum penalties to life in prison, require manufacturers to alert the FDA of a counterfeited drug within two days, and authorize $60 million annually for spot-checking counterfeits. Additionally, the country's second-largest drug distributor, CVS Corporation, has announced that it will no longer deal with secondary providers, fueling substantial anxiety and uncertainty in the wholesale sector.

WORK ENVIRONMENT

HOURS: **B-**   COMFORT: **C+**

Drug counterfeiters travel frequently to coordinate with manufacturing partners, establish distribution channels, and purchase ingredients or finished concoctions. Workplace conditions vary tremendously. Some drug counterfeiters work in extremely sophisticated, temperature-controlled laboratories and plants, while others endure long hours in the crudest of improvised repackaging facilities. Although mavericks and independents have enjoyed considerable success in this occupation, today's rapidly globalizing standout operations emphasize team coordination, delegation, and specialized division of labor.

FENCE

DUTIES: Fences commission thefts and buy stolen goods from shoplifters, burglars, pickpockets, muggers, auto thieves, art thieves, jewel thieves, and amateur abettors. They refurbish and repackage purloined properties and vend goods to retail and wholesale customers. Fences provide reliable, liquid markets for property theft professionals, and repurpose the pilferage of truck drivers, warehouse workers, security guards, salespeople, and other occupational opportunists. In one recent market survey, 57 percent of burglars reported regular commerce with fences, 36 percent sold directly to businesses, and 45 percent "laid off" to pawnshops and second-hand dealers.

Most fences operate legitimate *front* businesses in conjunction with their extracurricular market activities—up to 74 percent manage "straight" concerns, and as many as 64 percent own them. High cash-flow operations are particularly suited to supporting and disguising capital-intensive fencing transactions. Jewelry, gem, and convenience shops; auction houses; junk and scrap yards, pawnshops, and flea market stands are all industry favorites.

While traditional fences earn handsome livings vending used items liberated from residential and commercial properties, today's leading practitioners partner with Organizer Retail Theft (ORT) rings to wrest pristine, unused goods from retail outlets, warehouses, and other weak links in the supply chain. The FBI estimates that ORT is a $32 billion to $35 billion

Advil 8 ct. (yellow or blue)	Closed on	25¢	
Advil 24 ct. (yellow or blue)		50¢	
Advil 50 ct. (yellow or blue)	Sunday	$1.25	
Advil 100 ct. (yellow or blue)		$2.00	Open
Advil 165 ct. (yellow or blue)		$3.00	
Advil 250 ct. (yellow or blue)		$3.50	
Advil Cold or Sinus - 24 ct.		$1.00	Monday
Advil Cold or Sinus - 50 ct.		$1.50	
Afrin - 24 ct.		25¢	Thurs.
Anacin - 24 ct.		50¢	
Anacin - 50 ct. and 80 ct.		$1.00	Saturday
Anacin - 100 ct.		1.50	
Anacin - 200 ct.		2.00	1.00 P.
Anacin - 300 ct.		3.00	
Bayer - 24 ct.		50¢	
Bayer - 50 ct.		75¢	M
Bayer - 100 ct.		1.50	

ARE YOU THE ORGANIZED TYPE?
A "booster's" shopping list, created by a meticulous street fence.
Source: Food Marketing Institute, "A Report on Organized Retail Theft"

domestic industry. In most cases, *street fences* recruit, fund, and manage groups of professional *boosters*, training them to steal high-demand everyday products. Street fences typically buy directly from fifteen to thirty boosters, and settle debts in cash or drugs. They devote extreme effort to *cleaning* stolen goods (removing price and surveillance tags) and *freshening* them (applying counterfeit UPC codes with extended shelf dates) as well. Damaged or out-of-date products are consigned to flea markets, liquidators, or discounters. Prim, saleable goods are boxed, shrink-wrapped, and wholesaled to upper-level fences or directly to enterprise-scale *repackers*.

Upper-level retail fences deal in stolen cargo loads, illegally diverted brand lines, and bulk spoils of credit card scams and *bust-out* extortions. Typically, they interoperate with repackagers, corrupt wholesalers, and price-sensitive retailers to service an increasingly farflung base of end-consumers.

A Chicago-based ring that harvested goods from four states grossed over $18 million in one year by selling *directly* to the public, out of a single West Side grocery shop. The direct-to-consumer market is immature but full of potential. Only 13 percent of Americans admit to having purchased stolen goods, and only about 36 percent have been offered them.

COMPENSATION AND REWARDS EARNINGS: B+ PERKS: B+

IT FELL OFF THE TRUCK!

Assorted items recovered during Operation Enterprise, a 2004 sting that cost a Genovese family fencing ring $1 million

Stolen item	Market Value
294 boxes of thermometers	$89,000
115 hospital beds 119 cartons of nebulizers	$107,000
5,000 units of L'Oréal Line Eraser	$77,000
50,000 units of Bath Body nail polish	$500,000
6 pallets (5,000 units) GX jeans	$35,500
John Deere skid steer	$27,000
Forklift and electrical equipment	$55,000
Imported Italian marble	$37,000
Backhoe	$84,000
Car parts	$75,000

Source: U.S. Department of Justice

Theft of property is a mainstay of the underground economy, amounting to as much as 2 percent of our gross national product. Fences typically pay out 10 percent to 50 percent of an item's retail value, and mark up their merchandise by at least 50 percent. Slow-moving and unusually *hot* items command mere pennies on the dollar. Jewelry is often fenced at scrap rates.

Top retail fences have posted spectacular performance numbers in recent quarters. Phoenix's Jamal Trading Company netted $11 million in profits from stolen baby formula in just two years. High-end specialists selling out of their own domiciles can also do quite splendidly. A Miami fence, operating from his living room, cleared over $500,000 a year selling stolen designer suits to business honchos and small-time politicians.

ENFORCEMENT AND PENALTIES — ARRESTS: B SENTENCING: C

Clearance rates for property offenses remain near historic lows, and career fences rarely face arrest. Fencing is generally a low priority for overwrought urban enforcers, and cash-strapped constables can often be plied with small tributes in cash or merchandise. Organized retail theft, however, has caught the attention of the FBI. Willful disposition of more than $5,000 in ill-gathered goods is a federal felony, carrying ten years' bad luck. Major rings have also proven vulnerable to pesky racketeering and money laundering indictments.

STRESSES AND HAZARDS — DANGERS: B PRESSURES: C

Like all traders, fences wither or grow with their ability to balance supply and demand. If they misjudge the mood of the market, they may be forced to *sit on* hot inventory for an uncomfortable interlude. One pair of fences, recently decommissioned by the FBI, were found sitting atop nearly $2 million in unsold overstock.

As professional middlemen, fences are the public face of property crime, and long-term visibility can prove perilous. Snitches, moles, and stings are all ongoing causes for concern.

The great majority of known fences are middle-aged men (46.5 years on average), whereas their thieving accomplices average a wee twenty-eight years. Receivers of stolen goods—customers—are also a youthful and manly lot. Customers ages sixteen to twenty-four are four times more likely to buy than are those ages thirty-six to sixty. Men outspend women by more than two to one.

Fences can fly solo or front large organizations. Mom-and-pop storefront practices offer limited upside, but the stability and simplicity of a grassroots operation can be attractive. Upper-level fencing shops, repackaging houses, and corrupt wholesale distributorships offer a faster-paced, structured workday, significant advancement opportunities, and immersive indoctrination in industry best practices.

As usual, the Internet stands ready to "change everything." In 2004, a San Diego cop and his wife were accused of auctioning nearly $2 million in burglarized goods on eBay. The pair had been quietly selling eight hundred to one thousand items per month.

WAYNE J E BROWN
PO BOX 303
YORBA LINDA CA 92885-0303

WAYNE J E BROWN
PO BOX 303
YORBA LINDA CA 92885-0303

FIREARMS
TRAFFICKER

DUTIES: Firearms Traffickers divert new or secondhand guns from licensed owners and sanctioned sellers into the remunerative illegal resale market. Although corrupt federally licensed firearms dealers were implicated in fewer than 10 percent of recent trafficking investigations, these "power-sellers" account for nearly half of all guns illegally trafficked. The average crooked gun dealer misappropriates 350 guns in his moonlighting career: via sales to prohibited individuals (felons, mental patients, etc.), falsified recordkeeping entries, or illegal interstate transfers.

Gun shows and flea markets provide large-scale opportunities for unregulated transfers of illegal firearms by licensed and unlicensed traffickers. A useful loophole in federal law permits traffickers to vend weapons from their "personal collections" without subjecting privacy-loving purchasers to pesky background checks. Self-styled, undocumented dealers compose roughly one-fifth of the nation's illicit market for small arms, distributing over 20,000 guns per year. *Straw purchasers*—who leverage their own relatively clean legal pedigrees to secure guns for shadier clients and associates—are the most visible faces of American firearms trafficking. They are involved in almost half of all annual illegal transfers, vending an average of thirty-seven weapons per straw purchaser, for an estimated twenty-six thousand firearms a year.

The more than 300,000 U.S. firearms filched annually from licensed dealers, pawnbrokers, manufacturers, wholesalers, shippers, and individual owners compose a robust secondary supply channel for well-connected traffickers. Although deal-

HOT ROD HEAVEN
Crime guns come in many handy shapes and sizes
Source: FBI

ers are required to report all thefts to the Bureau of Alcohol, Tobacco, Firearms, and Explosives (ATF), federal law does not require individual firearms owners to report thefts or losses.

Traffickers furnish gangs and individual violent offenders with indispensable tools of their trades. In a recent national survey of jailed felons, 45 percent of respondents said they obtained their guns through trafficking middlemen. Sixty percent of those boasting gang affiliations obtained their most recent weapon through illegal means,

55 percent stated it was "easy" to acquire firearms illegally, and 34 percent believed they could get a serviceable gun in under a week. Traffickers also address substantial demand from the youth sector. In a 1996 survey of Los Angeles high school students, 25 percent believed they could obtain a gun for less than $50.

Firearms Traffickers cultivate relationships with felons from many disciplines, so it is little surprise that a quarter of all recently convicted traffickers were themselves previously convicted of other felonies.

COMPENSATION AND REWARDS — EARNINGS: **C+** PERKS: **D+**

The most industrious solo practitioners in this field vend impressive volumes of goods at high margin. Sean Twomey—a federal firearms licensee who forged a new license when his old one was revoked—sold more than 1,100 big-ticket

SHOOTING BLANKS
Gun-assisted crime has plummeted since the '90s crack boom

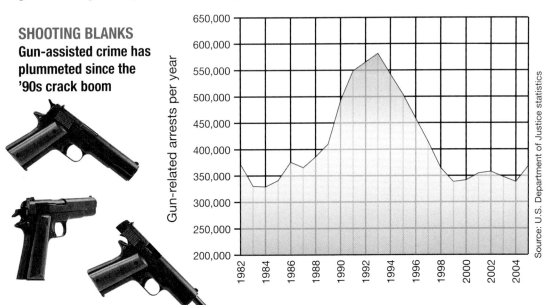

Gun-related arrests per year

650,000
600,000
550,000
500,000
450,000
400,000
350,000
300,000
250,000
200,000

1982 1984 1986 1988 1990 1992 1994 1996 1998 2000 2002 2004

Source: U.S. Department of Justice statistics

guns in the San Francisco Bay Area in less than two years. Twomey's "crime guns" were later traced to wide variety of West Coast infractions including murder, robbery, and drug dealing. Per-gun profits vary wildly. Independent straw purchasers often pass on their weapons to gang associates, friends, or family at purchase cost. Urban specialists may demand premiums of more than 500 percent for silenced and automatic wares.

ENFORCEMENT AND PENALTIES   *ARRESTS:* **B+**   *SENTENCING:* **C**

Almost 90 percent of all federal gun crime indictments center on possession of legal firearms by felons or the use of a firearm to abet felonies. Meanwhile, twenty other major federal gun laws are left obligingly underenforced. In 2003, the ATF inspected just 4.5 percent of all firearms licensees. Although they found a hardy 149,396 violations, they saw fit to revoke an anemic 54 licenses. The Justice Department seems similarly trade-friendly. In the same year, it tried just 188 trafficking cases, 532 cases of lying on a background check, and 32 cases against corrupt dealers nationwide. Out of the 4,923 mischievous Marylanders who lied on their background check, only 14 were prosecuted. The unlucky federally interdicted few, however, face 97 percent conviction rates and average sentences of nine years.

POPULAR USES FOR TRAFFICKED GUNS

Crime	Percent of total
Drug offense	27.5
Assault	25.2
Homicide	17.4
Robbery	16.5
Property crime	15.0
Juvenile possession	14.1
Sexual assault/rape	1.9
Other crime	5.4

Source: ATF, *Following the Gun*

STRESSES AND HAZARDS

Traffickers interface with the most volatile members of the underworld and conventional society. Almost 27 percent of all U.S. homicides, robberies, and aggravated assaults in 2003 were facilitated with a firearm. On-duty traffickers fall frequent victim to the crimes and criminals they abet.

Traffickers also face long-term economic uncertainty. Domestic production and sales of handguns have paralleled the historic downtrends in American crime. Pistol production is off more than 50 percent since 1992, and the number of federally licensed dealers has fallen from over 200,000 to 74,220. Additionally, after years of precipitous decline, national violent-crime rates have shown recent signs of stabilizing.

WORK ENVIRONMENT

Youths (ages eighteen to twenty-four) and juveniles (seventeen and under) participate in more than 40 percent of U.S. firearms trafficking activity. Though most involved youngsters are direct or straw purchasers, an increasing number are taking advantage of opportunities in gun theft and local distribution. Although this is a predominantly male occupation, college-age women are in high demand as presentable straw purchasers.

The highest-volume traffickers illicitly disperse crime guns from the comfort of their licensed establishments; journeymen vendors, on the other hand, frequently travel to out-of-state gun shows and gang strongholds. Almost half of ATF investigations involve interstate trafficking, whereas 11 percent center on international gun migrations.

FORGER

DUTIES: Forgers fabricate and vend artistic items that they humbly represent as the handiworks of others. Generally, forgers work in the style of deceased masters. (In a notable exception, Norwegian painter Kjell Nupen was dismayed to find forged copies of his own work hanging in a Swedish gallery in 2004.) Although some produce literal copies of existing or destroyed works, most create fresh masterpieces emulating the techniques, materials, and subjects of collectable artists, schools, movements, or periods. Forgers often create *pastiches*—new pieces blending elements from obscure existing works.

The line between legitimate copies and illicit forgeries can be rather fine. In 1996, France's Guy Hain was convicted of passing off $25 million in "fake" Auguste Rodin bronzes. The sculptures had been faithfully recast from Rodin's own molds but were falsely attributed to his original foundry. The exposure of this audacious fraud depressed prices for fine bronzes worldwide.

Forgers generally have extensive training in studio arts. The most successful are astute students of art history and tradition. Many are recognized artists in their own

ARE YOU A COPYCAT?
Though some artists enjoy imitation, others crave recognition and creative control.

right. The distinguished English painter Eric Hebborn minted more than five hundred Old Masters before his moonlighting was first discovered in 1978. Undaunted, he refined his techniques and created *another* five hundred paintings and sculptures over the next decade. "It gives me some satisfaction," he bragged, "to note that museums are still buying them." Before his unsolved murder in 1996, Hebborn shared his considerable erudition with the publication of his two-hundred-page training treatise, *The Art Forger's Handbook*. The landmark monograph demystifies the finer points of the forger's craft, delivering nuts-and-bolts advice on replicating period paints and varnishes, aging canvases, mimicking archaic brushwork, and hoodwinking self-satisfied academics and dealers.

Physical fabrication is only the first step in monetizing a forgery. If a new masterwork surfaces without previous paper trail or pedigree, cagier collectors are apt to suspect a rat. Forward-thinking forgers craft fictional paper *provenances*

for their work products. British art dealer John Drewe set the gold standard for historical fiction in what Scotland Yard called "the biggest contemporary art fraud the twentieth century has seen." In addition to forging certificates of authenticity and sales receipts for two hundred paintings, Drewe planted false records in the archives of London's Institute of Contemporary Arts and even bullied a Catholic order into vouching for his fakes.

According to the former director of the Metropolitan Museum of Art, Thomas Hoving, 40 percent of the works his museum considered for purchase were forged or "restored" beyond reasonable recognition. Depending on the genre and the artist, 10 percent to 40 percent of all major works are generally believed to be bogus. Modernist lithographs provide especially rich opportunities for subterfuge. Over 100,000 prints bearing the false signature of Salvador Dali have surfaced in the past fifteen years. A single seizure in Hawaii netted ten thousand illicit prints.

 COMPENSATION AND REWARDS   *EARNINGS:* **B+**   *PERKS:* **C+**

The wages of artistic sin range from a few dollars for a forged tourist curio, to a king's ransom for a major work. Elmyr de Hory, whose picture-perfect Picassos, Renoirs, Modiglianis, and Matisses fooled

the art elite for two decades, claimed to have placed $60 million in forged work between 1961 and 1967. In 1986, John Myatt placed a classified ad in a satirical London biweekly, offering "nineteenth-

and twentieth-century fakes for $240." John Drewe eventually commissioned him to concoct over two hundred Postimpressionist fakes. The industrious Drewe pocketed an estimated $1.8 million over the course of their association. He paid Myatt a penurious $165,000.

Cases involving sales of forged works typically are tried under general-purpose felony wire- or mail-fraud statutes. The owner of two exclusive Manhattan galleries was arrested in 2004 for substituting forgeries for legitimate masterworks he purchased at auction by Modigliani, Renoir, Klee, and Gauguin. Though Ely Sakhai faced up to twenty years for each of eight mail-fraud counts, he was sentenced to forty-one months in prison, forfeiture of eleven authentic works, and $12.5 million in restitution to the victims. Typical sentences, however, are much more palatable. Though art fakers have had great success in stymieing carbon dating, X-ray fluorescence, and infrared forgery detection methods, emerging techniques such as wavelet decomposition may prove challenging.

THE OLD SWITCHEROO

A classic substitution scam orchestrated by New York gallery maven Ely Sakhai

1990	Purchase Marc Chagall's authentic original *La Nappe Mauve* for $312,000
1993	Commission an expert forgery and vend it for $514,000
1998	Sell the authentic work for $340,000
Net gain	$542,000

Source: FBI

STRESSES AND HAZARDS

DANGERS: **B**   PRESSURES: **B**

Forgers work with a variety of solvents and other toxic, volatile substances, and their improvised studio spaces often lack viable ventilation.

Though their paintings may survive initial critical scrutiny, some forgers fret that they will someday be unmasked or, conversely, that their genius will *never* be recognized. Advances in detection technology can be vexing, as can stray words from coconspirators and close associates. John Drewe's elaborate back stories were summarily undone when his former girlfriend alerted police to a variety of incriminating documents she found in the couple's home.

WORK ENVIRONMENT

HOURS: **B+**   COMFORT: **B-**

Forgers work primarily indoors, in climate-controlled studios. Though some processes are time- and labor-intensive, the speediest artisans can complete a major work in under a day. China's legendary Chang Dia Chien (1899–1983) is believed to have completed more than thirty thousand paintings in his notorious career. For the most part, forgers set their own schedules, assignments, and work quotas, and enjoy considerable professional autonomy.

GANGBANGER

DUTIES: Since the early 1800s, street gangs have provided needy, curious, and restless youths with an intensive introduction to the criminal workplace. By the mid-1920s there were more than 1,300 gangs in Chicago, with a total of over 25,000 members. In 2002, the approximately 21,500 gangs in the United States had 731,500 active members. In that same year, 91 percent of cities with a population of more than 250,000 reported at least one gang-related homicide. Although exact definitions of street or youth gangs can be tricky, in the eyes of law enforcement, gangs are groups of three or more individuals whose members gather regularly, individually or collectively engage in criminal activity, adopt common *signs*, colors, or symbols, and maintain identifiable leadership and recruitment structures.

Most gangs adopt distinctive color themes and modes of dress to emphasize group unity and perceived size. Many gangbangers *flash* or *throw* specialized hand signals to communicate, identify themselves, or "dis" (disrespect) rival gangs. Gang symbols, displayed through tattoos, graffiti, and jewelry, are also widely employed for purposes of identification, communication, and intimidation.

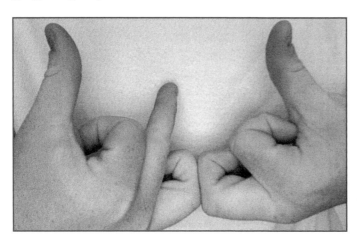

WHAT'S YOUR SIGN?
Can you tell what word these nimble gang fingers spell out?
Blood.
Source: Wikimedia Commons

A recent survey of over four thousand active gangbangers by the National Gang Crime Research Center provides unprecedented insight into this entry-level career option. Some 68.5 percent reported that their gang has written rules, 59.3 percent have a special language or code, 58.6 percent attend regular weekly meetings, 27.9 percent pay weekly dues, 84.3 percent answer to adult leaders who have been in the gang for many years, and 71.3 percent believe their gang has kept its promises to them. Some experts believe that more than 80 percent of gang members are functionally illiterate. Yet, many can earn the equivalent of full-time wages through part-time drug trafficking, illegal weapons sales, robbery, and theft. Fully 82.4 percent report that their gang has sold crack cocaine, 58.5 percent have committed a crime with their gang for financial gain, and 50.1 percent state their gang has ties to traditional organized crime. More surprisingly, 23.1 percent indicated they had worked for politicians, and 47.5 percent indicated that their gangs hold equity interests in legitimate business.

Gang structures vary significantly. The largest gangs, with more than two thousand members, subdivide into smaller units called *clubs* and *cliques*. Clubs are typically gang branches established in new towns or cities to capitalize on vertical drug-marketing opportunities. Cliques are often organized around shared interests of individual members (such as street combat, or breaking and entering). Most gangs are loosely affiliated with even broader-based groups known as *nations*. The four major recognized nations are Folks, People, Bloods, and Crips.

The most organized and established gangs have evolved impressive operational infrastructures. The Black Gangster Disciples, for example, employ a formal membership application, supplemented by a detailed background check. The Disciples operate under a written constitution and code of conduct; maintain a rigid, multi-tiered hierarchy; and regularly disseminate organizational memos and official minutes.

Some gangs operate like traditional corporations. A president heads up strategic planning, provides gravitas in dealing with senior executives and delegates of other organizations, and has final say over all matters of security. The vice president oversees field communications and general operations, via car phones, walkie-talkies, pagers, and beepers.

Although the rewards, prestige, and camaraderie of gang membership are compelling, prospective applicants should note that gang initiations can be rather taxing. Many gangs favor the traditional *beat in* (also known as the *act of love* or *jump in*), in which an inductee must endure a spirited beating by a standardized number of members for a predetermined length of time. Others require candidates to commit or participate in violent or dangerous crimes. Female members (composing 6 percent of all gangbangers in 2000) are often *sexed in* by having intimate congress with multiple gang members. A lucky few with familial or preexisting ties to the gang may be *blessed in* and excused from typical initiation proceedings.

Exiting a gang can be as unpleasant as joining. Many gangs mandate lifetime memberships; others offer a *beat out* option that is typically more injurious than the beating in.

BIRTH OF THE GANG NATIONS

Nation	Roots	Colors	Enemies	Friends
Crips	Formed in Compton, California, in 1968 by high schoolers Ray Washington and Stanley "Tookie" Williams.	Blue	Bloods, People	Folks
Bloods	Chartered in reaction to the Crips by Sylvester Scott and Vincent Owens.	Red	Crips, Floks	People
Folks	Started in the late 1960s by the founder of Chicago's Black Gangster Disciples, David Barksdale.	Blue and Black	People, Bloods	Crips
People	Founded by members of Chicago's Blackstone Rangers.	Red	Folks, Crips	Bloods

COMPENSATION AND REWARDS   *EARNINGS:* **C+**   *PERKS:* **B+**

As in other hierarchically organized businesses, the tangible fruits of gang life vary with work role, experience, initiative, and locality. Shares in drug profits are the mainstays of most gangs' compensation plans. The three-thousand-member Black Gangster Disciples are believed to generate over $100 million in annual narcotics-derived revenues, with as much as 10 percent of gross receipts being "kicked up" to a handful of senior managers. Street-level drug *runners* or *slingers* earn anywhere from $50 to $25,000 per week, with mean earnings of $1,631.41 per week. About one in five gangbangers participates in group-sponsored extortion, earning an annual average $8,696.09 in *street tax*.

Style-conscious bangers spend an average of $547.38 per month on clothing, of which $237.48 goes to gang-specific colors, symbols, etc. Some 58.8 percent of all gangs maintain a treasury, with an average on-hand balance of $34,920.71. Gangs reserve up to one-third of earnings to fund ongoing and onetime operational expenses, but hold monthly dues to a modest average of $36.87.

THE TOP TEN PRISON GANGS

Penologists have identified more than 1,600 gangs and Security Threat Groups in the U.S. correctional system, with over 113,000 incarcerated members. Here are the ten most popular U.S. gangs to "do your time" with!

GANG

1. Crips
2. Black Gangster Disciples
3. Bloods
4. Latin Kings
5. Vice Lords
6. Aryan Brotherhood
7. Folks
8. White Supremacists
9. Surenos
10. Five Percenters

Source: National Gang Threat Assessment 2005

Combating gangs is one of the nation's top three enforcement priorities, and more than 360 special police units have been created to dampen opportunities in this burgeoning sector of the underground economy. Frequent interactions with uniformed and unmarked antigang personnel are exacerbated by the mounting possibility of infiltration and arrest by undercover workers. To even the high-stakes playing field, 53 percent of gangbangers surveyed by the National Gang Crime Research Center report that their gang has active members working as moles within the criminal justice system.

On the other hand, a full 70.5 percent of gangbangers surveyed felt that shooting at a police officer "would be really stupid because of the heat it would bring upon my gang," yet 29.5 percent felt that this action would enhance their standing among peers, and 46.7 percent of the members of formal gangs had actually committed this high-status crime. Gangbangers apprehended in the course of their appointed duties can take solace in the knowledge that 33.1 percent of gangs tracked maintain a segregated account for the legal defense of their members.

THE WAY OF THE GUN
What 4,000 gangbangers said about their gun use

Popular gang activity	"I almost always use a gun!"	"I sometimes use a gun."	"I almost never use a gun!"
Felonious assault	31.8%	22.0%	6.4%
Homicide	30.6%	13.3%	5.2%
Drug sales (street)	19.1%	34.7%	9.2%
Drug sales (wholesale)	16.2%	23.1%	8.1%
Carjacking	15.6%	21.4%	6.9%
Intimidation and extortion	10.4%	24.9%	8.1%

Source: National Gang Threat Assessment 2005

Battles for territory, market share, and social status are endemic to this occupation. In 2003, juvenile gangs were credited with 819 confirmed killings, and 42 percent of local law enforcers surveyed believe that gang violence is generally "getting worse." Nearly half of all homicides in Los Angeles and Chicago are currently attributable to workers in this field. Though 54.4 percent of all active gangbangers have been beaten up by a rival gang, 35.1 percent report having been beaten by their own gangs in *violation* rituals sanctioned to address rule violations (16.8 percent report paying *fines* as an alternative penalty). Two-thirds of active gang members have fired a gun at associates of rival gangs and 50.8 percent believe their own associates are prepared to die for them. Loyalty, however, has its limits, and one-third to one-quarter of

REACHING OUT TO TROUBLED YOUTH
Gang Recruitment in U.S. Schools Remains Vibrant

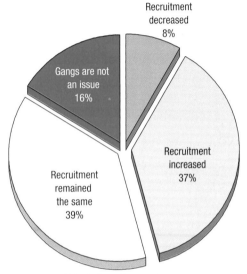

Source: National Youth Gang Survey

all gang members say that, for the right price, they are prepared to "rat on" fellow members.

This is a merit-based field where youthfulness is little barrier to professional achievement and acceptance. The average age of all gangbangers is just 18.6 years old, and the average age at first arrest is 13.8. The typical gangbanger spends 5.5 years on active duty. School-based outreach programs are essential in recruiting the standout practitioners of tomorrow. In 2003, over 37 percent of school-based police officers believed that gang activity was increasing in their schools, and 78 percent reported taking a weapon from a student on school property.

The atmosphere at gang-related workplaces is often convivial and informal. Over half of the workers identify themselves by nicknames chosen by co-workers or friends. Controlled substances are often used to cement social bonds, with 69.9 percent of bangers indicating they have five or more "close friends" who indulge in frequent drug use. Opportunities for mixing with the opposite sex (at sex-ins and less formal occasions) are ample, as 45.7 percent of gangs have female members. Gender-equity is limited in most gang circles, but 45.7 percent of gangs do have female members in middle-tier leadership capacities.

Technology is playing an increasingly important role in gang life. Cell phones and pagers have become ubiquitous, and 44.4 percent of members report having employed a police scanner in the commission of a crime.

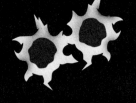

HIT MAN

RANK: 39 out of 50 **AVERAGE GRADE:** C

DUTIES: Hit Men commit or attempt murder for hire. Customarily, a hit man works under a *contract*, a semiformal, verbal agreement to expunge a third party (or parties) at the behest of a second. In one broad-based industry study, 96 percent of contracts stipulated the slaying of a single soul. All contract killings involve substantive remuneration. Paid *hits* are sanctioned by organizations or individuals with intractable interpersonal problems.

The most frequent reason for hired gunplay (about 19 percent of all corroborated cases) is the dissolution of an unrewarding romantic relationship. In many cases, an obsessive ex seeks to permanently check the future coupling of a former love mate. Alternatively, ex-intimates may wish to clear the way for their own recoupling, secure child custody, or deactivate a serial abuser.

Money-motivated murders account for about 16 percent of work assignments, target males disproportionately (more than 90 percent) and often entail the assistance of an associate offender.

Silencing of witnesses is a lucrative professional sideline, composing 13 percent of contract killings in one sample. Revenge is another solid standby (10 percent), with a somewhat senior "target" market (fifty to sixty-four years, on average).

MORTAL MOTIVATIONS
Why nice people hire paid killers

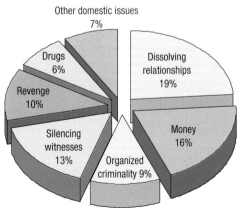

Other domestic issues 7%

Drugs 6%

Revenge 10%

Silencing witnesses 13%

Organized criminality 9%

Money 16%

Dissolving relationships 19%

Source: Australian Institute of Criminology, *Attempted and Completed Contract Killings: 1989–2002*

Initiating contact with a willing contractor—*putting out a paper* or *putting out the word*—can be perilous for underworld noninitiates. Established criminal concerns often have in-house assassins, standing relationships with freelancers, or junior aspirants anxious to undertake an assigned annihilation to "make their bones." Independent instigators typically approach amateur acquaintances with histories of antisocial violence, with requests for referrals or direct offers of employment. Amateur and semiprofessional eradication attempts are increasingly common and comparatively ineffective. Nine out of ten acquaintance-assisted attempted rubouts end without fatalities. Wiseguy wannabes frequently represent themselves as experienced expungers. James Edward Perry, a Detroit street ruffian, drew inspiration for his botched triple hit from *Hit Man: A Technical Manual for Independent Contractors*—a supposed insider guide actually authored by a middle-aged housewife.

Enforcement-funded decoys are also a perennial drain on potential assignments for credentialed death workers. Gary Johnson, an investigator for the Houston District Attorney's Office, has impersonated hit men on at least thirty-seven occasions. High-profile dupes include Qubilah Shabazz, the daughter of Malcolm X (who sought revenge on the man she believed deleted her dad), and rogue CIA spook Edwin Wilson (who proposed the perforation of two prosecutors in his case to an FBI-planted cellmate).

First contacts typically center on discussions of motives, locations, methods, timing, and fees. The identity of the intended is generally *not* disclosed until an in-principle agreement has been consummated. Most details are the prerogative of the purchaser, though professionals often evolve preferred methodologies. Richard "the Iceman" Kuklinski (credited with more than one hundred career kills) favored a "clean," in-your-face application of sprayed cyanide—causing death in under a minute and dissipating from the body after two hours. When a client required something "messier," though, he was always accommodating. After the would-be whacker has assessed the seriousness of the solicitor and the toughness of the task at hand, there is typically some back-and-forth over pricing and terms of payment.

The next step is *stalking*, which entails locating targets and assessing their movements. Working from these observations and other available intelligence, the hit man formulates a plan of action.

Finally, there is the "execution" phase. The majority of American murders for hire transpire after two A.M. at the home of the decedent. Handguns are the weapons of overwhelming choice in all categories of homicide, but are especially popular among paid practitioners. Bombs and incendiary devices are more common in high-level hits—particularly among Outlaw Bikers (see page 149) and certain mobsters. Top professionals may *stage* elements of the crime scene, to falsely indicate an accidental ending (e.g., cut brake line or drug overdose) or a precipitating crime-gone-wrong (rape, robbery, carjacking, etc.). Alternatively, seasoned pros may provide disposal options as value-adds to their service offerings. The Iceman, for example, learned his professional "chops" under the tutelage of a former butcher, and earned his nickname for his penchant for refrigerating concealed corpses.

COMPENSATION AND REWARDS   *EARNINGS:* **B-**   *PERKS:* **B**

Contract killing is a small and somewhat secretive specialty (less than 2 percent of the overall homicide sector), so data on domestic fees are fairly patchy. A 2003 Australian retrospective survey revealed average per-hit pricing of US$16,500—with individual Aussie-elimination fees ranging from US$5,000 to US$50,000.

The Iceman—who once described himself as a "hardworking expert of sorts"—earned a workmanlike $1,600 per liquidation. Yves "The Mad Bumper" Trudeau, a Hells Angels assassin-for-hire with forty-three admitted kills, demanded $200,000 for his high-risk double hit on the killers of Canadian biker chief Frank Peter "Dunie" Ryan. He needed the cash to fund his outsized cocaine craving, which reportedly exceeded $25,000 per week. Fellow Canadian biker Cory Patterson agreed to eliminate a family of Korean grocers for a comparatively paltry $2,000—even providing a payment plan.

Entry-level mob hitters—who often work gratis—trade upfront fees for downstream advancement and ongoing opportunities to "earn."

MAKING A KILLING?
A per-hit survey of professional fees

$11k–$20k
22%

$5k–$10k
54%

$21k–$50k
9%

More than $51k
6%

Less than $5k
9%

Source: Australian Institute of Criminology

Solicitation to commit murder is a Class A felony carrying recommended retribution of at least twelve years in prison, and successful murder-for-hire is a death penalty–eligible event for both contractor and solicitor. Overall homicide clearance rates have fallen by almost 20 percent since the seventies, to less than 65 percent. Decommissioning of contract killers, however, is far less common. At least half of all suspected murders-for-hire are unsolved, and the savviest slayers complete dozens of uninterrupted assignments. Though these high-profile hitters weather withering enforcement scrutiny, many remain surpassingly slippery. Once cornered, some celebrated shooters still have cards to play. John Mar-

GETTING AWAY WITH MURDER!
Homicide clearance rates hover near historic lows

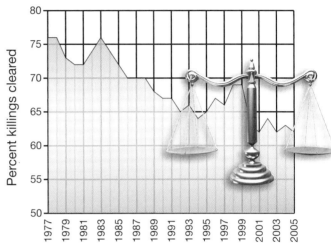

Source: U.S. Department of Justice

torano—a Boston tattle-tale with twenty confirmed hits—will serve just three years, thanks to his 2004 testimony against Beantown's most notorious cops and robbers.

STRESSES AND HAZARDS   *DANGERS:* **C-**   *PRESSURES:* **C+**

This is a technically demanding profession in which even small errors can result in irreparable nonloss of life. In 2005, for instance, an English hitter was sentenced to life for stabbing the wrong housemate. In retrospect, the slipup was potentially avoidable, as the victim was black, while the intended target was white. Even experienced enforcers have off days. Sixty-four-year-old hit man Frank Gambino had a senior moment during a routine 1996 drive-by shooting. He missed his seventy-six-year-old target completely, after he became distracted by a witness's shrill screaming and shattering shop glass. In 1994, two spooked Philadelphia hitters actually ran away from a work site when their target—whom they had shot in the head—rose up and chased them.

In many cases, hit men have more than ghosts to fear. Faced with imminent death, many victims fight quite tenaciously. A hit man dispatched to dispose of one of England's notorious Kray twins was, instead, sliced so severely that his liver dropped out on the spot.

WORK ENVIRONMENT

HOURS: **B** *COMFORT:* **C**

Freelance Hit Men enjoy considerable professional autonomy, setting their own risk parameters, hours, and fees. Salaried workers trade self-determination for job security. They may find themselves on call at inopportune hours, or could be compelled to accept unpleasant or ill-advised assignments.

Workplace comfort varies considerably from hit to hit. A long stalk could be tedious and uncomfortable in one locale, and scenic and stimulating in another. Although well-heeled hitters can afford top-flight conveyances and luxury accommodations, stolen cars and flea-bitten flophouses often are better suited to the sneaky business at hand.

HUMAN SMUGGLER

RANK: 27 out of 50   **AVERAGE GRADE:** C+

DUTIES: Human Smugglers transport undocumented aliens into the sovereign territories of the United States. Smugglers (usually known as *coyotes* or *snakeheads*) collect onetime fees for their assistance in cross-border entry, whereas Slave Traders (see page 211) seek long-term profits through the ongoing exploitation of the aliens they transport. The Census Bureau estimates that over 500,000 illegal immigrants enter the United States annually. Roughly 95 percent come via our border with Mexico. The U.S. Border Patrol thwarted 932,000 attempts to enter the southwest region in fiscal 2003. At least one-third of successful entries were assisted by coyotes.

As prices and profits in Mexican human smuggling have inclined, independent agents have largely been muscled out. The majority of the industry is thought to be controlled by roughly fifty major factions with as many as three hundred employees each. Many of these highly professional groups are thought to be intimately allied with Central American drug cartels.

CLAUSTROPHOBIC?
Work quarters can be rather tight.
Source: U.S. Immigrations and Customs Enforcement

Mexican nationals seeking a coyote's assistance—known as *pollos* (Spanish for "chickens")—usually make their way to border towns, such as Nogales. There, they entertain offers of transport from emissaries of competing smuggling enterprises. Once a deal is inked, would-be immigrants are driven to motels or safe houses in the staging town of Altar, awaiting recruitment of enough countrymen to constitute a full load. When a quorum is gathered, the group is driven sixty miles to the edge of the Sonora desert. From there a *guide*—specializing in Border Patrol evasion—will shepherd them on a multiday desert trek toward Arizona's Highway 86. To speed their perilous journey, human smugglers sometimes compel their charges to ingest energy-rich methamphetamine or cocaine.

At a preappointed hour, a short-haul driver is dispatched from the Phoenix area to pick up the pollos and transport them to a nearby safe house. Safe-house workers prompt each smuglee for the phone number of a U.S.-based sponsor who can wire them payment. Sponsors are subsequently instructed where to wire funds and *runners* are dispatched to discreetly retrieve the loot. If all goes as planned, the pollos bid farewell to the coyotes or await long-range transport to inland areas. In 2003 alone, an estimated $500 million was wired to Phoenix-based smugglers.

CARGO ECONOMICS
A look at the ledgers of Chinese snakeheads

Ledger item	Median	Range
Investment in smuggling business	$3,000	$0–$500,000
Smuggling fees	$50,000	$1,000–$70,000
Profit per client	$10,000	$117–$40,000
Annual income from smuggling business	$50,000	$0–$2,000,000

Source: National Institute of Justice, *Characteristics of Chinese Human Smugglers*

COMPENSATION AND REWARDS   EARNINGS: **B+**   PERKS: **C**

Global revenues from human smuggling are estimated to be at least $9.5 billion per year. The lion's share of fees from U.S.-bound émigrés are channeled to elite executives controlling the high-volume Mexico-to-America route. Ticket prices range from $500 for the Nogales-to-Phoenix junket to $3,500 for door-to-door transport from central Mexico to the American Midwest.

In the wake of 9/11, aspiring immigrants from nonadjacent nations have become increasingly dependent on the services of human smugglers, who typically demand substantial premiums. The going rate for Saudi Arabian human cargo is said to be $50,000. Chinese mainlanders pay up to $70,000 for subhuman transport via intermodal shipping containers. Pakistani import hopefuls should budget $15,000 to $30,000 per alien. A Canadian raft owner who piloted four Indian women across the Niagara River to the shores of Grand Island, New York, asked a comparatively reasonable $4,000 per passenger.

ENFORCEMENT AND PENALTIES   *ARRESTS:* **C+**   *SENTENCING:* **B-**

In fiscal 2004, more than 2,400 human-cargo workers were convicted under the federal alien-smuggling statute. The $7.3 million in smuggling-related assets seized did little to offset the $9 billion spent to police the southwest frontier. Though the ranks of the Border Patrol swelled from 3,651 agents in 1992 to over 11,000 in 2004, the smuggling labor force experienced parallel growth over the same period.

Human smugglers arrested in the United States currently risk a maximum of five years' incarceration. First-time offenders can expect probation or deportation. In Mexico, penalties recently have been increased to six to twelve years without bond.

KNOW THY FOE
The Border Patrol can be a tenacious adversary.
Source: U.S. Customs and Border Protection

The sharp rise in coyote fees that accompanied America's post-9/11 security crackdown ushered in an unprecedented era of violence in the industry. A new trade was born—*people rustler*. Most often, an employee of an established human-smuggling organization serves as a double agent, alerting accomplices where and when a convoy of pollos will be transported. The rustlers kidnap the hapless migrants, spirit them to their own safe houses, and phone their sponsors with demands for monetary satisfaction. If sponsors can't be contacted or persuaded, hostage situations ensue. Over 750 such rustled hostages have been rescued— and then deported—by federal agents. Violence between smugglers and rustlers peaked in 2003, with a gun battle near Phoenix that ended in four deaths and five injuries. Additional threats include the deployment of nearly five hundred self-styled civilian border patrol agents known as the Minuteman Project, and the passage of a 2005 congressional bill to construct 370 miles of new fencing and 500 miles of new vehicle barriers along the southern border of the United States.

AMERICA OR BUST
U.S.-bound cargo-persons face some of the highest fares in the world

Route/country of destination	Average fee
To the USA, depending on route and origin	$1,000–$100,000
From China to Italy	$13,000
From South Asia to Spain	6,000 Euro
From North Africa to Spain	4,000 Euro
Through Hungary (from Russia to Western Europe)	800–10,000 Euro
From Slovakia to Italy	$3,000–$4,000
For transit through Serbia and Montenegro	$1,000
Through Malta (from Africa to mainland Europe)	$800–$1,000
To/through Croatia	500 Euro
From Hungary to Italy	500 Euro

Source: The Financial Action Task Force

Latin American cartel–based coyotes are scrupulously scrutinized crime workers who answer to well-defined chains of command, adhere to complex schedules and budgets, and even maintain meticulous accounting records. A logbook recovered from an Agua Prieta–based group in 2002 details per-trip expenses for wages, vehicle purchase, housing, and food. "I didn't expect the really detailed record-keeping that they do," one investigating federal agent admiringly admitted. "It's a big money-making business, and they have to account for every expense in dealing with each other." Despite their immersion in some elements of traditional corporate culture, coyotes on the southern border battle extreme temperatures, rugged terrain, high-tech enforcers, and profit-hungry people rustlers.

Chinese snakeheads are a more independent lot. They typically work in egalitarian groups of ten or fewer core members, with clear divisions of labor but little hierarchy. The great majority remain in the business for fewer than six years. Cooperative cargo-handling among extended families and friends is common. Although a substantial majority of Chinese practitioners are male, the world's most illustrious snakehead, Cheng Chui "Big Sister Ping" Peng, is a woman.

IDENTITY THIEF

RANK: 4 out of 50   **AVERAGE GRADE:** B

DUTIES: Identity Thieves unlawfully obtain, transfer, or fraudulently utilize other people's personal data or identifying documents. Potential applications for appropriated personas are abundant and wide-ranging. Advanced criminal practitioners assume actual alter-egos to mask their misdeeds, or to obtain "clean" credentials to help them flee in case of sudden setbacks. In 2003, for example, a retired Englishman was arrested in South Africa when he was mistaken for a fugitive in a major Texas telemarketing fraud case who had "cloned" his passport. Terrorists (such as the al Qaeda cell interdicted in Spain in 2002) use hijacked credit accounts to finance operational expenditures, stolen phone cards to communicate securely, and assumed identities to obtain travel documents. The great majority of identity interceptions, however, are perpetrated for financial gain. Twenty-eight percent of FTC-reported work actions involve breach of credit card accounts with downstream purchases or cash advances. Twenty-three percent involve attacks on bank accounts or impostor-initiated loans, 19 percent center on false billing for telephone or other utilities, and 6 percent involve phony government benefit schemes.

Identity acquisition techniques vary greatly in sophistication and effectiveness. Physical collection methods are popular and accessible but tend to be rather labor-intensive. *Dumpster divers* rifle through residential or institutional refuse in search of revealing discards such as bills, bank statements, receipts, or—especially—unredeemed offers for preapproved credit cards. *Shoulder surfers* scrutinize the finger movements of payphone and ATM attendees to deduce phone card numbers and PINs. More evolved ATM artistes deploy fake machines, hidden cameras, or electronic monitoring devices to capture card and PIN data (see ATM Attacker). Postal specialists target ingoing and outgoing mail, whereas pickpockets, burglars, and muggers perpetrate traditional thefts with extended, identity-based afterlives.

IDENTITY CRISIS! Blockbuster personal data breaches of 2005		
Company	Millions of identities exposed	How did it happen?
Bank of America	1.2	Stolen backup tapes
DSW Shoe Warehouse	1.3	Hacking
CitiFinancial	3.9	Lost backup tapes
MasterCard	40.0	Processor security breach

Source: Privacy Rights Clearinghouse

Underprincipled employees are a rich and renewable source of confidential information in bulk. Security analysts estimate that 65 percent to 70 percent of identity thefts involve private information intercepted by employees or transaction participants. In a 2003 survey, two-thirds of workers and managers opined that their co-workers—not hackers—posed the greatest threat to customer privacy. In 2002 a help-desk worker at Teledata (a small Long Island company that provides credit report terminals to auto dealers) was charged with theft of more than thirty thousand identities. He partnered with a ring of Nigerian nationals, who paid him sixty dollars per deprivatized person. Identity donors in this landmark larceny have reported combined losses of $2.7 million, but the true take is believed to be tremendously higher.

The most spectacular penetrations of personal privacy are accomplished via the digital domain. In 2005, four separate security lapses netted more than 1 million electronic identities *each*. The most impressive breach leveraged a surreptitiously planted malicious program—*malware*—to transmit privileged information for approximately 40 million credit card accounts to an anonymous hacker. Consumer anxiety over breaches is so high that a hacker who stole 300,000 card numbers from Internet music meisters CDUniverse, requested a "ransom" of $100,000 to divest himself of the purloined digits.

Millions of individual PC-users have unknowingly participated in scaled-down versions of such hack attacks by downloading *Trojan horse* programs or pornography containing hidden *keystroke loggers*, *screen scrapers*, or other *spyware/crimeware* applications. Fiscal 2005 saw a huge increase in Web sites that exploit security holes in Internet Explorer to install *spyware* and *malware* without *any* action on the part of unsuspecting visitors.

Today's most audaciously innovative identity thieves, *phishers*, don't so much steal personal information as *ask* for it. They craft and broadcast official-looking

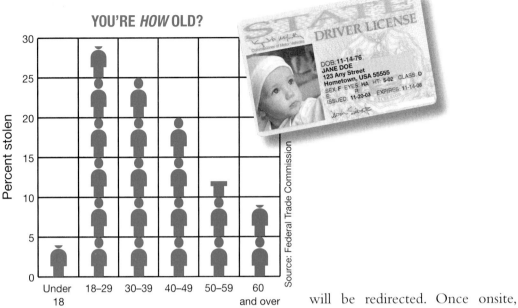

YOU'RE *HOW* OLD?

Percent stolen (vertical axis: 0, 5, 10, 15, 20, 25, 30)

Age of identities stolen (horizontal axis: Under 18, 18–29, 30–39, 40–49, 50–59, 60 and over)

Source: Federal Trade Commission

bulk e-mails purporting to originate from legitimate institutions, such as banks or brokerage houses, with which the recipients are affiliated. These "bait" e-mails—which adopt the exact look, tone, and apparent Internet addresses of their supposed senders—urge recpients to click on an embedded link to take some direly needed action at the site to which they will be redirected. Once onsite, they are prompted to log in— thus unwittingly submitting their username and password to an electronic angler somewhere in cyberspace. According to the Anti-Phishing Working Group, fifteen of 2005's top twenty phishing scams targeted online banks.

Phishing, which some term "spam's evil cousin," began in late 2003 and grew exponentially in 2004. The Gartner Group estimates that 57 million Internet users have received a phish, 11 million have "clicked through," and nearly 2 million have divulged damaging personal or financial information. The FBI recently described phishing as the "hottest and most troublesome" scam on the Web.

HIGH FIVE!
America's Hottest States for Identity Theft

Rank	Identity donor state	Identities lost per 100,000 population	Identities lost
1	Arizona	142.5	8,186
2	Nevada	125.7	2,935
3	California	122.1	43,839
4	Texas	117.6	26,454
5	Colorado	95.8	4,409

Source: Federal Trade Commission

Identity theft is one of the world's fastest-growing criminal careers. The U.S. Federal Trade Commission estimates that American thieves assumed 9.9 million false identities in 2004, with losses to impersonated individuals totaling more than $5 billion (and damage to domestic businesses exceeding $47.6 billion). Between 2002 and 2003, market coverage grew by more than 80 percent, with activity in the phishing sector alone topping $1.2 billion. Business has been brisk throughout the online banking segment, with over 5 million unauthorized balance transfers completed to date.

Top performers in this new-millennium mega-field earn superstar salaries. A twenty-four-year-old American and a twenty-five-year-old Scotsman operating out of England, for example, are alleged to have pocketed £6.5 million ($11.8 million) from their phishing and credit card cloning operations in just over a year.

No one in the industry, however, can hold a candle to Abraham Abdullah. In a six-month spree, he amassed over $260 million—by methodically researching and impersonating superrich Americans, including Paul Allen, George Soros, Bill Gates, Charles Schwab, Steven Spielberg, and Martha Stewart. An FBI agent who followed Abdullah's previous escapades for a decade called him a "pioneer when it comes to fraud."

At the low end of the scale, opportunistic offenders use casually clipped credentials to finance a plethora of incidental expenses.

In 1998, Congress enacted the burdensome Identity Theft and Assumption Deterrence Act, which carries a maximum term of fifteen years' imprisonment and forfeiture of all business gains. Additionally, interdisciplinary identity professionals may be subject to censure under state and federal statutes governing wire fraud, credit card fraud, bank fraud, computer fraud, viruses, and spam. There is, however, quite a bit of good news. Although the clearance rate for the overall property crime sector is a lenient 16 percent, fewer than 1 percent of identity compromising episodes end in indictments.

On average, federal white-collar prosecutions cost a prohibitive $11,443. The Secret Service, which has principal responsibility for combating identity thieves, expends an average of $15,000 per investigation and only accepts cases over $200,000 involving multistate hijinks. The FBI estimates its average cost per financial crime investigation at $20,000.

STRESSES AND HAZARDS

DANGERS: **B+**   PRESSURES: **B**

In many cases, interdicted identity thieves appear to be victims of their own heady success. In late 2004, a meth-fueled ring of Washington state mail thieves (who had stolen at least 250 identities) was toppled after one member braggingly wrote "the crime wave went from 100 crimes a month to 367 . . . I bet they're pretty pissed." The Teledata group, which pilfered 30,000 credit profiles, was foiled when they grew greedy and billed an implausible 15,000 reports to Ford's nationwide account. After he had safely socked away $260 million, über-thief Abraham Abdullah became obsessed with the goal of stealing $1 billion and felt no satisfaction when he initiated an ill-fated second wave of superscams.

For high-volume operators, frequent trips to far-flung banks can be burdensome, and pressing, repetitive paperwork can stack up quickly.

WORK ENVIRONMENT

HOURS: **B+**   COMFORT: **C+**

Data and document acquisition are undertaken at a wide variety of work sites. Electronic interlopers work almost exclusively indoors; in contrast, Dumpster divers, mail grabbers, and hands–on thieves may spend a significant portion of their workday outdoors or on the go.

In most cases, identity theft is a crime of opportunity, and tempting opportunities present themselves in a multitude of social and professional situations. Even public servants are subject to the pull of windfall profits.

In 2004, a New York municipal worker was arrested for vending some thirty-five thousand social security numbers and tax histories to a multimillion-dollar tax fraud concern.

Although the majority of identity theft workers have previous criminal backgrounds in substance abuse, narcotics trafficking, violence, or robbery, barriers to entry are actually quite low. The first person in the United States indicted for phishing offenses (in January 2004) was a seventeen-year-old California boy.

INDUSTRIAL SPY

RANK: 14 out of 50 **AVERAGE GRADE:** B-

DUTIES: Industrial Spies covertly collect and transfer proprietary materials or trade secrets from commercial concerns at the behest of other business entities or private sponsors. Industrial espionage is legally distinct from its criminal cousin, economic espionage, which involves clandestine gathering of economically actionable intelligence by foreign governments or their surrogates. With the abrupt end of the cold war, thousands of career and freelance *spooks* reentered the job market.

Many repositioned themselves as in-house intelligence and counterintelligence gurus for hypercompetitive U.S. corporations. Today, the Society of Competitive Intelligence Professionals has seven thousand members.

The financial stakes of the corporate neo–cold war are awesome. Half the companies on the Fortune 500 are believed to have suffered major industrial espionage. With intangible knowledge assets ac-

SPIES MAKING A DIFFERENCE
Three capers that spooked corporate America

Date	Target	Incident
2000	Microsoft	The company's network was hacked for two to five weeks. Elements of Microsoft's core source code were breached in an apparently professional attack.
2001	Lucent	Two of the company's top scientists joined with an outsider to steal source code for Lucent's flagship data and voice system. The thieves bragged that their joint venture with a Chinese partner would become the "Cisco of China."
1999	Caterpillar	Jack Shearer built an $8 million energy parts business, using information stolen from Caterpillar Inc. He paid three employees at the company's Solar Turbines subsidiary more than $100,000 to steal plans for oil-field and pipeline machinery.

counting for 50 percent to 85 percent of the overall value of U.S. companies, the American Society of Industrial Security pegs the combined impact of economic and industrial spying at $250 billion a year. Scores of overtly reputable consultancies have plunged into the murky-but-profitable waters of competitive intelligence (CI). Accounting mainstay Ernst & Young now boasts a sixty-agent intelligence unit. Rivals Deloitte & Touche—who themselves endured a multimillion-dollar 1998 software breach—have drafted a small army of former CIA agents. Aspiring suit-and-tie sneaks can even earn a four-year degree at Pennsylvania's Mercy Hearst College.

Although corporate CI executives perform a host of nominally legal activities, felonious misdeeds generally are subcontracted to specialists known as *kites*, to maintain plausible deniability. Kites bug phones, offices, and conference facilities; enter locked and unlocked office spaces; illegally obtain telephone records (*running tolls*); penetrate computer networks; copy or steal electronic and paper documents; recruit enablers; tender bribes; and conduct a variety of other *black ops*. In addition to technical trade secrets, targeted information includes corporate negotiating postures, pricing and cost structures, client lists, business plans, contract bids, and timetables for new product introductions. Most kites are generalists, but computer and telecommunications specialists are making major inroads in the increasingly high-tech espionage workplace.

Seventy percent of all domestic information security breaches are facilitated by former or current employees. The majority of big-league industrial escapades involve foreign interests targeting U.S. companies with outsize investments in high-tech

DON'T ASK, DON'T TELL
Why U.S. corporations don't report data security breaches

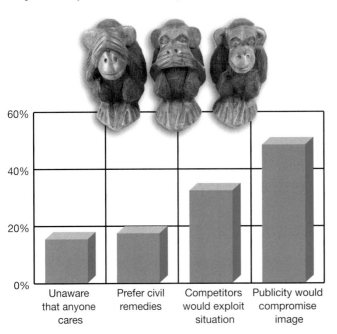

Source: 2004 CSI/FBI Computer Crime and Security Survey

research and development. In the manufacturing sector, losses per breached trade secret average $50 million. Technical subject matter experts (SMEs) often are recruited for extracurricular duty during overseas conferences and trade junkets. Motivators for such *moles* include naked greed, disgruntlement, loyalty to nations of birth, and extortionate threats. Low-level support staffers such as technicians, secretaries, and maintenance workers can also be highly effective operatives and are especially susceptible to economic incentives.

COMPENSATION AND REWARDS — EARNINGS: B   PERKS: B

It is no trade secret that pay scales in this field can be rather uneven and arbitrary. Midlevel corporate intelligence officers earn an average annual salary of $67,000. Senior "C-level" executives earn a handsome $300,000 to $600,000 per year. Some hardworking moles command a comparative pittance for their high-risk contributions. Ten Hong "Victor" Lee, a materials scientist for label maker Avery Denison, transferred an estimated $60 million in company secrets to Taiwanese rival Four Pillars. He received a mere $125,000 over eight years. Conversely, Deloitte & Touche consultant Mayra Trujilo-Cohen sought $7 million for a single software theft from *her* employer.

ENFORCEMENT AND PENALTIES — ARRESTS: B   SENTENCING: C+

Under the Economic Espionage Act of 1996 (EEA), individuals convicted of theft, purchase, or conspiracy to steal trade secrets are eligible for up to ten years of federal incarceration and fines up to $500,000. In practice, felony indictments are unusual and sentences of more than five years are quite rare. Restitution and civil damage awards, however, can be quite draconian. Multimillion-dollar judgments have become the norm. The majority of work efforts in this field are never brought to the attention of law officers. Fewer than one-third of large companies suffering serious electronic breaches in 2001 reported the attacks to the FBI.

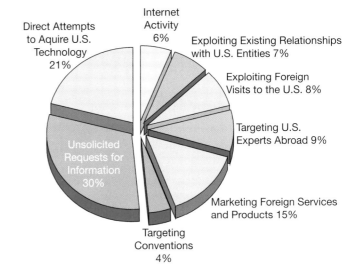

THE OUT-OF-TOWNERS
How foreign spies access U.S. trade secrets

Source: U.S. Department of Defense Security Service

Internet Activity 6%

Direct Attempts to Aquire U.S. Technology 21%

Exploiting Existing Relationships with U.S. Entities 7%

Exploiting Foreign Visits to the U.S. 8%

Targeting U.S. Experts Abroad 9%

Unsolicited Requests for Information 30%

Marketing Foreign Services and Products 15%

Targeting Conventions 4%

STRESSES AND HAZARDS   *DANGERS:* **B**   *PRESSURES:* **C**

Independent operators who lack pre-arranged outlets for their niche wares may find going to market a tad perilous. John Morris, a New York textile executive, thought he had found the perfect customer for information on his company's proprietary pricing, when he began corresponding with a representative of his company's rival for a major military contract. Instead he had struck up negotiations with an undercover agent for the Department of Defense. Other fledgling spies fail to grasp the necessity for discretion in their professional communications. A deceitful employee of Maine veterinary medicine maker Idexx Inc. was unmasked when an e-mail to her coconspirator was misrouted to a co-worker. "They know I've been stealing, so to speak, from the company and sending information to someone," she presciently wrote. "Can I go to jail for this?"

Freelance spies travel frequently and are expected to assimilate to a wide range of working cultures and conditions. Moles must balance moonlighting tasks with primary work responsibilities and may find the physical reproduction, annotation, transmission, and presentation of stolen technical information to be laborious and concentration intensive. Although senior employees have preferential access to market-worthy intelligence, opportunities abound for precocious self-starters. Igor Serebryany, a nineteen-year-old student at the University of Chicago, was able to parlay a summer photocopying assignment at an L.A. law office into a multimillion-dollar theft of trade secrets from satellite entertainment provider DirecTV.

JEWEL THIEF

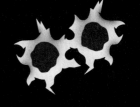

RANK: 26 out of 50   **AVERAGE GRADE:** C+

DUTIES: Jewel Thieves illicitly procure gemstones and assembled jewelry pieces via force, distraction, subterfuge, fraud, or employee pilferage. Traditionally, jewel thieves have been associated with highly skilled, stealthy extractions from fortified residences and institutions. The technical virtuosos of yesteryear posted enduring career records. Walter T. Shaw—who once rifled through Liberace's jeweled drawers—is credited with lifetime receipts of over $70 million, before becoming Ted Bundy's jailhouse chess partner. Mob freelancer Bill Mason nabbed $35 million in trinkets from such old-time luminaries as Phyllis Diller, Bob Hope, and Truman Capote. Today's biggest scores, however, are fast-paced ensemble efforts, emphasizing force over finesse. Since the early 1980s, highly organized teams of illegal aliens from Colombia, Ecuador, and Peru have been conducting lightning raids on traveling jewelry salespersons, who often carry hundreds of thousands of dollars' worth of lucre for their buyers' inspection.

Initially, these South American theft groups (SATGs) targeted the hotel rooms of sales reps attending trade shows. Today, eight- to twelve-member teams stage carefully choreographed, direct attacks on couriers. The team's *spotter* trolls major urban jewelry marts in quiet search of the ever-cautious jewelry salesman. Once a candidate is spotted, *stalkers* trail him or her to assess potential vulnerabilities. When an opportune moment arises, they phone or radio a nearby *attack team*. Typically, two car-borne attackers motor up to a parked salesperson. They break his or her window with brandished guns, snatch the victim's cell phone and jewels, and exit briskly. The spoils are relayed to yet another team, who divide them into preaddressed delivery cartons and ship them before the victim can alert police. Overnight, the jewelry travels to fences in exotic lands. Precious metals are melted, gems are recut, and the untraceable recyclables reenter the world market. Occasionally, *flying fences* travel to Los Angeles, Houston, Miami, or New York City to liaison directly with SATGs.

Although South American guests liberate up to $30 million a year from

CUT AND RUN—A coed Colombian team is credited with ninety thefts from retail jewelers in eighteen Eastern states, totaling over $3.5 million. Typically, chatty team members distract salespeople while their associates cut the silicone seals securing the tops of display case. They lift the glass, remove jewelry, and exit gracefully.

TEAMWORK IN ACTION
A female jewel thief distracts a salesman as her male accomplice opens the case, then heads for the door.

BUM RAP—In 2002, Keith McCloud, a Minnesota gangbanger, presented himself as a successful rapper shopping for stage-worthy "bling." As his associate was being buzzed out of the store's security door, Mc-Cloud bolted with the $27,000 watch he had been "considering."

THE PRINCE AND THE PAUPER—Nordine Herrena, a French national, "palmed" two diamond rings, valued at $1.5 million, from a Florida retail store, while making it appear that he had returned them to their box. He identified himself as a Saudi prince and, accompanied by a well-dressed blond female, wowed sales associates with hundred-dollar tips.

domestic salespeople, U.S.-born jewel thieves are far from idle. In 2001, the Chicago Police Department's former chief of detectives pleaded guilty to masterminding $5 million in thefts in seven states, over more than a decade. William Hanhardt, then seventy-two, used police databases to track the movements of more than one hundred salesmen and $40 million in jewelry, gems, and watches. His team, aided by two other active-duty Chicago officers, used electronic listening devices, smoke grenades, and fake beards to execute eight high-stakes attacks.

In April 2003, three masked Americans tunneled into San Francisco's Lang Antique & Estate Jewelry from a vacant business next door. The trio camped for the night, then forced arriving employees to empty safes holding $10 million in diamonds, rubies, and Art Deco jewelry. "I would like nothing more than to stroll into police headquarters, [but] I'll get stuck with the dimwitted lawyer from *My Cousin Vinny*," wrote the group's beleaguered leader in an open letter to *America's Most Wanted*'s John Walsh. "I'd rather take my chances with hypertension as a fugitive." (He was eventually captured at a New York City subway station.)

COMPENSATION AND REWARDS — EARNINGS: **A-** PERKS: **B**

In 2005, reported gross revenues in this sector totaled $111.5 million, with on-premises attacks yielding a handsome $80.1 million, and robberies of mobile workers (231) totaling $31.4 million. This actually represents a significant, recessionary down-turn from 2003's receipts of $130.6 million. On-premises activity dipped by 10.5 percent, while off-premises work fell an alarming 27.2 percentage points. On average, large-scale jewelry repurposers can expect to recoup 10 percent to 15 percent of wholesale value from reputable fences.

A GEM HARVESTER'S GUIDE

Extraction method	Average gain
Distraction	$40,000+
Grab and Run	$20,000+
Sneak theft	$15,000+
Diamond switch	$7,500+
Cut/lift glass	$60,000+

Source: composite

ENFORCEMENT AND PENALTIES — ARRESTS: **C+** SENTENCING: **C-**

Hardened, elite SATG workers enter the United States via fraudulent visas or human smuggling routes (see Human Smuggler) and commit their high-speed holdups sans disguises. If apprehended—unless a homicide count is involved—they promptly make and jump bail, and usually reemerge with freshly minted false identities. A host of venerable federal regulations apply to this enterprise when it involves interstate or international activities. Applicable statutes include Theft from Interstate Shipment; Interference with Commerce by Threats of Violence; Racketeer Influenced and Corrupt Organizations; and Interstate Transportation of Stolen Property. In addition to modest jail terms, convicted workers risk bulky restitution awards, which often erase their hard-won gains.

THE KING'S RANSOM
Elvis Presley's 41-carat star ruby diamond ring, stolen from a Las Vegas museum.
Source: FBI

STRESSES AND HAZARDS

DANGERS: C+ PRESSURES: C

Pistol-whippings and occasional homicides are par for this jewel-studded course, but sensitive souls may be cheered to learn that 2004's victim death toll (three) fell to the lowest level in twenty-five years.

Contractors for security-minded organized groups may face unhealthy scrutiny if apprehended. Legendary mob *lifter* Walter T. Shaw was sequestered in Florida State Prison's death row until he could arrange a reassuring "sit-down" with anxious mob dignitaries. Cop turned caper-meister William Hanhardt was his own worst enemy after capture, attempting suicide via painkillers.

WORK ENVIRONMENT

HOURS: C COMFORT: C

Spotters and stalkers for organized teams battle fatigue, boredom, and eyestrain as they search for and shadow their oft-elusive quarry. Attackers may enjoy high-adrenaline confrontations but find long waits between engagements to be tedious.

Balanced male-female ratios among distraction thieves provide potential opportunities for workplace romance; however, personal attachments can color professional judgments and impede self-interested escapes.

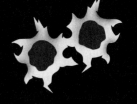

KIDNAPPER

RANK: 49 out of 50   **AVERAGE GRADE:** C-

DUTIES: Kidnappers take, transport, and hold persons against their will, by force, or using threats of force. Professional kidnappers demand financial remuneration—*ransom*—from hostages' families, associates, or intimates for their safe return. Amateurs are motivated by nonmonetary considerations including romantic and sexual obsession, desire for parental custody, and broad-based psychosis.

Ransom kidnappers identify, research, and maintain surveillance on prospective abductees, plan and execute human seizures, manage client communications, and

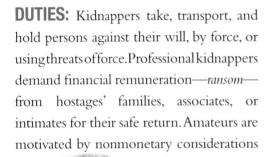

WHO YOU GONNA CALL?
The world's most-trusted names in kidnapping and ransom

CONTROL RISKS GROUP—An international consulting group that has handled more than seven hundred kidnapping, extortion, and illegal detention cases in seventy-nine countries. The group maintains bureaus in fourteen global hot spots, including Bogotá, Mexico City, and Moscow.

KROLL ASSOCIATES—A powerhouse New York security and investigative firm whose kidnap consultants have managed at least 120 incidents worldwide.

PINKERTON RISK ASSESSMENT—They earned their reputation busting bad men in the Wild West. Today, they employ crisis managers in thirty countries, deliver daily threat assessments on 230 nations, and maintain a database of more than 55,000 terrorist actions. Annual online subscriptions start at about $7,000.

TROUBLESHOOTERS—An elite group of former U.S. soldiers offering airborne hostage extraction and other specialized solutions on an à la carte basis.

arrange guest accommodations. They craft threats and demands, negotiate payments and terms, and guard against premature guest departure.

Kidnapping is a rapidly maturing criminal calling that is thriving worldwide. Over the last six years, ransom-bearing incidents have nearly doubled. In 2004, at least ten thousand for-profit actions were initiated globally. Sixty-seven percent ended in successful ransom extraction, with resultant revenues of over $500 million. More than 90 percent of these cash-bearing attacks took place in just ten nations: Colombia, Mexico, the former Soviet Union, Brazil, Nigeria, Philippines, India, Ecuador, Venezuela, and South Africa. The Latin American market is so overheated that it has given rise to so-called *fast food* kidnappings—an abbreviated variant in which seized subjects are forced to liquidate their own accounts, and are then immediately killed or released.

The U.S. market—with 100 to 150 reported ransom kidnappings per year—is relatively small but shows strong indicators of renewed growth. The current mini-boom began with the harvesting of some of the go-go eighties' most visible fat cats. First came the $5 million bid for Texas billionaire Robert M. Bass in 1990. His kidnapper selected him on the strength of his glittering profile in *Forbes*'s yearly list of the wealthiest Americans. The president of Adobe Systems was also drafted on the strength of favorable press notices, in 1992. He was liberated from a Jordanian abductor who had threatened to turn him into "shark bait," after four days in captivity. The president of Exxon, plucked from his driveway just two weeks earlier, fared worse. He died on the fourth day of his captivity. His acquirers—masquerading as radical environmentalists—continued their campaign for a $18.5 million stipend for another fifty-five days.

THE FACES THAT LAUNCHED A THOUSAND COPS
Napping famous kids can spell trouble.

Charles A. Lindbergh Jr.

Sources: National Institute of Standards and Testing, FBI

Patty Hearst

The year 1993 was marked by innovations. First, tuxedo tycoon Harvey Weinstein was buried alive in a four-by-eight-foot pit in a Manhattan rail yard. Then the daughter of casino magnate Steve Wynn was snatched by techie kidnappers with the aid of a cloned security remote.

The momentum continued in 1994 with a series of West Coast *doorbell abductions*. In these precision maneuvers, two abductors arrived at the home of a bank officer, one restrained his wife and/or children, and the other chaperoned the husband to rob his workplace. The attacks on bankers were followed by several roadside ambushes of Silicon Valley computer executives, who were forced to return to *their* workplace and facilitate bulk transfers of CPU chips and other high-tech valuables. These gave way to even more efficient attacks on the immediate families of—predominantly Asian—owners of chip storage facilities.

COMPENSATION AND REWARDS   *EARNINGS:* **B+** *PERKS:* **D**

Ransom demands have spiraled in recent years, with fourteen countries reporting snatchings with initial requests of $25 million or more. Typically, kidnappers settle for 10 percent to 20 percent of their initially inflated asking prices, though in some cases ransoms are violently nonnegotiable. Worldwide, ransom demands are met in 67 percent of cases, with payments averaging at least $500,000. The largest ransom on record was the $60 million paid for Hong Kong billionaire Wang The-huei in 1990. He was not released and his body has never been recovered.

THE GLOBAL KIDNAPPING MARKET

Europe and Former Soviet Union 5%

Africa 3%

North America 2%

Asia and Pacific 14%

Latin America 76%

Source: Composite

While worldwide apprehension and conviction rates are exceedingly slight, the FBI takes a keen interest in domestic kidnapping, and U.S. clearance rates approach 95 percent. Prison stays for ransom kidnappers begin at seven years and escalate with the previous work experiences of the perpetrator and the violence of the incident. Kidnappings terminating in an abductee's demise are death penalty–eligible offenses. In addition to conventional law enforcement,

K&R (kidnapping and ransom) insurance policies have become quite popular. Between 60 percent and 65 percent of Fortune 500 companies carry such coverage, which provides reimbursement for deployment of elite crisis management teams, as well as ransom money and miscellaneous expenses. One condition of all such policies is that the policyholder does not publicize his or her coverage, lest he or she attract undue attention from media-savvy kidnappers.

STRESSES AND HAZARDS | **DANGERS: C-** **PRESSURES: C-**

Mortal fear is a wonderful motivator, so kidnappers should never underestimate the determination or resourcefulness of their charges. In 2002, a seven-year-old Philadelphia girl gnawed through her duct tape restraints, kicked a small hole through a locked wooden door, and wriggled her way through to freedom.

Absolute discretion is also a must. The ex-con who planned to abduct David Letterman's twenty-six-month-old son in 2004 was foiled when he asked a loose-lipped acquaintance to "think about" the $5 million plot.

NOTA BENE
Handwritten notes can leave pesky clues.

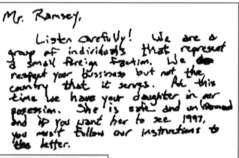

Source: FBI

A $118,000 demand to the family of JonBenet Ramsey.

Handwriting evidence in the trial of Bruno Hauptmann, the convicted Lindbergh kidnapper.

WORK ENVIRONMENT

HOURS: **C-** *COMFORT:* **C**

Most abductions take place in parking structures, driveways, or at intersections, where confined motorists can easily be approached, subdued, and packaged for transport. As the average kidnapping plays out over two weeks, establishing a secure holding spot for the detainee is of central importance. Basements and outbuildings are popular choices. Motel rooms and storage facilities are cheap and ubiquitous, but the convenience they provide may come at the risk of long-term imprisonment.

In 2002, a kidnapped Florida auto dealer was sequestered in an A-AAA Key Mini Storage unit, blindfolded, and gagged. While rolling around, he happened on a small screwdriver, freed himself, and summoned authorities.

LOAN SHARK

RANK: 35 out of 50   **AVERAGE GRADE:** C+

DUTIES: Loan sharks extend financial credit at usurious rates of interest, leveraging extortionate force or threats of force to collect legally unenforceable debts. Their crime, "extortionate extension of credit," involves loan amounts of at least $100 and annualized interest of more than 45 percent. Most loan sharks (sometimes called *Shylocks*, after a Shakespearean character who demanded a pound of flesh as collateral) insist on weekly *juice* (compounded interest) of 1 percent to 10 percent. This implies annual rates of 52 percent to 520 percent. Two exceptionally avaricious Chinese nationals who ran a boutique practice out of a southeastern Connecticut casino commanded annual premiums of up to 4,055 percent, backed by repeated threats of bomb use.

Loan-sharking has traditionally been closely associated with wagering. Financially strapped gamesmen who have exhausted traditional sources of short-term loans may turn to sharks as a perilously expensive last resort. Professional bookmakers (see Bookie) may also look to "the juiceman" for bridging funds in times of economic urgency. Though legitimate casinos serve primarily as centralized points for customer acquisition, they can also play a vital role in the laundering of windfall cash profits from loan-sharking (see Money Launderer). In November 2003, Susumu Kajiyama, Japan's reputed "Emperor of Loan Sharks," was charged with laundering several million dollars in Japanese juice at top Vegas casinos.

Organized crime families still dominate America's $10-billion-a-year illegal gambling industry, and their influence in loan-sharking is similarly profound. Our era's most telegenic crime figure, John Gotti, got his start in the late fifties collecting debts for Rockaway sharks and bookies with his bare fists. As he rose to *capo* and then *don, rent* payments from affiliated sharks remained a core component of his family revenues.

THE BIG FISH
Top Mob sharks of the twentieth century

Name	Alias	Headquarters	Family
Anthony Salerno	Fat Tony	New York City	Genovese
Anthony Accardo	Joe Batters	Palm Springs	Chicago
Gennaro Langella	Jerry Lang	Brooklyn	Colombo
Carmine Persico	Junior	Brooklyn	Colombo
Christopher Furnari	Christie Tick	New York City	Lucchese
Salvatore Santoro	Tom Mix	New York City	Lucchese
Philip Rastelli	Rusty	New York City	Bonanno
John Gotti	The Teflon Don	New York City	Gambino
Santo Trafficante	Louis Santos	Tampa	Tampa
Vincent Gigante	Chin	New Jersey	Genovese

Loan sharks often employ specialized *enforcers* to instill fear in borrowers and forcibly collect from deadbeats. Frank Calabrese Sr., who led a Chicago *street crew* with estimated loan sharking revenues of more than $2,600,000, counseled his enforcers to "do anything you have to do" to collect on nonperforming loans. Calabrese's star collector—former Chicago police officer Philip "Philly Beans" Tolomeo—went a bit too far by pocketing a fraction of the crew's juice for himself. Calabrese redressed Tolomeo's administrative misconduct by breaking his nose, taking title to his mother's home, and turning over the majority of his hundred *juice accounts* to junior associate Louis Bombacino (who was later convicted of threatening a prospective grand jury witness).

COMPENSATION AND REWARDS EARNINGS: B PERKS: B+

Like their namesakes, most sharks prosper by targeting lots of small fish. In 2002, Pasquale "Patsy" Fermo pleaded guilty to collectively extorting more than $250,000 from a whopping fifty fledgling Latino businesses in Corona, Elmhurst, Flushing, and Jackson Heights, New York. Occasionally, small accounts yield great dividends. If a business owner is delinquent in his payments, a farsighted shark may accept an equity stake in his business to offset the debt.

Partnering with otherwise legitimate enterprises offers great advantages, including access to healthy credit lines and plausible cover for money laundering. Frontline collectors for reputable crews can expect commissions of up to 25 percent on funds extracted.

ENFORCEMENT AND PENALTIES   *ARRESTS:* **C**   *SENTENCING:* **C-**

Extortionate extension and collection of credit are violations of Title II of the Consumer Credit Protection Act, and carry single-count penalties up to twenty years in prison and fines up to $250,000. Effective sharks mitigate their chances of prosecution and long-term incarceration by cultivating healthy levels of fearful respect among customers, associates, and potential jurors. Cases that reach the courtrooms have a discouragingly high conviction rate of almost 84 percent. Loan sharking indictments are often bundled with broader-based allegations of racketeering, bookmaking, and money laundering. In 1999, Genovese capo Joseph "the Eagle" Gatto negotiated a reduced sentence (four years) by detailing the elaborate interconnections between his sharking work and the family's gambling operations.

TOO LEGIT TO QUIT
The payday loan industry already dwarfs traditional loan sharking

Total U.S. payday lending	$25 billion/year
Average loan amount	$300
Total payday transactions	83 million/year
Average number of loans per borrower	11
Total number of borrowers	7.6 million
Percentage of borrowers caught in cyclic debt	66 percent
Total number of U.S. borrowers caught in cyclic debt	5 million

Source: Center for Responsible Lending

Some loan sharks become victims of their own success. Las Vegas's "Fat" Herbie Blitzstein was a well-known lieutenant for the late Chicago mob eminence Anthony "Tony the Ant" Spilotro (whose burial alive was immortalized in Martin Scorscese's *Casino*). For twenty years, Blitzstein traded on his former boss's fierce reputation, building an enviable loan-sharking practice. In 1997, emissaries from Buffalo, New York, and Los Angeles crime families asked Blitzstein to surrender his longtime business, and killed him when he refused. "Why me?" were his reported last words.

In recent years, many traditional loan sharks have had cause to ask "Why me?" as high-interest, quasi-legal payday loan operations usurped their markets and appropriated their methods. Since its humble 1993 beginning in rural Tennessee, payday lending has expanded to a $40 billion industry, with as many as 14 million of America's 105 million households in debt to payday lenders in 2003. Most payday loans carry effective annual interest rates of 700 percent to 2,000 percent—easily exceeding standard thresholds for usury. Such predatory lending schemes, however, have somehow secured the blessings of better government, with thirty-four U.S. states passing special authorization bills to ensure their continued legality.

WORK ENVIRONMENT *HOURS:* **B** *COMFORT:* **C**

Despite their brutish reputations, loan sharks are typically methodical businessmen who maintain predictable hours of availability, standardize their service offerings, and keep scrupulous records of payments and debts. Many still work out of shabby front businesses or vehicles, but computer-equipped offices are fast becoming the norm. The dawn of the information age has also brought new liabilities to loan-sharking. In 1999, FBI agents broke into the office of top Philadelphia shark Nicodemo S. Scarfo Jr. to plant a *keystroke logging* device on his PC. The logger enabled agents to intercept Scarfo's security password and decrypt his deeply incriminating loan-sharking records. Touchingly, his password ("nds09813-050") turned out to be the federal inmate ID number of his father, jailed Philadelphia–South Jersey Mob boss Nicodemo S. "Little Nicky" Scarfo Sr.

MARIJUANA CULTIVATOR

RANK: 29 out of 50   **AVERAGE GRADE:** C+

DUTIES: Marijuana Cultivators plant, tend, and harvest psychoactive strains of *Cannabis sativa* and *Cannabis indica*, dioecious annual herbs prized for their fibrous strength (in the form of hemp) and recreational charms. Typically, U.S. cultivators prepare crops for wholesale or retail distribution to domestic markets, though roughly 0.65 percent of America's 18 million monthly marijuana users grow plants for personal consumption. A small percentage of cultivators cater to the niche gray market for medical marijuana. Eleven states have passed legal medical exemptions since 1996, but federal enforcement agencies still regard all "grass roots" medical cultivation as illicit.

The coveted active ingredient in marijuana is THC (delta-9-tetrahydrocannabinol). In the 1970s, concentrations of THC in commercial-grade marijuana averaged less than 2 percent. Today's professional "green thumbs" coax average yields of 6 percent from their commercial buds, with premium sinsemilla (seedless) varieties yielding a dizzying 30 percent THC. Essential aids for world-class indoor cultivation include temperature- and humidity-controlled *grow rooms* and metal halide or high-pressure sodium lights. Early culling of male plants (*sexing*) and CO_2 supplementation are hallmarks of professional production. Growing tips, specialized equipment, and award-winning seed varieties are just a few clicks away at discreet mail-order Web sites.

The majority of America's high-grade cannabis still grows in the great outdoors. California and Kentucky lead the nation in outdoor cultivation. In 2003, 75 percent of the 466,054 cannabis plants seized in California were grown in isolated areas of public lands. Eighty-four percent of seized plants were controlled by the Mexican Drug Trafficking Organization (DTO), which often employs armed, undocumented workers to sit extended vigils at their remote, concealed *grows*. Mexico's narco-elite have embraced the laid-back California cultivation lifestyle as a low-stress alternative to the rigors of cross-border smuggling. In 2003, twelve

DTO-controlled grows boasted more than ten thousand plants each.

Kentucky's Daniel Boone National Forest accounts for 29 percent of all cannabis plants eradicated in our national wild lands. That state's mostly Caucasian citizen-farmers maintain smaller plots than their Mexican counterparts and frequently travel long distances to tend them. Smaller, family-based, vertical operations are the norm, reflecting lessons learned through generations of liquor bootlegging. In the late eighties, Kentucky gave rise to the so-called Cornbread Mafia, the largest domestic dope cartel in America's history. The group—which earned its name by planting pot between corn rows in dozens of Kentucky and Midwestern farms—functioned like most agricultural cooperatives, with affiliated growers pooling labor, equipment, and market intelligence. When the cookie finally crumbled for the Cornbread crew, they had stockpiled 180 tons of marijuana in nine states.

At least a half-dozen Kentucky sheriffs' departments have aided in the state's economic miracle over the past ten years. In Breathitt County, Sheriff Ray Clemons covered for a cultivation and distribution ring that included his own daughter. In Pulaski County, a hit on the incumbent sheriff was allegedly sanctioned jointly by his electoral opponent and the county's most prosperous grower.

The biggest story in North American marijuana cultivation, however, is the rise of Canada's indoor *grow-ops*. In January 2004, police seized thirty thousand plants (with an estimated street value of $30 million) from a single, factory-scale operation inside an abandoned Molson brewery in Barrie, Ontario. The sixty-thousand-square-foot facility included dormitory quarters for up to fifty workers. Canadian authorities speculate there may be up to fifty thousand grow-ops across the country, producing some of the continent's highest-quality cannibis.

COMPENSATION AND REWARDS — EARNINGS: **A**   PERKS: **B-**

Marijuana is America's number-one cash crop, with annual sales exceeding $32 billion. Prices for pot are much more varied than those for comparable agricultural commodities. Per-pound pricing ranges from $100 to $4,500 for commercial-grade, and from $900 to $8,000 for *sinsemilla*. Market prices reflect variations in potency, quantity, frequency of purchase, buyer-seller relationships, transportation, and proximity to sources of supply. With top-shelf wares, even modest operations can spawn wondrous profits. A seasoned Florida *hydroponic* grower generated $1.5 million in eighteen months from a single concealed room in her barn. Business was so brisk for her associates that they buried $2.2 million cash in Tupperware containers in their backyards.

HOW GREEN IS MY VALLEY?
Four states accounted for 80 percent of the $35 billion U.S. pot harvest in 2006

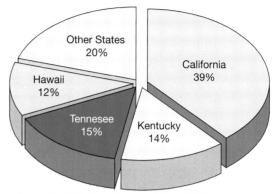

Source: The Bulletin of Cannabis Reform, Marijuana Production in the United States

ENFORCEMENT AND PENALTIES   *ARRESTS:* **C-**   *SENTENCING:* **D**

Taxpayers tender roughly $4 billion per annum to arrest, try, and incarcerate marijuana offenders. From 1992 to 2002, marijuana arrests rose from 28 percent to

HIGHER THAN EVER!
The average THC percentage of seized marijuana continues to rise

Source: Organization for the Reform of Marijuana Laws

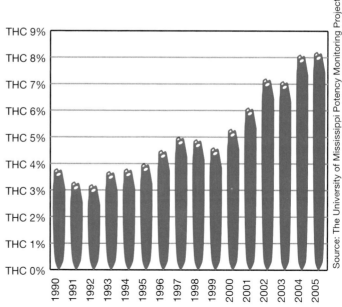

Source: The University of Mississippi Potency Monitoring Project

45 percent of all drug arrests. Fortunately for serious growers, 79 percent of these arrests were for casual possession, and only 6 percent resulted in felony convictions. Prestigious federal indictments are actually quite rare. There were only 711 issued by the Crime Drug Enforcement Task Force (OCDETF) in all of fiscal 2001.

Annual seizures and eradication of marijuana average more than 1,200 metric tons. Advanced interdiction techniques include aerial infrared detection and pinpoint application of environmentally friendly defoliants. In Kentucky, National Guardsmen fly five hundred helicopter-based burn missions each summer, rappelling with M-16s and Kevlar vests into booby-trapped pot fields. In the past decade they've put spark to $11 billion in backwoods combustibles.

STRESSES AND HAZARDS

DANGERS: **B-** *PRESSURES:* **C+**

Marijuana cultivators use public lands to obscure ties to their product and ensure ensure against judicial forfeiture of their own property. The remoteness of these public-private workspaces may make them difficult to defend, and worries over

GROWING RISKS
Recreational drug workers beware!

FIRE—High-powered grow lights, fans, and pumps consume vast amounts of power. Subcode wiring and illegal electrical meter bypasses frequently lead to unexpected flare-ups. In 2004, a small-time Philadelphia grower was charged with third-degree murder after two firefighters perished while extinguishing an electrical blaze in his basement grow room.

ELECTROCUTION—In British Columbia, an average of three growers are electrocuted each year.

TOXIC GASES—Large grows release major doses of carbon monoxide and carbon dioxide. Growers without protective gear run significant risks of short-term illness or even permanent respiratory disease.

BACTERIA—The same atmosphere that fosters high-quality buds also supports high quantities of germs and bugs.

pilferage or attack can prove taxing. To guard against inventory slippage, serious-minded farmers avail themselves of makeshift land mines, buried *punji* sticks, and— occasionally—poisonous snakes. Mother Nature can also be a clever thief, and droughts are a cyclical concern for growers who rely on natural irrigation.

WORK ENVIRONMENT

HOURS: **B-** *COMFORT:* **C**

Most marijuana cultivators enjoy considerable personal latitude in scheduling, hours, and work locale, but high-volume operations may demand long periods of sustained vigilance. Indoor grows generate substantial heat and odor, and can be quite unpleasant if adequate ventilation is not provided.

Outdoor cultivation inevitably requires exposure to a range of weather conditions.

In large measure, marijuana cultivation remains a young man's game. Fifty-seven percent of American cannabis professionals are less than twenty-four years old, and 87 percent are males.

BEER AND BUDS
A workplace tour of Barrie, Ontario's brewery/super-grow.
Source: Royal Canadian Mounted Police

MERCENARY

RANK: 48 out of 50   **AVERAGE GRADE:** C-

DUTIES: Mercenaries fight or assist in armed conflicts on behalf of foreign nations or groups with which they are not ideologically aligned—in exchange for payment or material gain. In addition to personal participation in land-, air-, and sea-based combat operations, modern *soldiers of fortune* assist in the training of military, paramilitary, security, and intelligence forces; provide strategic and tactical advice; arrange logistical support; and manage chains of supply. Beyond the battlefield, mercenaries often work to destabilize political regimes through acts of terrorism, or through the abduction, intimidation, or assassination of key stakeholders.

Interpretations of the legality of this time-honored field are in rapid flux. Mercenaries are explicitly outlawed under Article 47 of the Geneva Convention, and a 1994 UN resolution urges all nations to "exercise the utmost vigilance against the menace posed by the activities of mercenaries." Yet, the early nineties saw the dramatic rise of a new class of "supermercs" known as private military corporations (PMCs).

A Pretoria-based company set the model for this new breed of private army. In 1993, Executive Outcomes recruited nearly two thousand South African special forces veterans to fight UNITA rebels in Angola. EO eventually billed Angola more than $100 million for combat and security services, then went on to bill Sierra Leone $35 million for quelling a 1995 civil war with a mere 170 men and six aircraft. When South Africa and thirteen other African nations explicitly outlawed mercenary activity in 1998, EO conveyed many of its assets to England's Sandline International. Sandline's rogue operations in Papua, New Guinea, and Sierra Leone, respectively, toppled the standing government and nearly forced the resignation of the British foreign minister.

BIG BOYS' TOYS
Ready to step up to the real thing?

Today, PMCs employ an estimated ninety thousand combat-ready ass-kickers worldwide. The ratio of "contracted security personnel" to regular forces serving in Iraq is at least ten times greater than the ratio in the Gulf War, with an estimated twenty thousand contract workers in-theater in 2005.

Many of these outsourcing arrangements violate national or international laws. The widespread recruitment of soldiers in Fiji by U.S. PMCs, for instance, is overtly illegal under Fijian law. However, PMCs have been a boon for disgraced soldiers around the world, employing at least two confessed apartheid-era South African killers, an estimated five hundred Serbs who served under Milošević, and dozens of veterans of Chile's notorious Pinochet regime. Contract employees of CACI International and Titan Corp. have gone on to great distinction in their pivotal roles in prisoner abuse at Abu Ghraib. In Afghanistan, three American mercenaries (including ex–Special Forces member Jonathan K. Idema) achieved even greater notoriety in prisoner abuse, operating their own supposedly unsanctioned jail/torture chamber.

Although opportunities for gung ho independents are definitely on the decline, a 2004 coup attempt led by a former British officer and financed by the son of former British prime minister Margaret Thatcher, harked back to the glory days of "merc work." Mark Thatcher advanced $275,000 to his friend and Cape Town neighbor Simon Mann to launch a *Mission: Impossible*–style surgical raid into Equatorial Guinea and overthrow its ailing dictator, Teodoro Obiang Nguema Mbasago. Mann, who led a successful 2003 bloodless coup in the islands of São Tomé and Principe, was arrested at Zimbabwe's Harare airport with sixty-nine seasoned mercenaries. The police impounded Mann's $3 million 727 plane and $180,000 in cash, after learning that he planned to take a large cache of weapons on board.

COMPENSATION AND REWARDS   *EARNINGS:* **C+** *PERKS:* **C**

This is a demanding, specialized, and dangerous field, and mercenary "top guns" demand top pay. In Iraq, PMCs offer U.S. and European recruits up to $700 a day for high-exposure postings. Corporate mercs from developing nations receive considerably less. Former Chilean commandos employed by Blackwater USA to guard oil wells against insurgent attacks pocket a comparatively puny $4,000 per month. In its heyday, Executive Outcomes's pay scale ranged from $2,700 per month for basic infantrymen to $13,000 per month for bomber pilots, with life insurance coverage provided gratis. Enterprising mercenaries frequently supplement their incomes through looting, gunrunning, and drug trafficking.

ENFORCEMENT AND PENALTIES   *ARRESTS:* **B**   *SENTENCING:* **D+**

Captured mercenaries are subject to the prevailing laws of the lands in which they are detained, though they are occasionally extradited to their countries of origin. Daniel Gearhart, an American father of four who secured his posting in Angola through a classified ad in *Soldier of Fortune* magazine, was captured after three days in-country and executed by a firing squad. The three Americans who ran a private jail in Afghanistan received sentences ranging from eight to ten years. A panel of Kabul judges rejected their assertion that they were working for a secret Pentagon counterterrorist group.

OOPS!
Armed conflict does *have occasional downsides.*
Source: U.S. Department of Defense

STRESSES AND HAZARDS

DANGERS: **D-** PRESSURES: **D**

Although some military careerists never see a single day's combat, mercenaries seek out frontline, high-exposure assignments. As of June 2005, at least two hundred "security contractors" had been killed in Iraq. Mistreatment after capture is also a serious concern in this occupation. Amnesty International believes that Gerhard Eugen Nershz, a German national jailed for participation in Simon Mann's ill-fated 2004 coup attempt, was tortured to death while in custody in Equatorial Guinea.

WORK ENVIRONMENT

HOURS: **D** COMFORT: **D**

Extended visits to foreign lands can provide cultural enrichment, but battlefields are often uncomfortable places, and mercenaries typically work long hours under extraordinarily challenging physical and psychological conditions. Poor food, heavy packs, and public scorn are par for the bloody course in this unusual occupation. During cyclic periods of peace-related unemployment, adrenaline-addicted mercenaries may also experience feelings of agitation or alienation.

METH LAB OPERATOR

RANK: 44 out of 50   **AVERAGE GRADE:** C

DUTIES: Meth Lab Operators oversee clandestine facilities producing methamphetamine (meth), a versatile central nervous system stimulant that can be smoked, snorted, ingested, or injected. Methamphetamine—known by a galaxy of evocative street names including *crystal meth*, *crank*, *ice*, and *speed*—has quickly become America's most ubiquitous synthetic drug. Lab operators supervise or participate in the synthesis of meth from widely available chemical precursors—a process known as *cooking*.

Few clandestine lab cooks have formal training in chemistry. Most study under more accomplished offenders or sift among the hundreds of recipes available on the Internet. (On average, experienced cooks pass their knowledge to ten apprentices each year.) Most recipe ingredients can be derived from household staples: cold and allergy medications, rock salt, battery acid, iodine, lighter fluid, and drain cleaner. Items commonly repurposed as cooking gear include mason jars, rubber tubing, drink bottles, cof-

HOUSEHOLD HELPERS
Everyday Items Used in Methamphetamine Production

Acetone

Alcohol (isopropyl or rubbing)

Anhydrous ammonia (fertilizer)

Ephedrine (cold medications)

Ether (engine starter)

Hydrochloric acid (pool supply)

Iodine (flakes or crystal)

Kitty litter (clay)

Lithium (batteries)

Methanol (gasoline additive)

MSM (nutritional supplement)

Pseudoephedrine (cold medications)

Salt (table or rock)

Sodium hydroxide (lye)

Sodium metal

Sulfuric acid (drain cleaner)

Toluene (brake cleaner)

Trichloroethane (gun cleaner)

Source (photos): North Little Rock Police Department

fee filters, gasoline cans, and hotplates.

Small, portable setups are known throughout the industry as *Beavis and Butthead* labs. These tabletop labs can be fully provisioned at a big-box retailer for less than two hundred dollars. They can yield one to four ounces of methamphetamine per twenty-four-hour production cycle. *Superlabs* are professionally managed facilities yielding ten or more product pounds per workday. Although Beavis and Butthead operations are increasingly abundant, superlabs account for up to 80 percent of all production.

Historically, meth labs have been heavily concentrated in Southern California and Mexico. In recent years, Midwestern-upstart Illinois has been challenging California for leadership in domestic methamphetamine production.

Many lab operators do their own cooking. Others employ cooks on a contract or salaried basis. Top cooks freelance among multiple drug trafficking organizations and often are compensated with a percentage of the drugs they produce. Other key work roles include equipment setup and maintenance, chemical storage, property leasing, procurement, waste disposal, and facility security. Sole proprietors take on all these diverse responsibilities. Larger trafficking concerns tap immigrants (and other low-wage folk) to perform hazardous or distasteful duties. The informal sharing of men and materials is surprisingly common among midtier operators.

Lab operators acquire bulk quantities of restricted precursor chemicals through front companies, undocumented cash transactions, smuggling, forgery, theft, and bribery. They also trade in quantities just below government reporting thresholds—a practice known as *smurfing*.

Powdered methamphetamine is an enduring American favorite. Its crystalline cousin—ice—is a smokable Hawaiian variant that's starting to make a big noise on the mainland. Methamphetamine tablets, known as *yaba*, are popular throughout Southeast and East Asia.

COMPENSATION AND REWARDS   *EARNINGS:* **B**   *PERKS:* **B**

In 2003, 12.3 million Americans admitted having tried methamphetamine at least once, with 607,000 reporting having consumed a meth product in the last month. Hawaii's thirty thousand loyal users *alone* spend up to $1.8 billion annually to service $50-to-$170-per-day drug appetites. Pricing for DEA-seized powdered meth ranged from $3,000 to $13,000 per pound, $300 to $1,700 per ounce, and

BEAVIS 'N' BUTTHEAD
A very basic tabletop setup.
Source: West Virginia State Police

$40 to $125 per gram in 2002. That year, the average purity of street methamphetamine rose to 42 percent. Prices for rock candy–like ice were $1,200 to $70,000 per pound, $350 to $2,300 per ounce, and $120 to $500 per gram.

Although windfall profits in the U.S. methamphetamine sector were once largely monopolized by fearsome Outlaw Bikers (see page 149), since 1994 Mexican narcotics concerns have leveraged state-of-the-art supply chains and deep mastery of material sciences to usurp market leadership.

ENFORCEMENT AND PENALTIES   *ARRESTS:* **C**   *SENTENCING:* **D+**

Methamphetamine is classified as a Schedule II, high-abuse drug under the Controlled Substance Act. Its chemical constituents are monitored and restricted under the Comprehensive Methamphetamine Control Act. Each year, the DEA seizes 100 million to 150 million meth doses. In fiscal 2003, 4,456 practitioners were sanctioned by federal courts. Federal sentences for methamphetamine entrepreneurs average 88.5 months—compared with 115 months for crack dealers, 63.4 months for heroin vendors, and 38

months for marijuana specialists. Weapons are involved in 11.2 percent of meth-production-related convictions. Operators of motel-based labs risk extended sentences for imperiling public health.

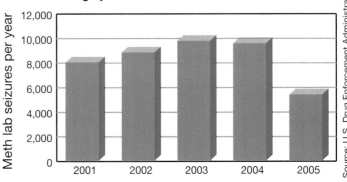

THE GREAT METH MIGRATION
Domestic production plummets, as enforcement matures and big operators head south of the border

Meth lab seizures per year

Source: U.S. Drug Enforcement Administration

Methamphetamine production involves extensive interaction with explosives, solvents, metals, salts, and corrosives. Each year, three to six clandestine-lab workers die from work-related explosions, fires, or inhalation of toxins. Cooks enamored of their own products often shun even basic laboratory precautions. One out of every five interdicted labs is revealed via explosion or fire. Forced entries by police frequently precipitate explosions—by accident or via booby traps. Poor ventilation exacerbates the risks of explosion and toxic inhalation.

Each pound of manufactured methamphetamine is accompanied by five to six pounds of hazardous waste. Cleanup costs for contaminated lab sites average $2,000 to $5,000.

Dangers of intentional methamphetamine abuse include addiction and psychotic features, including paranoia, auditory hallucinations, and suicidal thoughts.

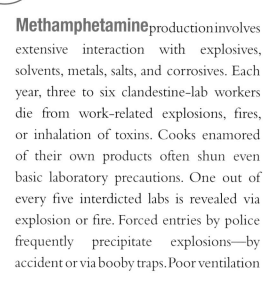

WORK ENVIRONMENT

HOURS: C-   COMFORT: D

Clandestine labs are sprinkled throughout America's cities, suburbs, and farmlands. They are sited in rental homes, apartments, motel rooms, campgrounds, garages, self-storage facilities, outbuildings, and vans.

Long shifts are the norm for production workers, and continued exposure to airborne irritants can lead to bleary-eyed moments.

Methamphetamine can be a powerful aphrodisiac, so sex toys and pornography are more common and better accepted at production facilities than at conventional work sites. Despite their decidedly adult orientation, more than 20 percent of the meth labs visited by law enforcement had children present.

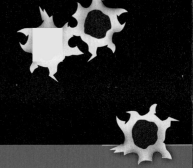

MONEY LAUNDERER

RANK: 23 out of 50   **AVERAGE GRADE:** B-

DUTIES: Money launderers conceal or disguise the nature, source, location, movement, or ownership of criminal proceeds. Launderers *wash* "dirty" money through a cycle of obscuring transactions, designed to make it appear to be legitimate, *clean* income. Although laundering can involve a galaxy of complex transactions, most schemes share three distinct stages: *placement*, *layering*, and *integration*.

THE WASH CYCLE
Stage 1: Placement

Ill-gotten greenbacks are deposited into institutions, traded for other currencies, used to purchase hard goods, invested in real estate, or smuggled abroad.

SMURFING—Numerous intermediaries, *smurfs*, are enlisted to deposit cash into their own accounts. Individual deposits are limited to $9,999—just below federal reporting thresholds. Funds are subsequently wired to a wrongdoer's accounts or subjected to additional obfuscation.

CASH SMUGGLING—The brute-force last resort for international transfers can be laborious and risky. One million dollars in hundred-dollar bills weighs at least twenty-two pounds, while the same sum in dollar bills weighs over a ton. Smuggler-launderers often trade bulky cash for more readily concealable or disguisable gems, precious metals, fine art, or rare stamps.

BANK COLLUSION—Banks or individual employees are bribed or coerced to overlook reporting requirements. In 2002, New York's Broadway National Bank pleaded guilty to failing to report $123 million in deposits for several major drug gangs and money laundering syndicates. The bank paid $4 million in fines.

TOO MUCH CASH CAN BE A BURDEN
When desperate times called for desperate measures.

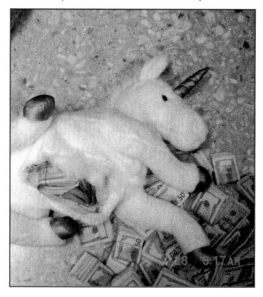

The old cash-in-the-unicorn gambit.
Source: U.S. Immigration and Customs Enforcement

Time for some belt-tightening.

Stage 2: Layering

Placed funds are routed through additional obscuring transactions, with the aim of rendering investigative backtracking effectively impossible.

TAX HAVENS AND OFFSHORE BANKS—Liberty-loving criminals favor jurisdictions with weak laundering controls, nominal taxes, and strict banking secrecy. In 2001, the Financial Action Task Force listed twenty-three such crime-friendly havens. After four years of intense international pressure, only three no-questions-asked, pariah nations remain: Myanmar, Nauru, and Nigeria. Launderers shuttle funds in and out of these enablers via electronic fund transfers to accounts held under anonymous shell corporations.

INTERMEDIARIES—Banks or individual employees are bribed or coerced to overlook reporting requirements or structure deposits to evade them.

Cleansed funds reenter the mainstream economy and commingle with legitimate monies to finance big-ticket commercial transactions, investments, and purchases.

BLACK MARKET PESO EXCHANGE (BMPE)—Executives of Latin American crime multinationals contract with specialized launderers to exchange dollar-denominated U.S. cash stockpiles for pesos redeemable in Bogotá (or other black-market hubs). BMPE brokers charge up to 30 percent for their transnational laundry delivery. They purchase wholesale U.S. goods with the dollars they take in, and vend them to legitimate Colombian businesses that they invoice in pesos.

PERSONAL BANKING—Power launderers disintermediate traditional financiers by setting up their own offshore "instant banks" or taking equity stakes in established institutions. In 1996, Mexico's famed Juárez cartel purchased a holding company with a controlling stake (20 percent) in Mexico City's Banco Anahuac. By 1998, the IRS alleged, the cartel had used the bank to transfer $30 million dirty dollars to five U.S. banks.

TRADE-BASED TRANSFER—Shell companies under- or over-invoice their laundering partners for shipments of actual goods, to provide cover for de facto cash transfers.

INTERNET PAYMENTS—Nonbank payment systems such as AnonymousGold, PayPal, and StormPay, and electronic currencies such as e-bullion, e-dinar, e-gold, and Evocash are used to anonymize international transfers.

COMPENSATION AND REWARDS   *EARNINGS:* **B+** *PERKS:* **B+**

Plausible estimates of global laundering range from $600 billion to $2.8 trillion annually. In 2001, U.S. law enforcement seized more than $300 million in freshly washed criminal assets. About 20 percent of the cases involved amounts over $1 million. Freelance launderers, black-market peso brokers, and gray-market intermediaries work for fees of 10 percent to 30 percent of assets under management. Do-it-yourselfers avoid commissions and potentially talkative middlemen by laundering their own dirty dollars.

Perks for offshore specialists include frequent junkets to tropical havens.

In addition to sanctions for their initial offending acts, launderers face bonus federal stays of up to twenty years and fines up to $500,000, or twice the value of the property involved. U.S. courts completed 1,420 money laundering cases in 2001. Roughly nine in ten of those defendants were convicted, and three out of four convicts received prison terms, with sentences averaging a tad over four years.

The U.S. Department of the Treasury has declared antilaundering efforts to be "integral to the war on terrorism." Since 9/11, 282 individuals and organizations have been chastised as Specially Designated Global Terrorist (SDGT) entities, and over $137 million in toys for terrorists has been seized.

MIXED MESSAGES
Federal indictments are up . . . but asset seizures are down

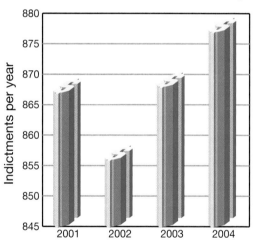

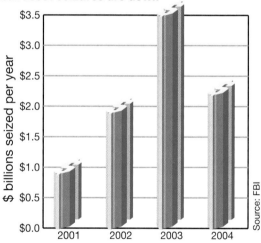

Source: FBI

Counterfeiters minted over 180 million bogus greenbacks in 2003, so funny money can spell serious trouble for duped launderers. Manual counting of large stacks of mixed-denomination bills often results in finger and eye fatigue, and counting discrepancies can lead to unpleasant disputes. Ongoing improvements in transnational intelligence sharing, control implementation, and financial transparency necessitate frequent reappraisals of tactics and institutional loyalties.

WORK ENVIRONMENT

HOURS: **C** *COMFORT:* **B**

Professional money launderers collude with a star-studded cast of international crime figures via prepaid cell phones, encrypted e-mail, and couriers. Frivolous face-to-face meetings are frowned upon, but major cash exchanges commonly mandate in-person character assessments or assurances. Initial implementation of layering schemes and cyclical recruitment of smurfs, coconspirators, and commercial dupes can be labor intensive, but online banking tools and electronic payment systems are alleviating the most tedious aspects of this field.

Professional attire is indicated for interactions with financial officers, but less formal, stylized costuming may be more disarming among criminal subculturists.

MUGGER

RANK: 41 out of 50   **AVERAGE GRADE:** C

DUTIES: Muggers—also known as *armed robbers*, *street robbers,* or *stickup men*—use force or threats of force to impel adjacent individuals to surrender valuables held on their persons. Most stickup specialists are short-term thinkers driven by very immediate desires for must-have street goods. A recent study of St. Louis armed robbery professionals found that 49 percent used their gruffly garnered funds to finance high-intensity bouts of drug consumption, gambling, or drinking. Twenty-five percent purchased status-enhancing tokens and totems, and fewer than 20 percent used their pocket plunder for so-called necessities. Secondary motivators include sadistic leanings, adrenaline addiction, effrontery at displays of wealth, and an enduringly countercultural dedication to *getting over* (avoiding the rat race).

Many muggers prey upon brother predators—particularly corner-side drug concessionaires who flaunt their Baggies, bank

SIGNS OF RECOVERY?
Street assault rates are holding steady

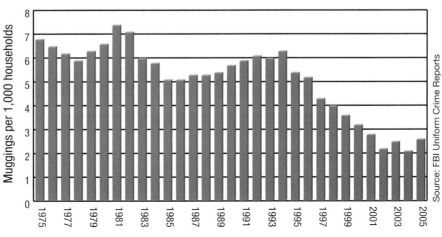

Muggings per 1,000 households

Source: FBI Uniform Crime Reports

rolls, and bling. Many see these acts as community services and just retribution against the keepers of the drug monkeys on their backs. Though peace officers, customers, and passersby are disinclined to agitate on behalf of dealers who get *jacked*, targeting substance slingers and other underground economists does entail an increased probability of violent retribution. The likelihood of retaliation increases as one moves up the food/drug chain. So most *drug robbers* primarily patronize entry-level street dealers who *front*—represent—that they are *hard*—tough.

Elderly quarry are prized for their low foot speed, limited fighting spirit, and well-founded fears of injury. Auto-based attackers favor work sites adjacent to major, free-moving thoroughfares for expedited exits. Conversely, pedestrian predators favor restricted-access parking lots and other barrier-rich environments tailored to retarding police pursuers. Surprisingly, conspicuous displays of police presence are little deterrent to determined muggers but *do* serve to lull potential prey into false perceptions of security.

The element of surprise is indispensable in denying the targets the opportunity to mount or even contemplate an effective defense. Most muggers approach with stealth or speed from the victim's rearward blind side, then mysteriously manifest, striking "out of nowhere." Others don nonthreatening, site-appropriate garb and directly *step to* their intended, choosing among a multitude of time-tested ruses. Requests for time of day and street directions are enduring classics. Fetching female accomplices are also particularly effective in distraction-based approaches. The ski masks, skull caps, and dark sunglasses so favored in armed institutional attacks are occasionally employed when seasonally sensible.

Efficient perpetrator-prey communications are the key to safe and successful streetside exchanges. Upon closing in on their quarry, perpetrators must quickly orient them to the nature, demands, and protocol of the event. Seasoned muggers strive to convey the instant impression of grave danger or imminent doom—"This is a robbery, mother …, don't make it a murder!" Often the initial utterance is coupled with the close-quarter application of an enabler weapon.

The next step—managing the full and efficient transfer of goods—is the most technically troublesome aspect of an attack. Felons fall into two camps, here. According to a St. Louis street worker survey, 47 percent of professional muggers directed their victims to extract and tender their own valuables—"If you want to survive, give me all your money. I'm not bullshitting!" This approach frees the mugger to watch for signs of danger but leaves some doubt about the completeness of the victim's disclosure. The "hands-on" camp prefers to forage for themselves, in hopes of liberating additional loot and preempting the surprise production of a small-caliber weapon.

COMPENSATION AND REWARDS

EARNINGS: **C-**   PERKS: **B+**

In the United States, a mugging is completed every fifty-one seconds. Street practitioners are the backbone of the industry, accounting for up to 60 percent of all productivity in this violent crime subsphere. Cash gains per grab tend to be petite, so volume is key. Most jobs net less than one hundred dollars. Only 9.4 percent of *all* robberies yield over $1,000 (this includes convenience stores, armored cars, etc.). In one study of street robbery professionals, 36 percent had completed fifty or more mugging assignments, and 71 percent had completed more than ten.

GOLDEN YEARS
Muggers' productivity peaks at an early age

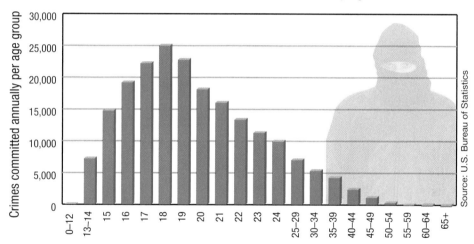

Crimes committed annually per age group

Source: U.S. Bureau of Statistics

ENFORCEMENT AND PENALTIES

ARRESTS: **B+**   SENTENCING: **C-**

If this accessible, entry-level crime appeals to you, the good news is that three-quarters of muggings go unsolved. The bad news is that the average prison sentence is ninety-four months, and more muggers are serving sentences of twenty years or more than any other group in prison. The key is to remain among the estimated 50 percent of career muggers who have never been convicted.

While robbery is a hybrid activity requiring skills in violence *and* theft, force is at the core of the mugger's mission. About 33 percent of all armed assignments result in victim injury and 8 percent end in felony homicide. Ten percent of *all* homicides, in fact, occur during unauthorized property extractions. Perpetration-place injuries are serious concerns for muggers at all levels.

Proper equipment selection is essential. Many workers prefer large-bore hand-guns for their stopping power and intimidation value. Knives are a controversial choice, as they can easily be turned back toward their wielder. In the end, though, the greatest hazard is the wild card of the human will. In 2005, German Centelles, an eighty-year-old New York City man, became incensed when a journeyman mugger attempted to relieve him of his cigarettes. He pulled out *his own* knife and stabbed the hapless attacker repeatedly, until two passing firemen pried him off.

THE YOUTH VOTE
Mugging is the favorite robbery activity among juvenile offenders

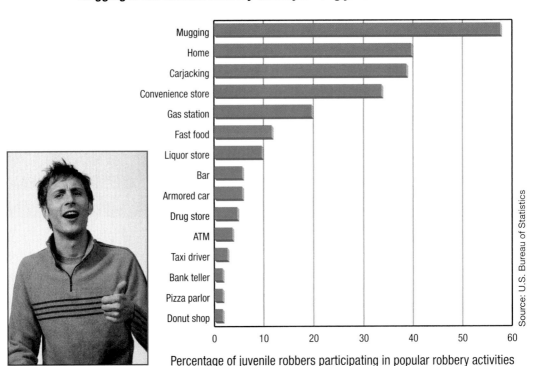

Percentage of juvenile robbers participating in popular robbery activities

Source: U.S. Bureau of Statistics

Muggers work primarily outdoors, stationing themselves at lurker-friendly lounging spots such as parking lots, shopping centers, and public streets. Areas around major city public transit stations are also perennial hotspots, with activity peaking about three-sixteenths of a mile from the station. A small minority of pocket predators specialize in indoor assignments at ATM locations and malls.

Roughly two-thirds of street robberies occur between three P.M. and midnight. Street action peaks in the November-December approach of the holidays. Typical commutes for muggers are mercifully short—as 40 percent of muggings take place within two miles of the robber's home.

Seventy-one percent of muggers consider themselves to be amateurs, 55 percent were drunk or high during their last robbery, and 18 percent say they would take on five or more people if they had a gun.

ORGAN BROKER

RANK: 3 out of 50   **AVERAGE GRADE:** B

DUTIES: Organ Brokers match human candidates for organ and tissue transplants with living and deceased donors. They co-ordinate transport of involved parts and parties, and contract with medical professionals and facilities to perform transplant procedures. Most U.S. brokers employ street-savvy local surrogates to identify and recruit healthy, impoverished donors in undernourished nations. Others import whole cadavers or choice subsections from tight-lipped donor dictatorships such as China. In the third world—where rates of hepatitis and serious infection are soaring—discriminating organ shoppers pay large premiums for living donors with well-documented medical histories. In 2004, 85,420 Americans anxiously awaited transplant surgery. Of these, 58,188 required a kidney. The previous year, more than 3,300 people died waiting for that prized part.

The commercial organ market took wing in 1983 with the establishment of the U.S.-based International Kidney Exchange. By 1994, when the Indian government outlawed outright organ sales, this service had helped facilitate some two thousand paid donations from living Indians.

India is still widely known as the "Organ Bazaar of the World." With wages averaging an anemic $11 a month, cash-strapped workers may be sorely tempted by the healthy stipends ($1,070 on average) offered for a "sponsored" nephrectomy (kidney transplant). The maturing market is dominated largely by accomplished heroin traffickers and influential owners of luxurious for-profit hospitals.

Gray-market brokers such as L.A.'s Jim Cohan—who prefers the title "international transplant coordinator"—are becoming increasingly geographically agnostic. They network with organ scouts in Pakistan, South America, Eastern Europe, the Philippines, Singapore, Iraq, and South Africa, and book operating rooms in nearly thirty nations.

China has emerged as the leading supplier to America's growing black market for body parts. Human rights monitors believe that China conducts more than fifteen thousand judicial executions

ANATOMY OF A WORLD MARKET

SOUTH AFRICA—The nation's famous Truth and Reconciliation Commission unearthed widespread allegations of organ harvesting at police morgues during and following the apartheid era. Today, moneyed foreigners enjoy four-star hospitality at a host of private transplantation clinics.

BRAZIL—Reports of child kidnapping, organ theft, and commercial tissue trade still abound, despite sweeping 1997 legal reforms.

IRAQ—Under Saddam Hussein, the going rate for a kidney was $2,000. In the recessional postwar climate, cost-conscious transplant candidates can obtain these items for as little as $700.

ISRAEL—The Holy Land lacks any formal prohibitions against organ trafficking and is home to Ilan Peri, thought to be the mastermind of the world's largest organ procurement ring. Peri's key associates reportedly include a former Israel police officer and a retired Brazilian military officer.

UNITED STATES—In 1997, the Los Angeles coroner's office sold more than five hundred pairs of corneas to the Doheny Eye & Tissue Transplant Bank. California's taxpayers received $335 per pair of corneas, which Doheny then resold for $3,400 per pair.

In 2004, the director of UCLA'S Willed Body Program was arrested for vending frozen body parts from research cadavers. Between 1998 and 2003, a middleman paid $704,600 for access to 496 human bodies in UCLA's freezer. A single, fully equipped corpse has a potential market value of up to $200,000.

UNITED ARAB EMIRATES AND OMAN—Over the course of five years, 131 oil-rich patients are known to have traveled to India, where they purchased kidneys from living donors for $2,000 to $3,000.

a year. The pace of prisoner disposal is so brisk that major courthouses are now accessorized with twenty-four-seat mobile execution vans. Assorted takeout portions of Chinese prisoners can be found throughout the world. A 1998 FBI sting netted two Queens, New York, brokers who contracted to sell "quality organs" harvested from prisoners executed on China's Hainan Island. One of the men produced documents identifying himself as a former deputy chief prosecutor at the island prison. A leaked directive from the publicity-shy Chinese government wisely warned "the use of corpses or organs of executed criminals must be kept strictly secret . . . to avoid negative repercussions."

Tales of stolen organs have long been derided as urban myths. Not so! The Brazilian underclass, for example, is particularly at risk. In 1995, a superficially injured Brazilian homeless man was counseled, "That damaged eye of yours isn't worth anything—let's just take it out!" The same year, a São Paulo woman discovered that one of her kidneys had been spirited away during surgery to remove an ovarian cyst.

In Romania and Moldova, meanwhile, surgery at knife- or gunpoint has become commonplace. Most amazingly, in the year 2000, the Russian public was stunned to learn that an elderly Moscow-area woman had contracted to "part out" her five-year-old grandson, Andrei, for $90,000.

COMPENSATION AND REWARDS — EARNINGS: **B+** PERKS: **C+**

Though corneas ($3,000 to $5,000 per pair) and other exotic items offer high profit potential, kidneys are the dominant commodity in global organ trade. The recent glut of discount Indian and Iraqi kidneys—with some breaking the long-standing $1,000 price barrier—has noticeably dampened kidney profits worldwide. However, prime kidneys still wholesale for up to $5,000 in Turkey and $20,000 in Israel. Israel's top broker, Ilan Peri, is said to have amassed over $4 million, by facilitating more than a hundred transplants. Recently, he quoted an American hopeful the kingly sum of $145,000 (cash in advance) for an all-expense-paid transplant tour of an undisclosed donor nation. Typical broker wholesale costs for transplant procedures range from $2,000 for a bare-bones Iraqi procedure to $20,000 for spalike pampering in South Africa. This represents a considerable savings over U.S. retail rates of $40,000 to $70,000.

PARTS IS PARTS	
Body part	Market rate
Heart	$11,000
Thigh bone	$11,000
Elbow	$9,500
Hip	$8,700
Achilles tendon	$3,700
Corneas	$3,000-$5,000/pair
Skin grafts	$1,000/square foot

Source: National Institutes of Health

ENFORCEMENT AND PENALTIES — *ARRESTS:* **A** *SENTENCING:* **B**

The 1984 *National Organ Transplant Act*—spearheaded by then senator Al Gore—mandates up to five years in prison and $50,000 in fines for patients or intermediaries who make substantive payments to organ donors. The intimidation value of this federal statute is somewhat diminished by the fact that, to date, no one has ever been convicted under it. The global community has yet to codify any clear international laws prohibiting the sale of human organs. The World Health Organization issued guidelines on the prevention of donor exploitation in the early nineties. Few of the 192 countries that endorsed the guidelines actively enforce them. In one signatory country, Iran, it is actually wholly legal to trade organs for profit.

STRESSES AND HAZARDS — *DANGERS:* **B-** *PRESSURES:* **B**

Owing to the vagaries of international attitudes on commercial transplantation, working trips abroad can be troublesome. Los Angeles broker Jim Cohan was arrested in Italy in 1999 when he flew to Rome to meet with an Italian transplant surgeon who had expressed interest in a potential partnership. The invitation was a setup. He was shackled as soon as he cleared customs, and accused of masterminding an international ring. He was left to languish in prison for five months until a court concluded that no laws were actually in place to try him under.

Brokers who take pains to project an aura of professionalism may be undermined by the excesses of their remote representatives. In 2004, a British missionary nun in Mozambique was murdered after campaigning against a local trafficking ring that kidnapped and killed local children for their organs. Earlier that same month, four other crusading nuns had narrowly escaped an armed ambush.

Most U.S. brokers are telecommuters who leverage their cell phones and PCs to "body surf" and connect consumers, suppliers, and enablers across the globe. Face-to-face meetings are still de rigueur for large-denomination transactions and partnering powwows, but virtual presence is definitely the trend. The Internet has empowered brokers to inexpensively market their specialized services and effectively broadcast targeted offers to an unprecedented base of potential donors. Type "kidney transplant" into any search engine and you will recognize the transformative role of the Web. Direct sales may be the final electronic frontier. In 1999, an unidentified eBay seller from Sunrise, Florida, offered bidders their choice of either of his healthy kidneys. The bidding started at $25,000 and topped $5.7 million before company officials shut down the auction.

OUTLAW BIKER

RANK: 3 OUT OF 50   **AVERAGE GRADE:** C+

DUTIES: Outlaw motorcycle gangs (OMGs) burst into the national consciousness in 1947, when a motley group of riders calling themselves the Boozefighters took drunken control of the sleepy town of Hollister, California: urinating into car radiators, drag racing in broad daylight, and towing an unconscious drunk in a wheelchair. The American Motorcycle Association issued a prompt denunciation of the incident, arguing that 99 percent of bikers are law-abiding citizens. In the coming decade, bike clubs sprang up across the country, modeling themselves on the "1-percenters" who chose to step outside the law in Hollister. By the 1960s, five regional supergangs had emerged: the Hells Angels (Northwest and South), the Outlaws (Midwest), the Bandidos (Southwest), the Pagans (East Coast), and the Mongols (California).

Today's Outlaw Biker is a multidisciplinary professional, participating in criminal activities that include, but are not limited to, the production, smuggling,

THE REBELS ARE COMING
Biking's Big Four have gone global

	Hells Angels	Bandidos	Outlaws	Pagans
U.S. chapters	62	80	67	41
Canadian chapters	35	5	8	0
Chapters in rest of the world	121	67	59	0
Total chapters worldwide	218	152	134	41
Founded	San Bernardino, California, 1948	Houston, Texas, 1966	McCook, Illinois, 1935	Maryland, 1955
Estimated membership	2,100	2,000	800	400

Source: 2005 National Gang Threat Assessment

transportation, and distribution of drugs; murder; assault; kidnapping; prostitution; money laundering; weapons trafficking; motorcycle and motorcycle-parts theft; intimidation; extortion; and arson. OMGs have evolved into hierarchical units rivaling the sophistication and reach of history's most venerated criminal conspiracies. They have written constitutions, bylaws, structured dues, and compulsory team-building meetings (referred to as "church"). American OMGs operate multinationally, with chapters in Europe, Australia, South America, and Africa. The Hells Angels lead the race toward globalization, with sanctioned offshoots in twenty countries, including Russia, Croatia, and the Czech Republic.

In contrast to traditional crime families, outlaw bikers flaunt their organizational affiliations through the charismatic displays of gang patches, colors, and tattoos (often incorporating Nazi, satanic, or pornographic imagery to maximize dramatic effect). Some OMGs have gone as far as to trademark their gang logo.

Although they do not typically conceal their outlaw alignments, established bikers employ a variety of surrogates to reduce their judicial accountability for crimes they commission. OMGs employ, direct, or control up to ten informal, street-level associates for each patch-wearing member. The Bandidos, for instance, delegate retail drug distribution to hang-arounds, prospects, and "puppet" support clubs, while members retain hands-on responsibility for drug wholesaling. In many areas, enterprising bikers have, in turn, successfully marketed themselves as value-added outsourcers and partners for Italian organized crime families.

OMGs are violently committed to operational diversity, yet drug trafficking remains the true engine of biker prosperity. The DEA regards the Hells Angels as the preeminent producers and vendors of illegal drugs in North America. This one gang controls double-digit shares of the markets for marijuana, methamphetamine, cocaine, hashish, heroin, LSD, PCP, and diverted pharmaceuticals. The Outlaws, meanwhile, have

THE BROTHERHOOD OF THE HOG
The other team rides Harleys too.
Source: New York Police Department

achieved outstanding brand equity in the methamphetamine sector but also maintain very creditable marijuana, cocaine, MDMA, and prescription operations. Two of their former international presidents, Harry "Taco" Bowman and James "Frank" Wheeler, were jailed for their tireless efforts in these areas. In recent years, law enforcement has substantially hobbled the Pagans' drug empire. However, some OMG experts believe that a return to full-scale trafficking activity is essential to finance the Pagans' escalating conflicts with the Hells Angels.

COMPENSATION AND REWARDS — EARNINGS: A- PERKS: B+

Over the last decade, outlaw bikers have reaped windfall profits in North America's booming domestic and export drug markets. The Hells Angels, for instance, are thought to control production and transport of nearly 60 percent of Canada's bounteous, indoor-cultivated marijuana crop. A single pound of "BC Bud"—high-grade British Columbian pot boasting an active THC content of up to 30 percent—retails for $6,000 to $7,000. Some estimates put the annual value of the Canadian crop at over $10 billion, with the lion's share flowing to a highly assertive cadre of outlaw bikers. BC Bud has proven so lucrative of late that recent Canadian wiretaps reveal it is being exchanged on a pound-for-pound basis for low-quality cocaine. The Angels' Canadian cocaine operation itself has estimated gross revenues of up to $5 million a day.

Money laundering (see page 134) has become an essential skill for today's biker-cum-executive. Prominent Hells Angels maintain interests in scores of strategically chosen legitimate businesses, including travel agencies, clubs, trailer parks, motorcycle shops, limousine services, trucking companies, groceries, and security agencies. Many grizzled veterans of this time-honored trade are experiencing tremendous upward mobility. Walter Stadnick and Donald Stockford, two leading members of the Hells Angels Ontario chapter, were credited by a Canadian court with net drug sales of more than $10 million and profits of almost $2.5 million over a nine-month period.

Briefcases of drug money may not await every new entrant in this field; however, modest opportunities abound for self-starters in such adjunct areas as extortion, prostitution, and robbery. Junior bikers from a Pagans chapter in Nassau, New York, for instance, were able to break in to the adult entertainment industry, extorting a very respectable $20 per-shift, per-stripper from area gentlemen's clubs.

Some gangs have biker-specific analogs to traditional unemployment benefits. The Outlaws collect money for their incarcerated members, known as Lounge Lizards, and encourage their "old ladies" and fellow Outlaws to send letters and care packages.

Most OMG chapters periodically procure accommodating females (venerated as "mammas" or "scooter trash") for the sexual gratification of the group or its individual members. This can be onerous

duty, as in the case of three seventeen-year-old girls drafted to service some three hundred bikers at an outdoor soiree hosted by Ontario's Outlaws and Red Devils OMGs.

SLEAZY RIDER
A coverage checklist . . .

Criminal activities	Hells Angels	Bandidos	Outlaws	Pagans
Drugs				
Production	x	x	x	
Smuggling	x	x	x	
Transportation	x	x	x	
Distribution	x	x	x	x
Weapons Trafficking	x	x	x	
Murder	x	x	x	x
Prostitution	x	x	x	
Money laundering	x	x	x	
Explosives violation	x	x	x	
Bombings	x	x	x	x
Motorcycle and motorcycle-parts theft	x	x	x	
Intimidation	x	x	x	
Extortion	x	x	x	x
Arson	x	x	x	x
Assault	x	x	x	x
Insurance fraud	x	x	x	
Kidnapping	x	x	x	
Robbery	x	x	x	
Theft	x	x	x	
Stolen property	x	x	x	
Counterfeiting	x	x	x	
Contraband smuggling	x	x	x	

Source: 2005 National Gang Threat Assessment

ENFORCEMENT AND PENALTIES — *ARRESTS:* **C-** *SENTENCING:* **C-**

The U.S. Department of Justice has selected the top five OMGs as principal targets of the National Gang Strategy (NGS), and major enforcement operations have recently been heating up. In June 2005, a sweep involving almost three hundred investigators across Washington, Montana, and South Dakota yielded a nineteen-count indictment against thirty Bandidos, including the club's international president, sergeant at arms, and the president of its linchpin Bellingham, Washington, chapter. Charges ranged from racketeering and witness tampering to drug trafficking and Harley theft. One year earlier, Frank Wheeler, the Outlaws' president, was sentenced to thirty years–to–life for racketeering, conspiracy to commit racketeering, and conspiracy to distribute drugs, in another multistate sting. OMG leadership has been, in fact, an iffy proposition for quite some time. Wheeler took over the reigns at the Outlaws after Taco Bowman went on the lam in the late 1990s, prior to receiving a life sentence for racketeering and conspiracy to commit murder.

STRESSES AND HAZARDS — *DANGERS:* **C-** *PRESSURES:* **C**

Biker violence has been escalating throughout the last decade as the major clubs fight to expand their memberships and market shares. By 2005, the Hells Angels' roster had swelled to 218 chapters—more than doubling in just five years. Between 1999 and 2000, the Bandidos tripled their bulk to 152 chapters and 2,000 members, rivaling the Angels' historic numerical dominance. The Outlaws added twenty-eight U.S. chapters between 1999 and 2002, bringing their membership to roughly 1,200, while the Pagans suffered net membership losses due to arrests and defections.

The carnage began in earnest in the early nineties, when the Bandidos induced the Rock Machine, a group of Montreal leather thugs, to forsake their allegiance to the Hells Angels. By the time Canadian police launched Operation Springtime—arresting Hells Angels' leader Maurice "Mom" Boucher and more than a hundred others—the Quebec biker war had occasioned 170 deaths, 84 bombings, and 130 arson attacks. Bloody skirmishes have become the norm, pitting the Angels versus every other major OMG.

In Scandinavia, Angels, Bandidos, and Outlaws fought in the streets with AK-47s. Violence there reached a crescendo when the Bandidos blew up the Angels' Copenhagen clubhouse with an antitank rocket.

In 2003, seventy-three Pagans attacked a Long Island, New York, catering hall where the Hells Angels were holding their annual Hellraiser Ball. One hundred police cruisers and two helicopters were dispatched to quell the battle. They confiscated nearly five hundred weapons.

Now, police are bracing for a major biker war in Philadelphia and renewed violence throughout Canada.

WORK ENVIRONMENT

HOURS: B   COMFORT: B-

Although most bikers still log considerable hours in seedy bars and atop their trusty "hogs," the newest club facilities offer huge advances in functionality and comfort. Clubhouses of major chapters incorporate reinforced walls, steel doors, razor wire, guard dogs, and video surveillance. On the very high end is the Hells Angels' $1 million clubhouse in Sherbrooke, Quebec—a sprawling estate complete with swimming pool, helicopter pad, luxury accommodations, and state-of-the-art electronic security. Bikers are also making inroads into the electronic workplace, embracing high-tech solutions for encryption of sensitive data, wireless communications, and Web-based project communications and public relations.

PAPERHANGER

DUTIES: Paperhangers perpetrate a rich variety of check-based fiduciary frauds. With 1.3 million bogus drafts (worth some $27 million) circulating daily, opportunities for ink-based enrichment abound in America. U.S. citizens sign 75 percent of the world's 90 billion annual checks, and more money is moved by this method than by cash and credit cards combined.

Kiters—also known as *bad* or *hot check artists*—account for 32 percent of all check-related chicanery. They knowingly endorse drafts against insufficiently funded or closed accounts, "banking" on the *float time* between deception and detection. Kiters typically establish accounts with false or stolen IDs. They inflate their apparent balances with rubber checks from other accounts, cashing out before the bogus deposits bounce back from their issuing banks.

Check washers use commonplace chemicals to remove payee and amount information from legitimately issued instruments, while maintaining the integrity of their preprinted backgrounds. Accomplished washers are ever on the lookout for alterable checks about to enter the U.S. mail. Some steal from residential mailboxes—whose red flags can indicate the presence of outgoing payables. Especially daring defrauders target public postal collection points.

CLEANING UP
Say goodbye to pesky ink with these check-washing supplies

Washing product	Application notes
Acetone	A volatile but effective organic solvent
Benzene	Carcinogen
Bleach	Laundry helper
Carbon tetrachloride	Carpet cleaning
Chloromice "T"	Bleaching baby diapers
Fox "IT"	Stamp collectors
Clear correction fluids	Typing mishaps

Check counterfeiters create or commission entirely new, unauthorized checks. Generally, they obtain specimen checks from well-stocked accounts, scan or photocopy them, then output an arbitrary number of accurate facsimiles. The most challenging assignments involve reproduction, simulation, or contravention of advanced security features, such as watermarks, microprinting, photoactive fibers, or hologram strips. Advanced practitioners use magnetic ink cartridges to *inaccurately* imitate the machine-readable routing numerals at the bottom end of each check. By routing checks to distant banks, a cagey counterfeiter can cause his paperwork to detour across the country, increasing the float by several days.

Check thieves acquire blank bankables by diversion, deception, or outright theft.

Organized paperhangers plant or recruit check-procuring moles within large companies or linchpin financial institutions. Enterprising independents *take over* individual accounts by impersonating account holders and having new negotiables sent directly to addresses of their choosing. The information extractable from a single discarded deposit slip is often sufficient for a phone-based takeover.

In *split deposit* or *less cash deposit* gambits, fraudsters use legitimate slips to deposit large, phony checks. The aim is *not* to cash the hefty decoys, but to secure a relatively small sum of "cash back" without being asked to present ID.

Identity thieves secure comprehensive credentials for unaffiliated individuals and misuse them to establish exploitable new accounts (see Identity Thief).

COMPENSATION AND REWARDS   EARNINGS: B   PERKS: B+

Attempted check fraud against U.S. banks alone topped $5.5 billion in 2003, and hard-dollar revenues extracted from banks exceeded $677 million. The *combined* check fraud take from banks, corporations, institutions, and individuals is estimated at over $12 billion per annum. In a 2004 survey by the American Banking Association, counterfeit checks yielded the highest average gains per incident

($3,059), followed by kited drafts ($2,566), and washed/altered items ($1,452).

Though duffers and dabblers content themselves with a few extra dollars or duty-free niceties, tight-knit ethnic enterprises employ hundreds of check procurers, counterfeiters, information brokers, and check passers, generating millions in annual revenue. Sophisticated soloists can do rather handsomely, as well. In 2003, a former Virginia CEO perpetrated a $2.4 million kiting attack against two local banks, while an insolvent Indonesian ex-tycoon passed $8 million in hot checks at two Vegas casinos.

Additional inducements in this rewarding discipline include frequent travel for serial check passers and an endless variety of freely obtainable goods and services.

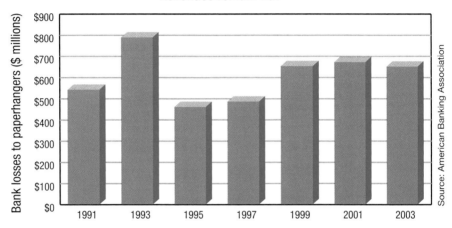

STALEMATE
Revenues remain flat

Source: American Banking Association

 ENFORCEMENT AND PENALTIES   *ARRESTS:* **A**   *SENTENCING:* **B**

Apprehensions and interdictions are refreshingly rare in this occupation. The overall clearance rate for check-related crimes hovers around 2 percent, and conviction rates remain historically low. In the late 1980s and early '90s, the majority of frauds against financial institutions was perpetrated by avaricious insiders. The rise of electronic counterfeiting has ushered in a new era of overpowering check-based outsider attacks.

According to the American Banking Association, major money center banks spend an average of $9.9 million a year on check-fraud prevention, detection, investigation, and prosecution. Regional banks budget about $1 million a year; small community institutions average a more manageable $5,000. In 2003, check fraud accounted for 43 percent of the suspicious-activity reports received by the fed's Financial Crimes Enforcement Network but consumed almost 90 percent of available investigative resources.

Sentences for paperhanging vary dramatically from state to state—and with the volume of the dollars debited—but are generally quite moderate for minor offenses. The most organized operators, however, risk indictments for racketeering, such as Denver's Marvin Holloman, who was sentenced to eighteen years for a $151,000 series of frauds against area businesses.

STRESSES AND HAZARDS

DANGERS: **C+** PRESSURES: **C**

Kiters are effectively high-stakes jugglers who risk arrest or penury should they drop a single logistical ball. All check passers face significant strain during face-to-face presentation of false payments, and these tensions often mount as the fraudster waits to gauge the success of his gambits. The rapid evolution of countermeasures also contributes to this overall climate of insecurity.

Serial exposure to benzene and other semisafe solvents could prove injurious to hands-on check washers over the long haul.

WORK ENVIRONMENT

HOURS: **C+** COMFORT: **B-**

Although paperhanging is a predominantly indoor, all-weather activity, amateur productivity inclines distinctly during the holiday run-up. The physical preparation and manufacturing of passable paper is typically a speedy affair, but foresting for washable or copyable checks, initiating multiple bank accounts, and placing checks in bulk can be quite time intensive. In large-scale ethnic counterfeiting organizations, these weighty responsibilities are distributed among teams of specialists. Leadership, procurement, production, and support positions in major Nigerian, Vietnamese, Russian, Armenian, and Mexican groups are reserved for security-conscious countrymen. Frontline check passers, however, are generally dispensable, low-profile locals who are privy to few organizational details. Typically, they travel incessantly, opening new accounts and transporting work proceeds. On average, they pass about 10 percent of an organized group's illicit output; the remainder is vended to other groups and individuals for 10 percent to 25 percent of face value.

PICKPOCKET

DUTIES: Pickpockets steal cash or other valuables from the person, clothing, or personal effects of their victims. They work by stealth, without force or threat of force. Pickpocketing is as old as money itself and is popular throughout the world. Although this skilled trade can take a lifetime to truly master, even youngsters and crackheads can conquer its basic challenges . . . with a little "hands-on" experience.

The simplest pickpocketing maneuvers—typically practiced by opportunistic dabblers—involve removal of property from loosely attached or adjacent bags. Students with backpacks and sleeping drunks are common targets for such low-level forays. Retrieving a wallet from the pocket or purse of a *mark* (a target for larceny) is a considerably more delicate affair. The basic approach is to mask the requisite illicit contact with apparently benign contact. On a packed subway, for instance, it is customary for passengers to brush against one another. Trained pickpockets exploit the indignities of modern transit to *bump and rob* with near impunity. Subway-based workers often bump their targets seconds before a train departs, then step off as its doors close. As the trapped mark travels toward the next station to report the crime, the pickpocket rings up credit purchases at in-station or nearby shops.

The *sandwich* is an ensemble technique employed to simulate the dynamics of a distracting crowd. In the standard two-man gambit, a *stall* stops abruptly in front of a

SWITCH HITTING
Skilled pickpockets are equally at home in pocket or purse.

mark, causing the mark to collide with him or her. A rearward *pick* subsequently bumps the mark from behind and extemporizes while removing his or her valuables.

Theatrically inclined pickpockets may evolve still more elaborate diversions. Staged fights are favored by teams of three or more to service larger crowds. Juvenile workers delight marks with drawings or toys. Attractive women feign flirtatious inebriation, and *splash and grab* artists leverage food or beverage spills for messy cover.

To allay suspicion, professional pickpockets frequently affect the dress and manner of affluent businesspeople. To conceal their hands, they employ newspapers, garment bags, or long-sleeved coats. Unabashed females occasionally use babies for this purpose. In inclement weather, pickpockets and victims don additional clothing. Multiple clothing layers minimize a mark's body awareness and help shield the pick's movements and conceal purloined items. On completion of a property extraction, some pickpockets shed their outermost clothing layer, revealing a very different garment beneath and stymieing victim identification.

Pickpockets patiently monitor potential victims. They wait for their bags to slip into accessible positions or for them to reveal the locations of their valuables. The great majority of victims expose their wallets minutes prior to the theft. When visual inspections fail, a pickpocket may *fan* a potential victim—casually brushing by to assess the location of his lucre.

COMPENSATION AND REWARDS   EARNINGS: B   PERKS: B

In 2003, the median gain per pocket picked was $166 (compared with $216 for purse snatchings). Only 10 percent of pocket picking assignments involve windfalls of $500 or more. Twenty-two percent yield less than $59. Reported annual revenues for this undertaking topped $20 million. Seasoned sole proprietors can expect sustainable earnings of up to $3,000 per day. Employees of organized rings take home up to $1,000 per day. Perks include complimentary jewelry and portable electronics, which are included in 5 percent of work assignments.

BIG PERKS . . .
SMALL PACKAGES

ENFORCEMENT AND PENALTIES ARRESTS: **B** SENTENCING: **B**

National clearance rates for this venerable property crime hover around 18 percent. In 2003, only 5.7 percent of reported incidents led to immediate arrest. Sentences for first-time offenders average a lenient 8.3 months, but a small minority of serial offenders may face greatly compounded penalties. A number of former pickpockets are serving life sentences under so-called "three strikes" laws. Yvonne Dockery, a heroin addict with convictions for shoplifting and pickpocketing, was recently liberated from *her* life sentence after tireless campaigning by a team of students at Fordham University's Law School.

STRESSES AND HAZARDS DANGERS: **C+** PRESSURES: **B-**

Physical retaliation from marks is an infrequent but serious occupational risk. Undercover transit officers posing as tourists or other favored marks can foster workplace anxiety. The mounting acceptance of surveillance cameras at public and commercial locations is also troubling; at some mainstay locations they have cut pickpocketing revenues by more than 50 percent.

WORK ENVIRONMENT HOURS: **C** COMFORT: **C**

Pickpocketing flourishes wherever large groups gather. Transportation terminals are perennial favorite locations. Department stores, casinos, and other well-patrolled commercial venues are generally avoided. The majority of pickpockets are male, but the majority of their targets are not. The average mark is thirty years old and uses the railroad/subway as a primary means of transportation.

Although this is a year-round occupation, activity increases during cold weather and may reach ten times normal levels during the holiday season. Rush hours and peak shopping times are also periods of intensive activity.

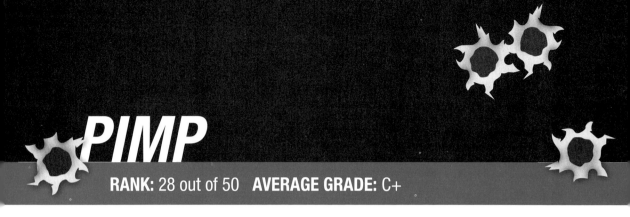

PIMP

RANK: 28 out of 50   **AVERAGE GRADE:** C+

DUTIES: Pimps recruit, train, deploy, and manage mobile or fixed teams (*stables*) of sex workers—known in the trade as *hos, hookers, streetwalkers, flat-backers,* or *whores.* Traditional work roles are blurring in the august prostitution services sector. *Pimping* has come to refer to a wide range of employer-employee arrangements in a diverse set of intimate venues: street corners, massage parlors, strip clubs, escort services, traditional brothels, etc. Traditional, *old school* pimping, however, revolves around economically exploitive relationships wherein the pimp derives prestige by pocketing the lion's share of his *bitch*'s proceeds.

The pimp's status among his peers in *the game* is a function of the size of his stable, the bulge of his bankroll, and the apparent ease of his lifestyle. *King pimps* or *macks*—known historically as *mack men*—field close-knit teams of seven or more hos. They often maintain establishments for indoor assignation and cultivate an understated air of carefree authority. *Players* are midtier street pimps with small-but-lucrative conjugal concessions. *Popcorn pimps* are unschooled, smalltime improvisers oft-derided for their evident lack of *game.*

For most pimps, the key to recruitment is a time-tested, persuasive *rap.* Uninitiated innocents usually respond best to love-based gambits. Typically, the charismatic *lover pimp* singles out an insecure adolescent female and lavishes her with short-lived affection and largesse. (Two-thirds of American street prostitutes enter the trade

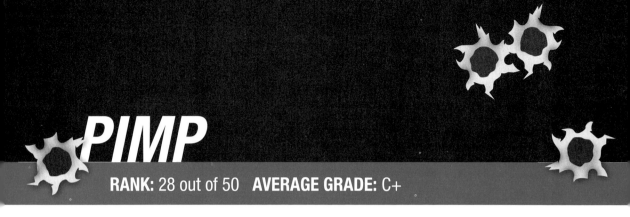

THE BLING THING
Subhead: In the pimp game, cars and clothes still make the man.

before the age of sixteen.) Once she has taken him unto her bosom and into her heart, he feigns situational insolvency. Then he tactfully suggests that she confirm her spiritual commitment by having onetime sponsored sex with strangers. When the waylaid waif realizes that the boyfriend-pimp's short-run cash shortage has morphed into a full-tilt franchise, he toughens his tactics. He may threaten to inform parents of their daughter's debasement, or to harm them or her directly. If threats fail, he may bust out the *pimp stick*—a wire hanger that has been unraveled and doubled over for maximal punitive effect. Although 76 percent of American prostitutes report that they have been beaten by their pimps, scheduled or corrective beatings are usually alternated with strategic helpings of kindness and generosity. This nuanced mixture of love and brutality defines the time-tested pimp-ho dynamic.

The *gorilla pimp* forgoes manipulative finesse and forcibly impels recruits into his erotic employ. His techniques range from credible threats to coldhearted kidnapping. The gorilla seldom prospers. He is scorned by high-class pimps and sought after by law enforcers. His *ladies* (and occasionally boys) harbor no loyalty and will abandon and betray him at the earliest safe opportunity.

Dealer pimps, conversely, have waxed as more pugilistic panderers have waned. Seventy-five percent of contemporary street workers are substance abusers. Enterprising narco-pimps often open their homes and drug *stashes* to early-stage addicts who have fallen out with parents and employers. Once the wayward guests have grown accustomed to the comforts of the house, their benefactors inform them that they must commingle with various cohorts to prolong their needle, pipe, or nose candy privileges. These transitional drugs-for-hugs exchanges are effective, desensitizing stepping stones to full-blown street prostitution. Dealer pimps continue the cycle of chemical control by supplying their substance-addled hos with wholesale pharmaceuticals at premium prices.

COMPENSATION AND REWARDS — EARNINGS: B PERKS: B+

The first rule of pimping is "the pimp must get paid." Master pimps set clear quotas and enforce them vigorously, demonstrating unequivocally that there is no "shame in their game." Typical commissions for pimps run 60 percent to 70 percent. Skilled managers can expect per-ho profits of $60,000 to $80,000 per year. Dealer pimps take less off the top but enjoy considerable recurring revenues from backend drug markups. Overall earnings in the U.S. prostitution sector are estimated at over $10 billion. Street vendors account for about 20 percent of all transactions, and 80 percent to 90 percent of those workers are thought to be affiliated with pimps. In some enlightened latitudes, pimps have become something of an anachronism. In San Francisco, 96 percent of prostitution providers operate independently.

ENFORCEMENT AND PENALTIES   *ARRESTS:* **B-**   *SENTENCING:* **C**

Although *pandering* (legal lingo for pimping) is a felonious offense in every state except Nevada, vice officers almost universally target labor (prostitutes) over management (pimps). Arrests of pimps are nearly always prompted by third-party complaints—usually by disgruntled prostitutes or unprincipled competitors. Pedophile pimps, however, can be lightning rods for scrutiny and scorn (see below). Once interdicted, pimps seldom quit the game. A short-lived Nova Scotia treatment program for convicted pimps boasted a perfect 100 percent recidivism rate.

JUVENILE JEOPARDY
Sentences for a group of ten cooperating Atlanta pimps convicted of underage offerings in 2002. Andrew Moore Jr. and Charles Pipkins—the leadership—were convicted on additional racketeering charges.

Defendant	Age	a.k.a.	Juvenile Victims	Prison Term
Andrew Moore Jr.	38	Playboy	14+	40 years
Charles Pipkins	55	Sir Charles	14+	30 years
Linda Moore	28		2	3 years 9 mos.
Michael Davis	45	Hollywood	6	5 years
Herman Hutson Jr.	32	Atlanta Redd	1	3 years 10 mos.
Dominic Terry	22	Little D	1	5 years
Bryant Weaver Bell	29	Worm	2	4 years 6 mos.
Terrence Anderson	29	Lance House, Scooby	1	6 years 6 mos.
Dwayne Comer	31	Julio	3	5 years
Deunbray Rucker	27	Poochie	4	5 years

STRESSES AND HAZARDS

DANGERS: **C** PRESSURES: **C-**

It is a well-known axiom that pimping ain't easy. Although the successful pimp projects a persona of carefree living and indulgence, providing for houseful of spirited hos, equitably apportioning one's affections, and maintaining an exuberant level of pomp can be exceedingly taxing. Furthermore, the conspicuously mon-eyed pimp is a high-profile target for all manners of predator. Beyond guarding the riches of the day, the wise pimp takes pains to secure his long-term treasures. Pimp-on-pimp ho pilferage is an integral part of the game. Professionals hold to the maxim "bros over hos" and settle their differences without violence or slander (a flat transfer fee is negotiated in the most civil circumstances). However, defections by Choosy Susies are at the root of many physical workplace unpleasantries.

WORK ENVIRONMENT

HOURS: **C** COMFORT: **B**

To maximize their prestige among peers and potential stable hos, old school pimps tend to adopt extravagant or expensive accoutrements. Luxury *rides*, free-flowing street pharmaceuticals, and ostentatious bling are the evident symbols of pimping success. To consistently attract, harness, and retain top *talent*, a pimp must keep up appearances. Although pimps strive to appear masterful and effortless in their stable-handling chores, workforce recruit-ment and supervision can be quite time-consuming.

Maintaining personally manageable staffing levels and sustaining team harmony are essential to long-term happiness and success in this endeavor. Proactive pimps empower senior sex-team members by del-egating certain managerial tasks and pre-rogatives. A pimp's most trusted assistant is his *main lady, bottom lady*, or *bottom bitch,* to whom he may be legally married. Often, he/she will be charged with managing ac-counts, training recruits, and fostering group discipline. A *wife-in-law* is a junior support staffer entrusted with similar duties.

CROSS TRAINING
The extensive criminal credentials of sixteen working pimps

Offense	Number who committed offense	Average age at first offense	Number who committed offense in last six months
Shoplifting	11	12	3
Possession of drugs	16	14	16
Burglary	13	15	3
Criminal damage	8	15	4
Robbery	12	17	10
Drug supply	14	18	12
Fraud	10	18	3
Arson	4	20	0
False imprisonment	7	21	2
Possession of firearm	12	22	10
Supply of firearm	8	24	1

Source: UK Home Office, *For Love or Money: Pimps and the Management of Sex Work*

PIRATE

DUTIES: Pirates track, intercept, board, and forcibly seize civilian maritime vessels for financial gain—*booty*. Sea-borne violence is enjoying a worldwide renaissance, with aquatic attacks tripling in the last decade. Global losses to new-wave *buccaneers* swelled to an estimated $16 billion in 2004, with 325 confirmed attacks and as least as many unreported incidents. Oil and gas tankers (67 attacks in 2004) and bulk carriers (53) have emerged as the professional pirate's targets of preference. Indonesia's treacherous seaways—most notably the Strait of Malacca—accounted for a phenomenal 91 attacks in 2004. India, Bangladesh, and Nigeria maintained their traditionally strong market shares, while Somalia showed impressive gains (especially against yachts and other smaller craft).

Maritime raiders board ships in port, at anchor, or underway in domestic or international waters. Opportunistic beginners often attempt stealthy in-port entry via gangways, mooring ropes, or small, silent *bumboats*. (Technically, thefts from moored vessels constitute *sea robbery*, rather than true piracy.) More seasoned *sea dogs* target large commercial vessels as they slowly navigate narrow sea-lanes. Frequently, high-powered boarding boats are disguised as harmless fishing craft. Sometimes a strong rope is strung between two light boats. The target ship unknowingly catches the rope across its bow, rapidly drawing the pirate vessels to either side of its hull. Other aquatic escapades leverage the cover of darkness and deficiencies in ship-to-ship radar. Grappling hooks, bamboo ladders, and planks are employed to facilitate energetic deckward passage.

ROUGH SEAS
Nine hot spots accounted for two-thirds of world piracy in 2005

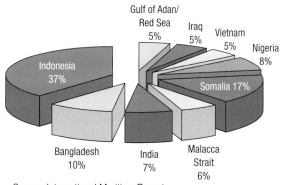

Gulf of Adan/Red Sea 5%
Iraq 5%
Vietnam 5%
Nigeria 8%
Indonesia 37%
Somalia 17%
Bangladesh 10%
India 7%
Malacca Strait 6%

Source: International Maritime Report

More than 80 percent of piratical outings culminate in *maritime muggings,* brief engagements whose primary purpose is to harvest cash from the vessel's safe, personal effects from crewmen, and reusable equipment from the ship. The remainder of water-based assignments involve hijacking. Some hijackers seek ransom money from ship owners and intimates of the crew. Somali pirates, who are renowned for this subspecialty, seized a UN-chartered tsunami relief vessel in 2005 and demanded $500,000 ransom from the World Food Program. In the first six months of 2005, 176 crewmen were taken hostage worldwide.

More audacious hijackers aim for permanent usurpation of target ships and their contents. Coveted cargoes include diesel fuel, palm oil, rubber, and copper concentrates. Snatched ships are routinely repainted while still under steam. After their bulky booty is offloaded to a buyer- or accomplice-ship, they sail to one of twenty-seven nations that offer no-hassle, "flag of convenience" registration. Their crews are set adrift, slaughtered wholesale, or coerced into servitude.

Transnational crime syndicates employ rechristened *phantom* ships for major cargo scams and high-volume smuggling of human beings (see Human Smuggler and Slave Trader). In the first case, they solicit legitimate cargo loads, then illegally vend them at unscheduled ports. In trans-oceanic, *snakehead* smuggling operations, Asian crime families exact up to $70,000 per expat for cargo-class passage to the United States or other greener pastures.

COMPENSATION AND REWARDS　　　*EARNINGS:* **B+**　*PERKS:* **B+**

Maritime commerce is a $2 trillion global industry, and tributes to pirates amount to just thirty-two cents for every $10,000 of goods shipped. Nonetheless, gains for professional pirate crews can be gigantic. Chew Cheng Kiat—a senior executive for a Hong Kong-based multinational crime concern—is credited with coordinating twenty-two hijackings in the South China Sea and the Strait of Malacca. Just one of these attacks, against a tanker laden with diesel and jet fuel, netted $2.3 million in 1998. The ship's Indonesian second engineer, whom Kiat recruited as a sleeper agent, earned $4,000 for his well-timed tip-off call.

AAARGH!
Anti-piracy technology comes of age

SECURE-SHIP—This nonlethal, electric perimeter fence surrounds the entire ship and delivers a 9,000-volt pulse to deter boarding attempts. Also activates floodlights and sets off a very loud siren.

INVENTUS UNMANNED AERIAL VEHICLE—A state-of-the-art flying wing reconnaissance system that covers a large ocean area and relays real-time data to ground stations or seagoing vessels. The Inventus is fully autonomous and flies in all weather conditions.

SHIPLOC—A satellite tracking system allows owners to monitor fleet locations via the Internet. Distress feature sends SOS signals that cannot be detected onboard or by ships in the vicinity to owners and authorities.

ENFORCEMENT AND PENALTIES   *ARRESTS:* **C+** *SENTENCING:* **C-**

BIG BOOTY ALERT
Today's super tankers can be huge treasure chests.

The Geneva Convention on the High Seas calls for signatories to "cooperate to the fullest possible extent in the repression of piracy." Yet, only forty-three nations have ratified another convention banning sanctuary for pirates and mandating strict maritime enforcement. Liberty-loving pirates concentrate 80 percent of their efforts in coastal waters of nations with minimal enforcement, questionable stability, and limited resources. Nations actively opposing modern piracy have had limited success.

Thailand's $13 million antipiracy unit hasn't made an arrest in eleven years. Judicial rebukes for "washed up" pirates can, however, be rather daunting. Several nations still have death penalties on the books. The United States, in fact, mandates this punishment for pirate attacks resulting in deaths.

STRESSES AND HAZARDS

DANGERS: C-   PRESSURES: C

Violence in this traditionally rugged field is on the incline. In their continuing quest for tactical supremacy, well-funded pirates have traded handguns and long knives for rocket-launched grenades, recoilless rifles, and incendiary bombs. Friendly-fire incidents are common, as are injuries from close-quarter combat and boarding mishaps. Although pirates killed thirty seamen in 2003, professional sailors are notoriously reluctant to resist them once they have boarded. Amateur skippers, however, are much more prone to panic and fire on approaching pirates. Military retaliation is rare, but the Indonesian Navy did succeed in sinking a hijacked ship bound for Malaysia in 2005 and arresting the three pirates who had seized it.

WORK ENVIRONMENT

HOURS: C+   COMFORT: C-

Pirates brave rough seas, inclement weather, and increasingly hostile crewmen. They often work in minimal light and must maintain forward momentum as they are met with small arms and high-pressure water hoses. Although traditional maritime hierarchies mandate rigid discipline and centralized command and control, pirate crews are granted unusual personal autonomy to respond to chaotic, rapidly evolving conditions. While seamanship and violent physicality are still paramount in the pirate workplace, high-tech skills are invaluable in disabling shipboard communications and tracking systems, and eavesdropping on maritime satellite communication networks.

PIRATE RADIO OPERATOR

RANK: 43 out of 50   **AVERAGE GRADE:** C

DUTIES: Pirate Radio Operators assemble, maintain, man, and broadcast over unlicensed AM, FM, and shortwave radio transmitters. Radio pirates broadcast in opposition to Federal Communications Commission (FCC) regulations on licensing eligibility, frequency, and transmitter wattage. The great majority of U.S. pirate stations (more than one thousand by most estimates) utilize the FM band, but shortwave activity has spiked in the last few years. The recent arrival of high-power AM transmitters, which appear exempt from FCC licensing, could trigger interest in that area of the spectrum, as well.

Most workers in this field assume a challenging combination of on-air, administrative, and technical duties. Though one-man operations are common, management by small groups of ideologically- or musically-connected individuals is the emerging norm. Key responsibilities include content creation, program and resource scheduling, equipment selection and upkeep, fundraising, and promotion.

The FCC mandates licensing for any FM transmitter emitting more than .25 watts (the power of a typical baby monitor). In 1978, the agency rescinded all licenses under 100 watts, forcing U.S. micro-power broadcasters to go silent or take up the pirate flag. Today, a complete FM broadcast package can be purchased for as little as $700, via the Internet, and installed with little technical expertise. Though the FCC reinstated limited micro-power licensing in 2000, just a handful of licenses have gone to former pirates, and clandestine stations are on the rise.

A substantial minority of pirate stations operate from known, fixed locations, in open defiance of FCC enforcement. Stations of this class are often operated by organizations with deeply held interests in free speech, media diversity, political activism, or public affairs. To combat increased FCC enforcement and tough new anti-piracy laws, such as Florida's SB 2714 (which classifies pirate broadcasting as a third-degree felony), politically savvy pirates have lobbied local governments to intercede on their behalves. In the last two years, San Francisco Liberation Radio (93.7 FM), Free Radio Santa Cruz (96.3 FM) and Vermont's Radio Free Brattelboro (87.9 FM), all secured official resolutions of support from their respective city councils. The FCC, however, was relentless; only the Santa Cruz station remains on the air.

Most pirate stations, however, operate from undisclosed, concealed, or mobile locations. The history of Boulder Free Radio (KBFR 95.3 FM) illustrates the spectrum of available clandestine options. Colorado's KBFR (tagline: "Radio so good it's illegal") had broadcast from a Boulder home for three months before receiving an FCC first visit—known as "The Knock"—in 2001. Taking the FCC's hint, Boulder Free Radio dismantled its stationary equipment. Within weeks, an oddly familiar station calling itself "Free Boulder Radio" began broadcasting from a van, changing location frequently to avoid easy FCC detection. Eventually, the pirates tired of mobile operation and devised a novel scheme. They leased a room at a local garage, parked their transmission van outside, and began broadcasting from their garage room/studio via a 2.4 GHz wireless Wi-Fi network. When FCC field agent Jon Sprague came knocking again in 2002, he found a van and transmitter, but no studio. He left behind a business card and e-mailed a warning to the group's Yahoo! address. Next, KBFR embraced

PIRATE HAVENS
Ten most pirate-infested states
(FCC charges 2000 to 2004)

State	Pirate Incidents
Florida	100
California	40
New York	25
Michigan	23
Texas	14
Washington	13
Colorado	10
Illinois	11
Ohio	9
Minnesota	9

Source: DIY Media, "FCC Watch"

the timeshare model with the van shuttling among a small circuit of listener-provided fixed antenna. For a time, the van could even be reached for song requests. As of September 2005, KBFR had gone dark. Its main organizer, Monk, had disappeared amid rumors of renewed FCC shenanigans. Fellow pirates fear this may—finally—be the end.

The latest innovation in pirate radio isn't exactly radio at all. In 2003 the U.S. Library of Congress announced that operators of Internet radio stations would be required to pay the Recording Industry Association of America (RIAA) a $500 annual minimum to play music online, plus 7 cents per listener, per song. Stations such as San Francisco's popular SomaFM.com, which drew more than a thousand listeners a day at its peak, went offline within days of the decision. Now, an English game designer named Ian McLeod has created Streamer, a program that enables would-be Internet Radio Pirates to build virtually untraceable online stations, with no technical expertise.

COMPENSATION AND REWARDS — EARNINGS: **B** PERKS: **B**

For most, pirate radio is more an avocation than a vocation. Although some pirates secure minor compensation through fundraising or organizational subsidies, as a rule, most are unpaid. A notable exception to this rule, Doug Brewer, the notorious "Tampa Party Pirate," claimed advertising revenues of more than $1,000 a month and vended T-shirts boasting "License? We don't need no stinking license!" In November 2003, however, a helicopter-based FCC SWAT team staged a surprise raid at Brewer's home, seizing more than $100,000 worth of stationary and portable equipment.

In supplement to substandard pay and benefits, Pirate Radio Operators enjoy unusual levels of notoriety and street credibility among listener constituencies. Indeed, the pirate mystique often offers clear social and sexual advantages. Meetings and collaborations with fellow workers in radio, independent media, and activism afford moderate opportunities for work-related travel.

ENFORCEMENT AND PENALTIES — ARRESTS: **A-** SENTENCING: **C-**

Although arrest and conviction rates in this field remain quite low, enforcement actions have been climbing in recent years, and multithousand-dollar fines are becoming more commonplace. On the bright side, almost 30 percent of the FCC Enforcement Bureau's field staff is currently eligible for retirement, and the bureau estimates that by 2011 its presence will dwindle to half of today's level. Further, a 2000 audit by the FCC's inspector general found that the commission collected on only a quarter of the fines it issued. Equipment and fleet maintenance are also major concerns for the bureau: 90 percent of FCC radio-detection vehicles are more than six years old, and half are more than ten years old.

THE AIR WAR
The FCC's battle with low-power insurgents drags on

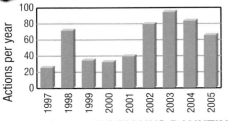

Actions per year

1997, 1998, 1999, 2000, 2001, 2002, 2003, 2004, 2005

ENFORCEMENT REMAINS DAUNTING
FCC anti-piracy actions.

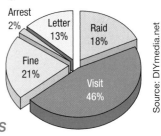

Arrest 2%
Letter 13%
Raid 18%
Fine 21%
Visit 46%

Source: DIYmedia.net

WHAT HAPPENS WHEN THE FCC TUNES IN?
Type of FCC enforcement.

STRESSES AND HAZARDS   DANGERS: C-   PRESSURES: C

Though construction tasks—such as antenna installation—can be physically strenuous, radio piracy is a largely sedentary occupation. In fact, DJs and engineers who sit for hours on end should adopt a regimen of stretching and exercise to avoid spinal discomfort or injury. Prolonged exposure to loud music via headphones is also commonly linked to long-term hearing loss. In addition to dangers of FCC equipment seizure, penalties, and fines, Pirate Radio Operators face eviction or censure if their activities become known to their residential or commercial landlords. Repetitive struggles to raise operational funds can also take a heavy psychic toll.

WORK ENVIRONMENT   HOURS: B-   COMFORT: D

In businesses that reward stealth and concealment, working quarters are often utilitarian and tight. Shoestring pirate budgets also spell bad news in the creature-comfort department. Though Pirate Radio Operators are largely self-managed and maintain flexible hours, the multidisciplinary requirements of this field can be time-consuming. Party promotion, tape duplication, IT troubleshooting, and interactive support can all be time eaters. The defiant individualism that draws many to this field must be tempered with respect for co-workers in more democratically organized Pirate Radio workplaces.

POACHER

RANK: 15 out of 50   **AVERAGE GRADE:** B-

DUTIES: Poachers hunt or capture wildlife in contravention to legal limitations on species sought, numbers killed, catch size, catch age, licensing, equipment, protected lands, or seasonality (see Rustler, for related opportunities with domesticated animals). Though die-hard amateurs still poach for subsistence or sport, this lucrative field is rapidly professionalizing. Poachers pursue a rich spectrum of wildlife for a variety of market applications. They capture live animals for exotic pets and research; slaughter others for medicines, food, clothing, and accessories; and harvest wild plants for use in botanical and pharmaceutical preparations. Worldwide trade in illegal wildlife and wildlife products is believed to total at least $10 billion and involve more than 350 million plants and animals. The United States imports an estimated $300 million worth of illegal wildlife every year and is fast becoming a major exporter, as well.

Next-generation poachers manage large, horizontally integrated organizations with sophisticated capabilities for materials processing, transportation, wholesale, and retail distribution and money laundering. Even small-scale senior poachers often delegate mundane or hazardous chores to junior workers. Florida poachers of sea turtle eggs, for example, minimize personal law enforcement interactions by subcontracting crack-addicted pieceworkers to perform high-exposure, low-skill harvesting tasks.

Although poaching has been traditionally associated with rural regions, California's Bay Area is emerging as a major alternative employment center in this field. Entry-level workers fish the San Francisco bay for the giant sturgeon, whose protected eggs fetch $100 per pound on the growing Russian black market for caviar. More advanced practitioners don scuba gear to harvest red abalone, a snail-like shellfish, which sells for up to $80 to $100 per fish on the Asian black market. Another urban maritime center, Seattle, also presents outstanding opportunities for entrepreneurs. A noted poacher of the geoduck (pronounced "goo-ee-duck"), the world's largest burrowing clam, was recently found in possession of over $2 million of the coveted mollusks.

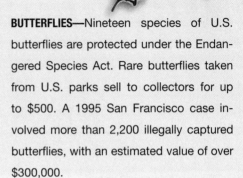

AMERICAN BLACK BEAR—In Asian cultures, salts from bear gallbladders are prescribed for intestinal, liver, and cardiac-related illnesses. In the U.S. and Asia, gallbladders sell for as much as $10,000. Bear paws are also prized for folk remedies, while bear hides and heads remain popular as trophies and decorative accents.

WILD AMERICAN GINSENG—The U.S. herbal remedy market has more than tripled in the past decade, with powdered ginseng root emerging as the first choice of new users. Wholesale prices for wild ginseng top $1,000 a pound. The American ginseng belt stretches from Maine to Alabama and New York to Oklahoma, but the Smoky Mountain National Park region holds the bulk of our nation's buried ginseng riches.

BUTTERFLIES—Nineteen species of U.S. butterflies are protected under the Endangered Species Act. Rare butterflies taken from U.S. parks sell to collectors for up to $500. A 1995 San Francisco case involved more than 2,200 illegally captured butterflies, with an estimated value of over $300,000.

ELK, DEER, BIGHORN SHEEP—A trophy-sized set of elk antlers goes for $12,000 to $20,000. Trophy whitetail or mule deer antlers fetch $5,000. Fees for guided hunts for bighorn sheep in the Yellowstone region average $20,000 to $25,000.

QUEEN BEES—A black market for exporting live queens to Canada has been growing quickly since Canada banned the import of them from the United States in 1987.

COMPENSATION AND REWARDS   *EARNINGS:* **B**   *PERKS:* **B-**

Potential rewards for poachers are great, but vary considerably across specialties/species. Annual earnings of $60,000 to $100,000 are common among divers and experienced ginseng diggers, but elite specialists can earn several times this amount. Unskilled, temporary workers can expect results-based stipends of $100 or less. Poachers travel moderate distances by car, boat, or small aircraft in pursuit of quarry. Advanced poachers travel nationally and internationally to negotiate transactions and bring their goods to market.

BEWARE OF DO-GOODERS
A sign of the times?
Source: Alberta Department of Infrastructure and Transportation

ENFORCEMENT AND PENALTIES   *ARRESTS:* **B+**   *SENTENCING:* **A-**

Legal controls, sentencing, and enforcement have long been lax in this field. The last decade has seen tightening of penalties and true innovation in enforcement. Along with increases in manpower and budgeting, new tactics include sting and mole operations, use of robotic decoys, and widespread deployment of motion detectors, remote cameras, and seismic monitors.

OK, FINE!
Financial penalties against poachers have increased dramatically

Type of action	2003	2004	2005
No. of violations	9,339	10,691	11,111
Fines	$7,905,138	$3,654,427	$22,216,189
Prison (years)	33	55	62
Probation (years)	545	500	677
Civil penalties	$8,572,534	$945,629	$1,445,280

Source: U.S. Department of Fish and Wildlife Legal Actions

STRESSES AND HAZARDS

DANGERS: C   PRESSURES: C

Physical challenges include extended stays in crouching, kneeling, and confined positions, and hauling of heavy specialized equipment. Deaths from drowning and decompression sickness (the bends) are becoming frequent among West Coast poacher-divers. Injuries from accidental firearm discharge or friendly fire are also common during fast-paced, clandestine hunts. Some frontline poachers are adopting the use of body armor, as armed confrontations with law enforcement continue to rise.

Poachers work within narrow windows of enforcement-free opportunity, and pressure from deadlines and quotas can be significant.

WORK ENVIRONMENT

HOURS: C+   COMFORT: C

Poachers work primarily outdoors, under a range of challenging conditions. Low light, extreme weather, and rugged terrain are endemic to this occupation. Boat- and scuba-based assignments have become common, while helicopters and bush planes are gaining acceptance among big-game poachers in wide-open areas such as Alaska and Montana. Frequently employed special equipment includes night vision and high-powered lighting, automatic rifles, telescopes and binoculars, powered digging tools, small explosives, advanced fish finders, and hunting dogs.

Poachers frequently adjust their working hours to avoid park rangers, game wardens, licensed hunters, and passersby. Generally, poaching is seasonal work, with shorter-than-average working weeks. Seasoned abalone divers, for example, earn a full year's pay for roughly two months' work. Most contract poachers enjoy considerable autonomy in quarry and route selection, evasion tactics, scheduling, and shifts.

PRISON WIFE

RANK: 50 out of 50   **AVERAGE GRADE:** D+

DUTIES: Prison "Wives" provide sexual and domestic services to fellow incarcerees, in exchange for physical protection, canteen supplies, drugs, and other valuable considerations. The pressures on *fresh meat*—newly arrived prisoners—to *hook up* can be intense in today's fiercely physical correctional community. Although just 10 percent of state inmates sustain treatment-worthy fighting injuries, penal pundits say up to 70 percent square off each annum. At least 20 percent of convicts have been coerced into a sex act, and 10 percent to 20 percent have been raped.

Under "protective pairing," a potential big-house bride-to-be (commonly referred to as a *punk, catcher, bitch,* or *kid*) acquiesces to the exclusive advances of a dominant *daddy*—also known as a *pitcher, jocker,* or *booty bandit.* Demand for datable detainees far outweighs supply, so competition for new conscripts often begins immediately. Aspirants to this prostrated position should take the courting process into their own hands, before some ill-suited suitor forces his affections. Jockers range from supportive helpmates to sadistic serial batterers. Seasoned punks rapidly assess the character, capabilities, connections, and commitment levels of prospective predators, and negotiate favorable terms of servitude. In a seller's market, the frequency and variety of intimate acts can often be negotiated along with levels of secondary service—such as cleaning and backrubs.

FROM CELL MATE TO SOUL MATE
Inside the shut-in singles scene.
Source: Office of Management and Budget

Most important, the *catcher* must ascertain whether the *pitcher* intends to lend or sublease him to his associates or the general prison population. Catchers who are put *on the block* are prostituted for their pitchers' enrichment. *Riders* are indentured to multimember gangs or cliques and may also be sold to outsiders. Ideally, a punk negotiates an exclusive arrangement with a formidable daddy, sheltering him from additional unprotected acts of forcible intimacy. Thenceforward, those wishing to harm or woo him do so at the mortal risk of offending his *man*. Though his largesse may extend to gifts of money, cigarettes, drugs, or affection, protection is a pitcher's primary obligation.

Inmates averse to the charms of penitential pursuers must fight or flee. A successful first rebuff might yield lasting *cred* but might also serve as a dark prelude to deadlier duels. Internees who request transfer to protective custody (otherwise known as *PC* or *Punk City*) can expect the howling derision of cell mates and guards alike. At best they look forward to twenty-three-hour lockdown, sanity-testing seclusion, and enduring ostracism. At worst, their requests are refused and they are turned back, into the waiting arms of assailants eager to *turn them out*.

Some jockers befriend boyish lawbreakers, advancing them funds or pharmaceuticals. Soon, the newcomers are apprised that they are expected to repay these advances plus compounded interest of 100 percent per day. Lacking the necessary funds, they are obliged to pay with their fundaments.

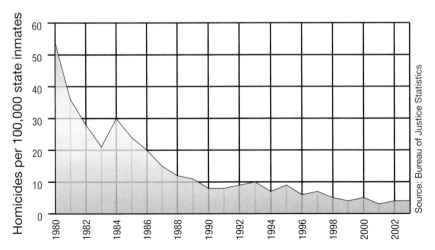

WHO SAYS INCARCERATION IS MURDER?
Prisoner-on-prisoner homocide is at twenty-year low

Homicides per 100,000 state inmates

Source: Bureau of Justice Statistics

COMPENSATION AND REWARDS   EARNINGS: **F+**   PERKS: **B**

Although the tangible rewards of prison matrimony—coffee, cigarettes, and occasional cuddling—are token, the potential health benefits are priceless. Survival enthusiasts implicitly conclude that a single *shanking* or gang shagging avoided is worth years of indignities. For-profit pitchers typically charge $2 to $5 for oral trysts with their bitches, and $5 to $10 for services at the opposite "end" of the sexual spectrum. Some incarcerated pimps pair up solely to procure resalable tail.

ENFORCEMENT AND PENALTIES   ARRESTS: **B**   SENTENCING: **B-**

Sexual contact among convicts is unlawful, so ill-camouflaged coitus could lead to a longer sentence. Generally, security arrangements are the province of the alpha-male aggressor. Although some jailhouse "screws" (guards) take a violently hard line on inmate intimacy, most recognize its moderating effects on prisoner-to-prisoner pummeling. In fact, all but the most celebrated sodomites are usually grudgingly tolerated by prison staff.

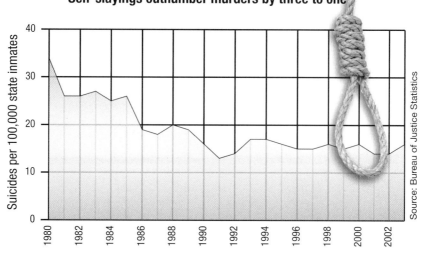

SUICIDAL PRISONERS CAN BE THEIR OWN WORST ENEMIES
Self-slayings outnumber murders by three to one

Suicides per 100,000 state inmates (y-axis: 0, 10, 20, 30, 40)

x-axis: 1980, 1982, 1984, 1986, 1988, 1990, 1992, 1994, 1996, 1998, 2000, 2002

Source: Bureau of Justice Statistics

STRESSES AND HAZARDS

The quality and character of inmate-mates varies greatly. The best are fine providers and protectors, for whom one may develop sincere affection. The worst are sociopaths and sadists, from whom one may develop a serious infection. Though AIDS is three to twenty times more prevalent in prison than in the general populace (depending on region and institution type), only six U.S. institutions allow the distribution of protective prophylactics. Improvised alter-natives include latex gloves, plastic bags, and plastic wrap.

The vast majority of catchers (and pitchers) strongly self-identify as het-erosexuals, so acclimating to the role of state-housed sex slave can be traumatic. Self-esteem often suffers, and suicides re-main commonplace. Juveniles in adult jails exercise this untenable option 7.7 times more frequently than do their peers in youth institutions.

WORK ENVIRONMENT

Prison wives work primarily indoors, on a 365-day basis. Typically, they are housed on the same cell blocks as their jocks, affording enhanced security and extended alone time. Custodial courtships between cell mates provide unparalleled privacy, but turning the communal sleeping space into a sexualized work site may erode essential labor/leisure boundaries. Outside-the-box thinkers may chafe in the ritualized role of *bottom man*.

PROSTITUTE

RANK: 45 out of 50   **AVERAGE GRADE:** C

DUTIES: Prostitutes perform a variety of common and specialized sex acts in exchange for cash, drugs, or other valuable considerations. Street prostitutes—vernacularly referred to as *hookers, streetwalkers, whores,* or *hos*—solicit passersby while stationed at street corners or ambling casually. Street hookers often signal their availability by donning suggestive, minimalist garb. After a *john* (customer) initiates contact, a pre-agreed-upon intimate act is performed in his car, an accommodating alley, or a rented room.

Streetwalkers often work in association with Pimps (see page 162). Pimps demand a percentage of gross receipts in exchange for nominal physical protection from other pimps and predators. They may also provide or procure drugs (75 percent of street workers are substance abusers); furnish food, transportation, or shelter; or offer emotional nourishment. Many, however, are manipulative and abusive sociopaths.

Street prostitution flourishes in marginally rundown neighborhoods with steady flows of unattached males. Typically, *red-light districts* are situated near industrial areas, declining residential zones, major thoroughfares, transportation hubs, convention centers, or hotels. Close proximity to open-air drug markets is also desirable and extremely common. Street prostitution accounts for 10 percent to 20 percent of the overall intimate-services market in our major metros, and as much as 50 percent in small cities with limited indoor venues.

Call girls—also known as *escorts* or *outcall girls*—schedule trysting appointments via phone, e-mail, or Web-based forms. Although the prices for their services are usually quoted on a flat-rate *session* basis (hour or half-hour), exotic, elaborate, or distasteful acts may trigger additional charges. Call girls generally administer their sexual services via house call.

Call girls often work through *escort services.* Customarily, they identify such opportunities through advertisements in regional newspapers. To effectively "service" a deep client base, escort agencies maintain databases or *stables* of procurable sex workers. They generally specialize in a single gender—male, female, or transsexual. Some cater to niche requests for a given body type, ethnicity, fetish, or age group. In addition to regional print ads and Yellow Pages listings, many services maintain Web sites with alluring photo catalogs. Clients initiate the ordering process with a call to an agency. The agency relays the client's contact information to an appropriate vendor who then negotiates the sexual and economic specifics of the *date*. This indirection ensures plausible legal deniability for the referring agency. As a security precaution, most escorts phone their services upon date initiation and consummation.

Brothel-based workers are permanently stationed at massage parlors and other semiconcealed dedicated locales. Other names for a brothel include *bordello,* *whorehouse,* and *cathouse.* The sex workers here are employed by *madams,* facilities managers who set pricing, provide security, and collect fees. Contrary to popular belief, not all madams are female, nor are all pimps male. In fact, the majority of West Coast brothels are operated by male-dominated Asian crime syndicates, which employ Asian gang members as enforcers and collectors. Many of these operate out of chiropractic front businesses, with the chiropractor of record receiving $200 to $1,000 a month for misuse of his credentials. Others are housed in quiet residential areas, to make law enforcement street presence easy to spot. A large percentage of girls working in Asian chiropractic brothels and "happy ending" massage parlors are illegally trafficked into the country and kept as indentured sexual slaves (see Slave Trader).

THE WIDE WORLD OF SEX WORK
Can you see yourself in the picture?
Source: Wikimedia Commons

Earnings and fees vary sharply with gender, vendor type (e.g., street/escort/brothel worker), locale, age, attractiveness, experience, presentability, and other intangibles. Male street workers (called *hustlers, rent boys, punks,* or *trade*) earn a weekly average of $600 to $800, compared with $1,800 to $2,000 for their female counterparts. Transsexuals—*shemales, he-shes,* or *trannies*—command substantial premiums. Crack-addicted discounters often key their fees for oral sex to the market price for a single crack rock. Rates for escorts range from $100 per hour to over $1,000. Associates of reputable agencies may receive perks, including subsidized gynecological care, chauffeured transport, and per diem food allowances.

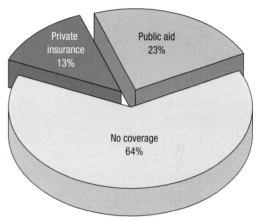

FULLY COVERED?
Even among well-paid indoor workers, health insurance is a rarity

- Private insurance 13%
- Public aid 23%
- No coverage 64%

Source: Sex Workers Project at the Urban Justice Center 2005

ENFORCEMENT AND PENALTIES   *ARRESTS:* **C+** *SENTENCING:* **B**

Though prostitution was outlawed in most states of the union between 1910 and 1915, it is legally regulated in ten of Nevada's seventeen counties. Nevada brothel associates work twelve-hour shifts, with an average of seven customers per shift, for three weeks at a time. It most other states, prostitution is an un-derenforced misdemeanor, though Alabama still classifies it as a felony. Nearly 85 percent to 90 percent of prostitutes arrested are street workers, though they represent only 20 percent of the work-force. Urban anti-prostitution budgets range from $1 million (Memphis) to $23 million (New York).

COMBAT FATIGUE?! Most prostitutes exhibit clinically recognized symptoms of post-traumatic stress	
Occupational Hazard	Frequency of occurrence
Trouble sleeping	59%
Irritability and outbursts	63%
Trouble concentrating	62%
Hyper-alertness or on-guard state	78%
Jumpy and easily startled	67%
Physical reactions to past stresses	63%

Source: Melissa Farley, Ph.D., and Howard Barkan, *Prostitution, Violence, and Post-Traumatic Stress Disorder*

STRESSES AND HAZARDS

DANGERS: **D** PRESSURES: **D**

Dangers abound in the erotic workplace. Seventy-nine percent of street prostitutes have been physically assaulted by customers, 76 percent have been beaten by pimps, and 50 percent have been abducted by pimps. Furthermore, 83 percent have been threatened with a weapon, 73 percent have been raped on the job, and 27 percent of those rapes involved four or more assailants. The most virulent occupational hazards, however, are actually sexually transmitted diseases and suicide. Fifteen percent of all American suicide victims are prostitutes, and 75 percent of all prostitutes have attempted suicide.

WORK ENVIRONMENT

HOURS: **D** COMFORT: **D**

Common work sites for indoor sex work include massage parlors, health clubs, hotels, motels, strip clubs, go-go bars, and peep shows. Other adult venues include makeshift brothels in gambling halls and trailers servicing rural work camps. U.S. military bases are often ringed by R&R clubs resembling those found at foreign posts—replete with trafficked Asian workers. In many American urban markets, the great preponderance of indoor sex work is controlled, financed, or backed by organized crime groups.

In some cities, more than 70 percent of female street workers are represented by pimps. In liberated San Francisco, however, 96 percent of female prostitutes work for themselves, about 30 percent of the city's prostitutes are male, and roughly 25 percent are transgender. Nationwide, males account for about 10 percent to 15 percent of the sex workforce.

Though hours and shifts vary tremendously, respondents in one large industry survey worked an average of twenty-two sex sessions over a six-day week.

PROTECTED WITNESS

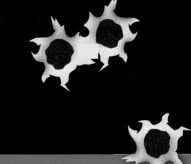

RANK: 25 out of 50   **AVERAGE GRADE:** B-

DUTIES: Federally Protected Witnesses give damning testimony against federal and state malefactors posing plausible threats of violent retaliation. Workers in this elite discipline receive physical protection, reductions in sentencing, financial entitlements, and specialized assistance in relocation and identity reassignment. Only 6 percent of protected witnesses are civic-minded innocents; the field is dominated by accomplished criminals proactively redressing career crises.

Typically, a well-established evildoer facing imminent indictment or irrevocable bodily harm is approached by court officers who have targeted his notorious senior associates for spirited prosecution. They apprise him that they he may qualify for relocation under the Federal Witness Security Program (WITSEC). In return he must lend his wholehearted cooperation to ongoing official animosities against his former crime-kin. If this is palatable, the prosecuting agencies tender an official request for protection to the Justice Department's Office of Enforcement Operations (OEO). The report highlights the scope and import of the applicant's potential testimony, the threats likely to arise from such tale-telling, and the potential harm the judicial Judas might visit on his new community. The OEO passes outstanding applications to the U.S. Marshals Service, which conducts preliminary briefings and administers

A WITSEC inspector blending in at a hearing.

SOME SUITS NEVER GO OUT OF STYLE
A convoy of feds moving their marked man.
Source: U.S. Marshals Service

THE PICKETER, THE POLITICIAN, AND THE PENIS
The lighter side of life and death

THE PICKETER—James Cardinali, a confessed quadruple-killer, was drummed out of the program for revealing his true identity to a girlfriend. He protested by standing vigil outside a federal courthouse with a sign reading MOB STAR WITNESS.

THE POLITICIAN—John Johnson, a New Jersey mob witness, was successfully re-settled in Austin, Texas. He blew his own cover by circulating copies of his lengthy rap sheet and running for mayor. It's better to elect a former crook, he told voters, than a future one. He received 496 votes.

THE PENIS—Before testifying, an important witness became clinically impotent and chronically depressed. To restore his confidence on and off "the stand," WITSEC paid for him to receive a penile implant.

psychological evaluations for all potential protectees over eighteen years of age.

If the U.S. Attorney General gives his blessing, the witness and his endangered family sign a *memorandum of understanding*, stipulating their informed consent to enter the voluntary, highly restrictive "program." Marshals then typically whisk the entire entourage out of the *threat area* to a tackily appointed *neutral zone* (usually a motel-esque safe house full of scrupulously segregated witnesses and handlers). Witnesses' families usually remain under the twenty-four-hour protection of WITSEC inspectors (specialized marshals) throughout pretrial and trial proceedings. Key witnesses are shuttled to and from courtroom threat areas by armed convoys, helicopters, and disguised vehicles. Communications with former associates are sharply limited or forbidden outright.

Most protected turncoats adapt quickly and enthusiastically to their new work responsibilities, and are highly effective on "the stand." Since the program's inception in 1970, 89 percent of the cases involving its witnesses have ended in convictions. Many witnesses forget their long-held distaste for snitchery and take evident pleasure in their contributions to "the team." Far-thinking finks, however, withhold a few names or incriminating nuggets as bargaining chips for a rainy day.

After trial, each witness or witness family is paired with a long-suffering WITSEC inspector. His oft-thankless chores include identifying an unsuspecting host community, hunting down housing stock, briefing psychiatric social workers, and doling out "subsistence" checks to protected payees. Witnesses choose their own new names. Most maintain their initials or

OLD DOG, OLD TRICKS

Fewer than 10 percent of protected witnesses return to their former lives of crime. Here are a dedicated few who refused to let the dream die

WITNESS: Marion Albert Pruett

QUALIFICATIONS: Killer, bank robber, kidnapper

DEAL: Testified against a fellow inmate for a jailhouse murder Pruett himself had actually committed

NEW LIFE: Dump truck driver

GLITCH: After murdering his wife in a drugged rage, Pruett set out on a multi-state mad-dog spree. He killed seven more people, kidnapped two, and robbed six banks. He was executed in 1999.

WITNESS: Joseph "The Animal" Barboza

QUALIFICATIONS: Respected homicide professional with twenty-six completed assignments

DEAL: Received immunity for sending four associates up the river for life

NEW LIFE: Cooking school, Merchant Marines

GLITCH: Returned to "the life," stole $300,000 in bonds, murdered a drug dealer, and went to prison. In 1972, he won temporary release by testifying that Frank Sinatra was a mob puppet. Got paroled, shook down San Francisco bookies, then finally got whacked.

WITNESS: Arthur Katz

QUALIFICATIONS: Crooked Kansas City attorney

DEAL: Rolled over on insurance fraud cohorts

NEW LIFE: Joined the civil service, day traded stock

GLITCH: Lost millions in the 1987 stock crash. Visited his broker's office with a .357 Magnum and "offed" the office manager and himself.

WITNESS: Peter "Big George" Yudzevich

QUALIFICATIONS: Extortionist extraordinaire

DEAL: "Ratted-out" two Gambino family associates and a corrupt mortgage broker for a "pass" on money-laundering charges

NEW LIFE: Bouncer

GLITCH: Dropped out of the program in late 1988. Turned up at a California "adult entertainment" venue with three bullets in his head in early 1989.

first names, so their new handles don't ring entirely false. Once a witness receives his new identification, his inspector is tasked with bringing him at least one solid employment opportunity. To date, WITSEC has successfully repotted 7,500 witnesses and more than 9,600 family members or associates.

WAYNE J E BROWN
PO BOX 303
YORBA LINDA CA

COMPENSATION AND REWARDS

EARNINGS: **B-**   PERKS: **B+**

Subsistence payments to witnesses average about $60,000 a year. Generally, Uncle Sam tries to wean suckling tattletales from the public teat within two years of the cessation of courtroom contretemps. For expert manipulators like Jimmy "The Weasel" Fratianno—who helped convict six major mob bosses and dozens of foot soldiers—the program represents a much broader-based opportunity. Fratianno stayed on the dole for ten years, pocketing nearly one million tax dollars, publishing two profitable books, and eventually collecting major appearance fees.

Almost 80 percent of current WITSEC cases are linked to narcotics. Lucky trafficker-informants can "double-dip" by negotiating large, performance-based "rewards for information" in DEA investigations (see Snitch). In one celebrated case, an ex-biker (who once cooked eggs while his partner beat an elderly man to death) received a briefcase stuffed with $30,000 in DEA cash—the night before he was to testify in a landmark drug trial against the Hells Angels.

Additional job benefits include subsidized health care, individual and family counseling, and free travel to a new city in the event of a "blown cover."

ENFORCEMENT AND PENALTIES

ARRESTS: **B**   SENTENCING: **B**

Ethically flexible indictees prepared to "name names" receive absolution, immunity, and reduced indemnity for a host of felonious sins. Many protected witnesses dodge detention entirely, whereas some serve time in special WITSEC wings of federal prisons, before being paroled to the program and relocated.

Others enter the program *from* prison. State or federal prisoners with need-to-know info on jail-yard crimes or preincarceration capers can petition the Bureau of Prisons for reassignment to a high-security WITSEC cellblock. Each year, the DEA tenders about 150 requests for such prisoner-witnesses to be furloughed. Furloughed prisoner-moles earn major sentencing reductions in exchange for high-risk participation in undercover drug buys.

STRESSES AND HAZARDS

DANGERS: **C+**   PRESSURES: **D+**

No witness who followed the letter of the program's strict law has ever been slain, but at least twenty strayed lambs have gone to the slaughter. Most recently, Brenda Paz—a seventeen-year-old who testified against the hyper-violent Salvadoran street gang MS-13—was murdered after she fled her safe house and returned to her old gang haunts in Virginia. Her case underscores the isolation and homesickness experienced by workers at all levels in this field. Culture shock is common, mistrust is advisable, and identity issues are inevitable.

"Protected" marriages are actually quite vulnerable to the stresses of the program, and breakups are commonplace. On more than one occasion, the principal cause of marital friction was the fact that the mistress had been relocated along with the wife. Divorces often precipitate the separation and independent relocation of family factions, who may no longer be trusted to have each other's best interests at heart. Enforcement of child support obligations is a perennially thorny issue.

WORK ENVIRONMENT

HOURS: **D+**   COMFORT: **C**

Preparation for racketeering cases often entails months of close-quarter coaching at flea-bitten motels. Takeout food fatigue and temper tantrums are to be expected, as weary wiseguys pine for their days on the dais. During trials, tedium gives way to claustrophobic fear as witnesses contemplate the possibility of en-route ambush on their overland outings. When the gavel

falls, quality of life inclines emphatically. In a 2004 survey of 168 WITSEC participants, 112 said no to the question "Have you or your family experienced problems under this program that could have been avoided"; 154 said that WITSEC is a worthwhile program; and 133 said they would enter the program again, given the same strange circumstances.

RUSTLER

RANK: 6 out of 50   **AVERAGE GRADE:** B

DUTIES: Rustlers covertly snatch living members of resalable species. As ever, the iconic cattle rustler is the main mover in the American market for secondhand meat. The age of Atkins brought record beef prices along with stampeding cholesterol counts, creating ample motive for a new generation of cow-centric criminals. Opportunities abound for livestock liberation in our vast, unattended outdoors. Most critters meander unsupervised, gates are rarely locked, and ranchers' when- and whereabouts are easily monitored. Small undercounts of cattle are often attributed to bovine wanderlust or poor fence-mending. The loss of ten calves from a two-hundred-head herd could go unnoticed for months.

Most cattle rustlers creep into barns or pastures late at night, then herd up to ten head into a lone trailer. The most practiced rustlers head directly to out-of-state livestock sales, where problematic pedigrees or paperwork are oft overlooked. In 2003, an outfit implementing this just-in-time approach successfully marketed 147 head of misbranded cattle. The group netted over $100,000 at old-fashioned sales across Iowa, Minnesota, Nebraska, and the Dakotas.

The largest scores are inside attacks. When two hundred head of cattle—worth $200,000—went AWOL from Peter Marble's 71 Ranch in northern Nevada, suspicion quickly turned to his former foreman. The disgruntled cowpoke and his wife had allegedly diverted the herd to their own nearby spread.

OPPORTUNITY ON THE HOOF
Most livestock remains udderly underguarded.
Source: U.S. Department of Agriculture

Rustlers favor unbranded calves, which—short of DNA testing—are essentially untraceable. Alternatively, they will superimpose a simple new shape over an existing brand mark. In one recent grisly case, a rustler skinned existing brands off living livestock, waited for the wounds to heal, then rebranded them.

In the late eighties, emus and ostriches were big-ticket targets of choice as prices soared up to $50,000 per big bird. By the height of the farm fad, injectable identification chips had turned the tide. Two million dollars' worth of tagged avian abductees were recovered in 1993 alone.

Since California banned horse slaughter in 1998, horse theft nationwide has dropped by 34 percent. Still, roughly fifty-five thousand horses are heisted each year in the United States. Many are marketed for their meat value. Horse rustlers are often accomplished makeover artists who dye, cut, style, bleach, and rebrand hijacked horse flesh.

Cactus rustlers seize high-demand succulents for live resale to foreign aficionados and ecologically inclined domestic *xeriscapers* (proponents of self-sustaining landscaping techniques). Nearly 100,000 wild cacti were illicitly harvested from Texas between 1998 and 2001. The U.S. Fish and Wildlife Service estimates that over 30,000 rustled plants from sixteen species were illegally exported from Mexico to Texas in the same period.

COMPENSATION AND REWARDS   EARNINGS: **B+**   PERKS: **C**

Beefy profits, indeed, lie ahead for America's top steer-stealers. With prices at historic highs, a single trailer of stolen stock can yield $20,000. Between 2001 and 2002, rustling activity in South Dakota increased by 300 percent. At any given moment, roughly $12 million worth of South Dakotan cattle are missing in action. In 2004, the Texas and Southwestern Cattle Raisers Association investigated 1,214 cases and located livestock and loot worth more than $4 million. In 2001, a Denton County couple trusted throughout the Texas ranching community lost three thousand head of cattle they had been paid to watch over during a drought; the heisted heifers were worth over $2 million. Cactus-cornerers cadged an estimated $3 million in plants from Texas parklands between 1998 and 2001, and smuggled an estimated $1 million in Mexican pricklies across the Rio Grande.

ENFORCEMENT AND PENALTIES   ARRESTS: **A-**   SENTENCING: **C-**

In most critter-crowded states, *cattle theft* and *horse theft* are Class 4 felonies punishable by up to ten years' imprisonment.

THE PROFITS ARE SPIKING
The prickly pear is a favorite target of cactus rustlers.
Source: U.S. Department of Agriculture

Clearance rates for these crimes are not centrally collected. However, brand inspectors (antirustling enforcers) in Nebraska, North Dakota, Colorado, Oregon, and Idaho say that suspects are caught in fewer than 10 percent of all open-range robberies. The giant scale of the great outdoors, the ubiquity of transport trailers, and the rise of the absentee cowboy conspire to keep this criminal activity comparatively safe. DNA sampling, networking among state brand databases, and computerized ID tags are starting to make a high-tech impact. As an optimistic Colorado brand inspector recently put it, "We're kind of coming out of the rock-and-stick age."

STRESSES AND HAZARDS

DANGERS: **B-**   PRESSURES: **B+**

Though modern rustlers are no longer hanged, some are still shot. Edward Lee "Ed" Cantrell—a former range detective who once beat a first-degree murder charge for slaying an undercover agent in an apparent fast-draw incident—is a hired gun for rustler-weary ranchers. The sixtyish Cantrell hones his handgun skills daily, as he keeps watch across a ten-thousand-square-mile stretch of southwestern Wyoming. "I can't remember ever backing off anything," Cantrell boasted in a 2001 NBC news interview. "I've shot two people here in Sweetwater County."

Established cattlemen who turn corrupt may experience unacceptable levels of community scorn and enforcement ardor when their exploits are unveiled. When cops came for Bob Harold Leach—a trusted Texas rancher who had incorrectly corralled two thousand head of cattle—he went ballistic, kidnapping a former girlfriend and heading for the high plains in a stolen SUV. After his initial capture, Leach participated in a spectacular jailbreak/standoff. It ended when he shot his fellow escapee, allowing two hostages to go free. He's currently serving a life sentence for the kidnapping plus twenty years' bonus time for the jailbreak.

WORK ENVIRONMENT

HOURS: **C+**   COMFORT: **C**

Livestock rustlers work primarily out of doors, under cover of darkness, in mostly remote regions. Cactus rustlers typically harvest for rare specimens in the searing heat of the Chihuahuan Desert or Texas's 800,000-acre Big Bend National Park. Top-tier livestock-lifters avail themselves of all the essential tools of the modern roundup, including motorcycles, lookouts with radios, and trained dogs. Portable corrals and double-length trailers are favored for long-distance hauling.

Although access to specialized equipment and familiarity with niche resale practices can pose significant barriers to entry, the fundamentals of this ancient trade are quite accessible. In 2005, a precocious sixteen-year-old boy single-handedly liberated eight cattle from a seventy-six-year-old rancher in California's Calveras County.

SAFECRACKER

DUTIES: Safecrackers unlawfully open or enter safes and vaults or remove them from their original locales to take, tamper with, or ascertain their contents. Today's leading *box men* draw from a rich tradition of time-tested *attacks* to select the tools and techniques suited to the conditions at hand. Any safe can be accessed by a properly equipped technician in the event of a malfunction or a lost combination or key. Given sufficient knowledge, tools, and time, expert safecrackers can get through any locking mechanism.

Combination deduction is the savvy safecracker's first line of attack. All safes are sent from the factory with *tryout combinations*. An astounding percentage of safe purchasers never reset these tryouts, which

IT'S WORTH A SHOT!
Tryout combinations for popular safes

The dialing guide indicates the direction and number of required dial turns.

Example: L4-R3-L2-R with a combination of 15-25-35 means LEFT four turns stopping at 15, RIGHT three turns to 25, LEFT two turns to 35, then RIGHT till the wheel stops.

Brand of safe	Dialing guide	Combinations
American	R4-L3-R2-L	30-20-10, 40-10-50
Chicago	R4-L3-R2-L1	7-8-2-1, 35-71-39-7
Diebold	L4-R3-L2-R	45-70-35, 60-20-40
Mosler	L5-R4-L3-R2-L	64-95-60-5, 91-39-76-59
Schwab	L4-R3-L2-R	15-75-0, 75-50-0, 40-70-35
Victor	R4-L3-L2-R	0-12-82-92, 1-13-89-93

are widely known by locksmiths and safe-crackers. Moreover, Memory Lane can be a winding road, so forgetful people often write their combinations on a nearby wall or scrap of paper. Others base their combinations on easily deducible numbers, such as their birthdate (e.g., "12-17-41"), anniversary, or social security number. When a combination is not readily visible or deducible, safecrackers often resort to surveillance via naked-eye, video, or telescopic means. If these gambits fail, in-the-know safecrackers will check if the safe is on *day lock*. This is a daytime convenience feature that allows safes to be opened by merely dialing the final number of their combination. If a safe is on day lock, the cracker turns the dial to the left until resistance is felt. Then he turns the dial to the right one number at a time until the safe handle "gives" under pressure.

Underwriters Laboratories rates safes according to the time required to complete a drill-based attack under ideal laboratory conditions. The best safes are rated at a mere sixty minutes, but real-world, onsite penetration with portable tools can take several times longer. In the great majority of attacks on freestanding safes (versus in-floor or in-wall safes), safecrackers remove the safe, then compromise it at a well-equipped, concealed location. To complicate removal and transport, modern safes are designed with sloping bottoms and hinges to thwart leveraged lifting via jacks or wedges. They are often secured to floors via reinforced bolts and may contain substantial ballast to increase their overall weight.

Drill-based attacks have become very popular. The most basic method is to drill into the face of the lock to access its lever, or *drive cam*. The safecracker then employs a *punch rod* to push the cam out of the path

TIPS FROM THE VAULT

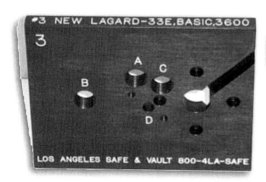

Drilling templates take the guesswork out of "boring" attacks.

Electronic locks present high-tech challenges.

of the main securing bolt. Higher-end safes employ cobalt plates to counter frontal drilling attacks. Given titanium or diamond bits, several drills, and extensive access time, a very determined cracker can eventually defeat a cobalt plate. Safecrackers typically forgo this option and drill above the cobalt plate, at an angle. Then they manipulate the locking mechanism aided by a fiber-optic viewer called a *borescope*.

The most sophisticated safes and vaults employ *relockers*, which are activated when a drill bit breaks through a glass or plastic barrier layer. The relockers trigger a very hardy auxiliary locking device. Relockers, in turn, can be defeated by a variety of precision back- or side-entry drilling techniques. Veteran safecrackers—like most skilled tradesmen—respect the value of the right tool and typically employ portable drill presses from specialized manufacturers.

At a sufficiently high temperature, any metal will burn. Oxy-acetylene torches are cheap and readily available but are not enough to work efficiently on better-fortified safes. More expensive plasma cutters and thermic lances (*burning bars*), on the other hand, can make short work of the peskiest safecracking assignment. Burning attacks generate lots of heat and smoke, so care must be taken to avoid barbecuing the safe's contents or triggering fire or smoke alarms.

Explosives are also quite popular among advanced practitioners. Traditionally, *safeblowers* (historically known as *peter men*) have em-ployed nitroglycerin-based *jam shots* to blow the doors off safes. Jellylike nitroglycerin "grease," however, is alarmingly volatile, so many have moved on to moldable, high-tech explosives, such as C-4, PETN, and RDX.

Lock manipulation is the process of opening a safe without defacing it in any manner. The scientific underpinnings of this family of attacks were first detailed by Harry C. Miller in 1940. In modern practice, safecrackers use stethoscopes, audio amplifiers, or electronic sensing devices to identify the sonic signatures of a safe's contact points and determine how many wheels it has. Contrary to most fictional portrayals, thieves must actually graph their results to determine potential combinations. Lock manipulation is favored by damage-averse locksmiths but is generally shunned by time-strapped safecrackers.

The current generation of electronic locks can challenge even the most seasoned safecracker. One company recently developed software that can interface with an electronic lock via a wireless connection with its programming port and deduce its combination through a high-speed sequence of trial-and-error attempts. Another particularly inspired attack involves covering doorknobs or handrails near the target safe with ultraviolet powder, then later illuminating the keypad with a black light to determine which keys were subsequently pressed.

COMPENSATION AND REWARDS EARNINGS: **B** PERKS: **B**

Hollywood safecrackers are forever pursuing one "really big score," but champion earners in the real-world learn that persistence and volume are the most reliable keys to success. Connecticut's dozen-man Haverill Crew, for example, pulled off more than six hundred jobs over a ten-year period. They are estimated to have earned more than $1.5 million during 1993 to 1996 alone. David Thomas Hughes, a former locksmith who learned to defeat alarms and safes while in prison, earned more than $2 million cracking at least two dozen safes in Texas after his release.

ENFORCEMENT AND PENALTIES ARRESTS: **B** SENTENCING: **D**

Safecracking is prosecuted as a separate and distinct crime from burglary or felonious larceny. Repeat offenders in this occupation should expect unusually stern sentences, though a 1978 ruling did establish that one safecracker's fifty-year sentence constituted cruel and unusual punishment.

In many cases, the mere possession of safecracking tools is an offense. Most state laws hold that entering premises with intent to crack is the same as actually violating a loaded vault. On a more positive note, apprehension rates of safecrackers have historically averaged less than 20 percent.

STRESSES AND HAZARDS DANGERS: **C** PRESSURES: **C-**

This is a technically and physically demanding line of work, and professionals must maintain constant vigilance to keep the "safe" in "safecracking." Beyond the obvious dangers of high-speed work with explosives, power tools, torches, and battering instruments, safecrackers often contend with noxious vapors and dangerously high noise levels. The severe time pressures of this position can also be taxing in the long term, and frequent armed interactions with police, private security, business owners, and other stakeholders pose much more intense, immediate risks.

UNSAFE AT ANY SPEED
A cautionary tale

Some wildcard hazards can't be predicted. After cutting a hole in the roof of an Illinois office building, two crackers battled a small safe for forty-five minutes with a sledgehammer and blowtorch. When they failed to crack it, they shoved the three-hundred-pound box out the window.

They loaded the safe onto the back of their truck and drove it straight into the path of an oncoming train. Miraculously, the pair managed to drive away, but a witness had already jotted down their license plate number.

WORK ENVIRONMENT

HOURS: B-   COMFORT: C-

This is a year-round occupation offering extensive opportunities in most moderately to densely populated areas. Daytime attacks on commercial establishments are unusual, but safecrackers who prefer a more traditional workweek may find satisfaction by specializing in residential assignments (where 60 percent of attacks occur in daylight). Nearly 90 percent of known safecrackers are male, but some exceptional women have gone on to distinction in this field. Before finding Jesus, Mary Kay Mahaffey earned a coveted spot on the FBI's Most Wanted List for her outstanding career achievements in safecracking and bank robbery.

SCALPER

RANK: 24 out of 50   **AVERAGE GRADE:** B-

DUTIES: Scalpers resell tickets to concerts, sporting events, theatrical performances, museum exhibits, and other high-demand public proceedings in contravention to state, municipal, venue, league, or team regulations. *Street scalpers* vend genuine, counterfeit, and stolen tickets mano a mano, in close proximity to venues or major pedestrian hubs. On event days, they generally service *both* sides of the market: snapping up surplus inventory from overstocked fans and exacting last-minute premiums from deep-pocketed procrastinators and impulsive passersby. Scalpers must be conspicuous enough to catch the eyes of prospective transaction partners while evading the unwanted attentions of guards, undercover agents, staffers, concessionaires, security cameras, and uniformed police.

Scalpers provide eleventh-hour liquidity while assuming "big-ticket," unhedged risks. They balance pricing levels and on-hand inventory against rapidly evolving developments in supply and demand. Once the first spitball is spat or the fat lady sings, spot prices head swiftly south. *Ticket brokers* operate off-site and generally deal in larger volumes than their street dealing brethren. Some maintain storefront pick-up spots. Others deal primarily via phone, the Internet, or mail order. Some brokers operate completely within the canons of law and decorum; however, a great many obtain tickets illicitly and mark them up at premiums to legislated maximums. The latter frequently collude with street scalpers to move excess merchandise and service the man on the street.

Both brokers and street agents employ *diggers* or *droids*—paid surrogates who brave long, rowdy lines to retrieve

SAY THE SECRET WORD
A typical Web site CAPTCHA, a security device used to defeat automated online ticket "Droids."

tickets or event bracelets. The largest operations field up to two hundred diggers, who are hired and herded by *crew bosses.* Stipends for diggers can climb as high as $60 per wait, but eager homeless applicants can often be retained for far less. Diggers also work phone "lines," furiously dialing for just-announced show dates. Sophisticated brokers leverage multiline computerized dialers to circumvent limits on phone-based purchases. Some also deploy state-of-the-art *bots* to harvest hundreds of Web-vended tickets in minutes. One $20,000 hacking program's sole function is to defeat Ticketmaster. com's CAPTCHA system (Completely Automated Public Turing test to tell Computers and Humans Apart), which requires users to prove their humanity by typing in a password embedded in a distorted picture.

Brokers typically credit the extraordinary quality and quantity of their offerings to brute-force *digging.* Most, however, rely heavily on bribes to ticket-distribution insiders—a practice historically known as *ice.* Ice-capade cohorts include box office employees, venue managers, employees of Ticketmaster or Telecharge, concert promoters, and security staff.

Scalpers refer to their relations with

BIG TICKETS FOR 2005
The year's biggest paydays for scalpers

Event	Price	Notes
Rolling Stones	$7,410	One pair, front row
U2	$4,250	One pair
Madonna	$14,000	Second row
NCAA Final 4	$3,000–$7,000	

Source: Ticketsnow.com

venue and distribution insiders as *hooks.* Payouts to New York hooks for prime Broadway tickets average 50 percent to 100 percent of face value. It is often claimed that ice paid on *The Phantom of the Opera,* over its ten-year run, exceeded the net profits paid to investors. On Broadway, ice is often a family affair. In one unlikely case that attracted the attention of New York's attorney general, five brothers worked at five Broadway box offices.

Although most insider trading involves the illegal redistribution of reserved house seats, subscription seats, and other segregated ticket blocks, scalpers are also forging lucrative relationships with retail ticket outlets. A New York investigation found that 70 percent of the tickets issued at certain Ticketmaster outlets were diverted into the resale market. One Long Island, New York, outlet officially recorded forty transactions during a period when only seventeen people actually entered the store.

Educated estimates of the secondary ticket market range from $10 billion to $25 billion a year. Scalpers and brokers are thought to control 10 percent to 15 percent of available Super Bowl seats and 30 percent of tickets to major rock shows. The gray and black markets are fragmented and regionalized, with no single entity controlling even 1 percent of trading volume. Even so, the most aggressive brokers boast seven- and eight-figure incomes. A well-known New York securities firm paid one New Jersey broker more than $360,000 in a single year.

Compensation for ice vendors varies with the volume and nature of the items offered. John Tironi, the former ticket manager for the Cleveland Browns, received a stipend of $5,000 per month for diverting seat licenses and tickets to Mark Klang, owner-operator of Amazing Tickets. While insider Tironi banked nearly than $60,000 between 2002 and 2003, his scalper accomplice netted $134,000. Generally, top-tier tickets trade at three to twenty times their face value, but erratic event economics can trigger windfalls or wipeouts.

PURCHASE TICKETS HERE

STATES WHERE A SCALPER *COULD* GET SCALPED

State	Maximum penalty
Connecticut	Felony
Louisiana	Imprisonment: 30 to 90 days
Massachusetts	Imprisonment: Up to 1 year
New Mexico	Imprisonment: Up to 1 year
New York	Felony
Pennsylvania	Imprisonment: Up to 2 years
Wisconsin	Imprisonment: 60 days

Source: National Conference of State Legislators

Twenty-two states have statutes on the books that outlaw or regulate scalping, but enforcement is patchy, and penalties are fairly mild. In recent years, however, New York, Connecticut, and Massachusetts have taken increasingly hard lines with scalping scofflaws. In 2001, New York's then attorney general, Eliot Spitzer, convinced state legislators to elevate participation in ice schemes from a misdemeanor to a felony. In 2005 Mike Tice, coach of the Minnesota Vikings, was fined $100,000 for selling some of his twelve Super Bowl tickets to a broker. Tice, the lowest-paid coach in the NFL, was saddled with the largest fine the league had ever levied. He got off lightly compared with the Browns's Tironi, who faces five years if convicted of the single conspiracy count against him.

STRESSES AND HAZARDS

DANGERS: C   PRESSURES: B-

This is a fast-paced, cash-intensive business, where greedy greenhorns can get *themselves* scalped. The economic hazards of the trade were underscored in 1997 with the suicide of Allen F. Caldwell III, a high-society golf promoter and ticket broker in Augusta, Georgia. Caldwell had invested $380,000 to market luxury golf tours centered on Augusta's Masters Tournament. When market rates for tournament badges soared to $7,000, Caldwell was unable to deliver the centerpiece of his offering, lost his shirt, and took his life. Fan animosity is also a serious concern, particularly at some of America's more beer-soaked ballparks. The typical cat-and-mouse between scalpers and stadium operators took a "big-brotherly" turn at baseball's 2005 Major League All-Star Game. U.S. Immigration and Customs agents used 120 eye-in-the-sky security cameras to stake out Detroit's Comerica Park and electronically bust scalpers and bootleg vendors.

WORK ENVIRONMENT

HOURS: C+   COMFORT: C

Grassroots scalpers confront punishing weather extremes, surly street denizens, and a wide variety of unfriendly authority figures. Diggers suffer similar indignities for sharply limited potential upsides. Although work windows are typically quite brief, the rigid deadlines and constant quotas endemic to this field can be depleting. Seasonal downturns are the rule, so poor planners may be compelled to travel to warmer climes, or to moonlight.

Corrupt ticket brokers enjoy somewhat cushier indoor conditions. Many work from *boiler rooms* packed with phone-covered tables and collegial coconspirators. Cyber-scalpers reap the fruits of the Internet revolution while working from the safety and comfort of home. Ticket volume on eBay is growing by almost 200 percent a year, and online ticket aggregators now empower independent brokers to post their own inventories for a 10 percent to 15 percent commission.

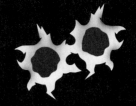

SHOPLIFTER

RANK: 16 out of 50 **AVERAGE GRADE:** B-

DUTIES: Shoplifters intentionally remove goods from retail establishments without tendering full payment. Although shoplifting has long been regarded as the province of juvenile amateurs and drug-addicted opportunists, adults compose at least 68 percent of today's rapidly professionalizing shoplifting workforce. Rings of seasoned *boosters* or *sweepers* account for just 20 percent of all current U.S. shoplifters but nearly 80 percent of goods lifted.

Sophisticated shoplifters target retailers with frequently replenished supplies of household commodities and trendy consumer goods. These can be inconspicuously resold through traditional fencing operations, flea markets, and complicit storefront and wholesale operations. High-demand targets for 2005 included over-the-counter medications, razor blades, film, batteries, videos, DVDs, smoking cessation products, and infant formula.

Organized boosters visit as many as twenty shops in a single day of spree "shopping" and often return to a victimized establishment in as little as an hour after an initial visit. Successful shoplifters select target stores for ease of access and escape,

FLYING OFF THE SHELVES
Shoplifters now account for one third of America's $47 billion in annual retail shrinkage.
Source: Center for Studies in Criminology and Law

Total U.S. Retail Shrinkage

- Employee theft 47%
- Shoplifting 32%
- Inventory mistake 15%
- Vendor fraud 6%

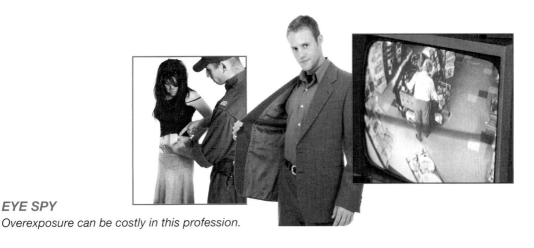

EYE SPY
Overexposure can be costly in this profession.

defeatability of security measures, and proximity to repackaging, distribution, and resale facilities. Professional boosters travel in vans or large passenger vehicles provided by sponsoring fences or wholesale distributors. Reimbursement for gas, meals, and incidentals is becoming customary.

Though solo *shelf sweeping* is common, gambits involving two or more cooperating lifters are gaining ground. A Utica, New York–based mega-ring would dispatch one employee to fill a cart with clothing items, then stash dozens of CDs or DVDs under the concealing bed of cloth. After abandoning the cart at a predetermined spot near an exit, the first team member would leave the building. Minutes later a second booster would locate the cart and cram the merchandise into a baggy coat lined with tin- or lead foil. Then he would rendezvous with his partner at the getaway vehicle. Metal-shielded garments and containers— dubbed *booster bags*—are extraordinarily effective in preventing stores' electronic

article systems (EAS) from detecting tags affixed to exiting items. As EAS systems evolve to counter existing booster bag designs, shoplifters are turning to high-efficiency tag removal devices.

U.S. retail "shrinkage" totaled more than $47 billion in 2003. Though this figure includes "inside" theft by employees and fraud by vendors, shoplifting accounts for at least 32 percent of all inventory shrinkage and $10 billion to $13 billion a year (roughly equivalent to national losses from auto theft). With shoplifters staging an estimated 330 million to 440 million theft attempts annually, retailers are constantly on watch, so workers in this field must identify and consistently evade electronic surveillance systems (visible or concealed closed-circuit television cameras) and loss prevention personnel.

Boosters identify low–visibility in store locations to transfer items from carts or hangers to booster bags, underwear, or interior clothing pockets. Display units make ideal blind spots, providing security workers with deceptively reassuring views of a booster's upper body while concealing the thief's below-the-waist activities.

The majority of today's high-volume, professional boosters honed their sleight-of-hand skills through earlier training and work as Pickpockets (see page 159). Some experts believe that up to one thousand rings of skilled former pickpockets from Colombia, Chile, Equador, and Peru are currently operating in the United States. The FBI has termed these organized retail theft gangs *South American theft groups*. Loss prevention experts have assembled dossiers on more than 2,500 South American shoplifters arrested at least once within the United States. The vast majority of those identified entered the country illegally; virtually all have multiple identities provided by gang organizers.

Although stealth is the preferred mode of most professionals, some maverick veterans achieve enviable results by sprinting through unobstructed exits with armfuls of lightweight, big-ticket items—a technique known as *dashing*. Security officers are generally barred from engaging in "hot pursuit," owing to the substantial possibility of injury to the officer, onlookers, or the offender. Thus, the possibility of apprehension for brazen dashers is substantially lower than might otherwise be thought.

COMPENSATION AND REWARDS — *EARNINGS:* **B-** *PERKS:* **B+**

WHAT'S HOT IN RETAIL?
The nation's ten most stolen items

Rank	Product name
1	Advil tablet 50 ct
2	Advil tablet 100 ct
3	Aleve caplet 100 ct
4	EPT pregnancy test single
5	Gillette Sensor razor refill 10 ct
6	Kodak 200 film 24 exp
7	Similac w/ iron powder case
8	Similac w/ iron powder can
9	Preparation H 12 ct
10	Primatene tablet 24 ct

Earnings vary considerably with the size and sophistication of the shoplifting organization. Independent part-timers seldom steal more than thirty dollars' worth of merchandise per incident. They often keep lifted items for personal use—or vend them on the street for mere cents on the dollar. Low-level professionals are still generally motivated by the immediate need for drugs and typically steal only enough to cover one day's self abuse. Workers at this level typically receive 20 percent to 30 percent of the retail value of stolen merchandise from street fences or unprincipled retailers. Gross daily harvests for low-level boosters range from $1,000 to $2,000, yielding $200 to $600 in net revenues.

Mid-tier rings employ five to twenty-five shoplifters under the supervision of street fences who control store targeting and item selection. Annual earnings of $100,000 to $200,000 are common at this level.

High-level rings maintain sophisticated repackaging/relabeling centers or function as large-scale illegitimate wholesalers (often masking their illicit operations by purchasing smaller volumes of legitimate merchandise). High-level shoplifting rings can net

ENFORCEMENT AND PENALTIES ARRESTS: C+ SENTENCING: B

In most states, shoplifting is prosecuted as a misdemeanor variant of petty larceny with first offenders generally receiving small fines. In a few jurisdictions, high-value or organized thefts may be prosecuted as felony burglary or felony shoplifting. One unlucky three-time loser, Leandro Andrade, was sentenced to fifty years–to–life under a very rare three-strikes scenario, but penalties in this field are generally quite minimal compared with the potential rewards. A bill recently introduced by Senator Larry Craig (R-Idaho) would make organized retail theft a federal crime, punishable by up to ten years' imprisonment. In one exceptional case, New York's then attorney general, Eliot Spitzer, was able to bring a federal case against an organized retail theft ring by invoking the RICO (Racketeering Influenced Corrupt Organization) statute.

On the more lighthearted side, it is now a crime in Colorado and Arizona to wear aluminized underwear with intent to steal.

In 2003, retail security personnel apprehended 336,956 shoplifters and recovered over $46.4 million in goods and restitution.

STRESSES AND HAZARDS DANGERS: B+ PRESSURES: C

Shoplifters must maintain constant vigilance at the work site, which can promote anxiety or paranoia over time. Employees of mid- and high-level rings enjoy little autonomy in their work routines and are subject to physical intimidation or violence if they skim merchandise or cooperate with law enforcement. Although detention and arrests are relatively infrequent among top boosters, violence and injuries are quite common in the course of attempted escapes by lower-level practitioners. In one recent case, a suspect who fled down the street with a stolen television died after being pinned by two Wal-Mart guards. On the upside, a significant number of guilty shoplifters have recently received large civil settlements for abuses or injuries sustained during in-store detainment. Other accused shoplifters who were subsequently acquitted have secured huge judgments for false arrest.

WORK ENVIRONMENT

HOURS: **C+**   COMFORT: **B-**

Although shoplifters spend much of their workdays in well-maintained, temperature-controlled retail environments, frequent entries and exits from crowded vehicles provide little comfort and potential exposure to inclement weather.

Shoplifters enjoy steady employment, as demand for shoplifted goods is fairly constant throughout the year. March and December are peak months, but activity in those months is only 3 percent higher than in the slowest month. Similarly, 17.7 percent of shoplifting apprehensions are made on Saturday, the busiest day of the week, but the least frequent day (Sunday) is only 5 percent lower. The majority of shoplifters are male, but the workplace is fairly balanced, with 45 percent females on the job.

SLAVE TRADER

RANK: 33 out of 50   **AVERAGE GRADE:** C+

DUTIES: Slave Traders recruit and transport persons for the purposes of involuntary servitude or sexual slavery. They use fraud, force, or coercion to induce vulnerable, gullible, or desperate individuals to participate in commercial sex work or submit to long-term forced labor. Each year, 600,000 to 800,000 human beings are *trafficked* across international borders for illicit exploitation. The United States imports a respectable 50,000 to 100,000 enslaved women and children per annum—primarily from Latin America, Southeast Asia, and countries of the former Soviet Union.

American slave traders, popularly known as *human traffickers* or *sex traffickers,* lure impoverished young females to our gilded shores with false promises of gainful employment, educational opportunity, citizenship, or matrimony. In 1996, for instance, a Maryland-based trafficking group advertised for Russian waitresses and au pairs in a Saint Petersburg newspaper. When the eager-but-penniless recruits arrived—from a homeland where 25 percent of the population is destitute—they were pressed into prostitution at a Bethesda massage parlor.

Some traffickers obtain tourist, training, or educational visas for target persons, then coerce them to outstay their legal welcomes. One group imported twenty-five Russian women, representing them to immigration authorities as exchange students at the University of Illinois. Instead, the crafty sponsors immediately confiscated

THE SUPPLY CHAIN
Leading exporters of U.S. slaves

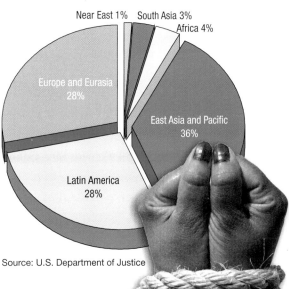

Near East 1%   South Asia 3%
Africa 4%

Europe and Eurasia
28%

East Asia and Pacific
36%

Latin America
28%

Source: U.S. Department of Justice

the women's passports and forced them to dance nude—ten hours a day—to pay down their travel expenses. When one of the women asked to quit, her captors demanded $5,000. After she failed to make payment, they dispatched a Russian co-conspirator to threaten her family with early termination.

Traffickers in the employ of organized Russian crime concerns go to extraordinary lengths to identify exploitable females in search of better lives abroad. They data-mine Internet matchmaking, modeling, and employment sites, advertise incessantly, and even set up "career day" booths at universities and vocational institutes.

When real or fraudulent immigration papers cannot be obtained, slave traders collude with Human Smugglers (page 93) to spirit their live cargo across U.S. borders. Asian smugglers, known as *snakeheads*, charge retail fees of up to $70,000 per person for air- or sea-based passage to North America.

Importers of Asian sex slaves typically negotiate discount rates of $10,000 to $15,000 per smuggled girl. These package fees usually include a $1,000 commission for a local recruitment agent, and an additional $1,000 honorarium for a *jockey* who shepherds the slave past immigration and customs enforcers. On arrival, the girls are advised that they must "service" debts of $30,000 to $60,000 each through a variety of sexual chores.

Frequently, Asian slave girls are recruited "to order." Older immigrants—laboring under an ancient belief in the restorative powers of underage intercourse—pay huge premiums for newly arrived neophytes. Alternatively, underfunded cargo persons may directly indenture themselves to a transporting snakehead, without the involvement of a third-party slave importer. Satisfaction of such debts is ensured through traditional kinship networks; threats of deportation; physical and cultural isolation; or overt forcible confinement.

COMPENSATION AND REWARDS   EARNINGS: A-   PERKS: B

According to FBI reports, the global market for trafficked slaves exceeds $9.5 billion a year. The lion's share of the spoils is controlled by diversified transnational crime syndicates, who view the slave trade as a low-risk, synergistic adjunct to their investments in narcotics and arms distribution.

An exemplary operation, funded by Asian organized crime dignitaries, rotated up to one thousand Chinese, Korean, Malaysian, Thai, and Vietnamese women through a sixteen-state network of brothels. The most active of the brothels grossed over $1.4 million in a twenty-eight-month period.

Tight-knit family operations have also posted some impressive gains. Seven members of southeastern Mexico's Cadena-Sosa family socked away over $2.5 million in just two years. The affluent-appearing elder women of the family lured young neighbor girls with promises of respectable jobs as nannies and waitresses. Then they smuggled them into the United States to work at trailer-based family brothels, sited at migrant worker camps in South Carolina and Florida.

ENFORCEMENT AND PENALTIES   *ARRESTS:* **C+**   *SENTENCING:* **D+**

The United States has frowned upon involuntary servitude since 1865, when we enacted the 13th Amendment. The Victims of Trafficking and Violence Prevention Act (2000) raised the maximum penalty for use of forced labor to twenty years in prison, criminalized psychological coercion, and strengthened the national enforcement framework. Between 2001 and 2004, the Department of Justice prosecuted 121 slave trade professionals, a nearly threefold increase over the preceding three years.

The courts have taken a stern tact on sentencing, as well. A Nigerian husband and wife convicted of holding a young girl as a domestic servant in their New York City apartment were sentenced to eleven and twelve years' incarceration, respectively, and ordered to pay over $250,000 in restitution. A Berkeley, California, landlord who sexually abused undocumented Indian girls, while exploiting them for cheap labor, was rebuked with a dispiriting $2 million in restitution payments.

STRESSES AND HAZARDS   *DANGERS:* **C**   *PRESSURES:* **C**

Maintaining a 24/7 vigil over restless captives can be taxing and anxiety-provoking. In 2000, a group of six men lured forty desperate Mexican migrant workers from Arizona to Buffalo, New York, with promises of highly paid farm work. The underdocumented aliens were ferried in seatless, unventilated vans, then advised that they each owed $1,000 for their deluxe transportation. The contractors posted armed guards and made grave threats to ensure repayment of these "debts." Yet, ten of the ungrateful workers escaped and eventually filed felony charges.

AMERICAN SLAVE QUARTERS
A work site tour

UNITED STATES V. BRADLEY & O'DELL

TYPE: Toolshed

LOCATION: New Hampshire

FUNCTION: Forced labor

LABOR TYPE: Tree cutting

CONTROL METHODOLOGIES: Passport confiscation, false promises, confinement

SLAVES: Up to sixteen

NATIONALITY: Jamaican

UNITED STATES V. KIL SOO LEE

TYPE: Factory

LOCATION: American Samoa

FUNCTION: Forced labor

LABOR TYPE: Garment

CONTROL METHODOLOGIES: Passport confiscation, deportation, threats, armed confinement, beatings, and bludgeonings

SLAVES: 250-plus

NATIONALITY: Vietnamese and Chinese

UNITED STATES V. SOTO

TYPE: Trailer camp

LOCATION: Texas

FUNCTION: Sex slavery and forced labor

LABOR TYPE: Domestic

SLAVES: One hundred–plus smuggled humans per month and four full-time sex slaves

NATIONALITY: Central American

Sources: U.S. Department of Justice, FBI

Working conditions for slavery professionals vary considerably. Enforcers and facilities managers for Asian brothels, who constitute a substantial percentage of the full-time workforce, must contend with rampant overcrowding, substandard amenities, and little or no natural light. A routine 1994 housing inspection of a brothel in New York's Chinatown revealed fifty Thai women living behind barred windows at the behest of armed enforcers.

Asian brothels are typically littered with takeout containers. Enforcers, who are responsible for doing food runs, may employ chains to restrain their captives during their absences, if threats against a captive girl's family have proved ineffective against attempted escape.

Some enslavers work from the relative comfort and informality of home. In 2004, a middle-aged Long Island couple and their twenty-something daughter were found to be holding sixty-nine Peruvians as de facto economic hostages at their small suburban homes. The family charged each immigrant an initial smuggling fee of $6,000 to $7,500. Then they ratcheted up the supposed debts with hefty surcharges for accommodation in their unheated garages and toolsheds. They forged credentials for their permanent houseguests, got them jobs at nearby factories, and pocketed their collective pay.

SNITCH

RANK: 20 out of 50 **AVERAGE GRADE:** B-

DUTIES: Snitches aid in the surveillance, apprehension, and prosecution of criminal wrongdoers. They provide insider intelligence, collect evidence, abet peace officers and moles, and tender actionable tips and testimony. Snitches—more politely known as *confidential informants* or *cooperating witnesses*—tell incriminating tales in exchange for leniency, exemption from enforcement attention, or personal gain. Jailhouse snitches cultivate the confidences of fellow detainees, extract confessions, elicit compromising admissions, and tender damning testimony. In the absence of *actual* incriminating utterances, slammer-based snitches often fabricate false statements for attribution to incarcerated intimates. Clarence Zacke slew the brother of a Florida assistant state's attorney, then ordered a hit on the star witness in his trial. He trimmed an unwieldy 180-year sentence to just twenty-three years by recounting imaginary courtyard confessions from suspects in two unsolved cases. One man he framed served twenty-two years before being exonerated by DNA evidence. The other died in prison, though Zacke had confessed to bearing false witness against him at the behest of two Florida state's attorneys.

TEE-D OFF

Pro-criminal activists have popularized "Stop Snitchin'" T-shirts, which have been donned in courtrooms nationwide to intimidate potential witnesses. Clever law-and-order killjoys have countered with their own "Stop Stop Snitchin'" apparel.

Trafficker-informants leverage their professional networks, infrastructure, and expertise to aid drug warriors in consummating deals and building career-boosting cases. Many trafficker-informants volunteer their services at the sunset of their narco-careers, to shore up dwindling revenues or head off imminent indictments. In addition to upfront infiltration fees and de facto investigatory immunity, they receive sizable commissions on assets seized from brother-vendors. When "legitimate" drug deals prove too nettlesome to transact, manufacturing evidence and false testimony against unseasoned innocents can be equally remunerative. Even offenders of the first order sometimes cultivate sidelines in snitchery. Boston's Irish mob kingpin, "Whitey" Bulger, forged an early-life alliance with rising FBI star John Connolly.

Bulger helped the bureau bust out Boston's entrenched Italian Mafia, and they tipped him on upcoming stings and shielded him from prosecution. The notorious killer and his federal handlers traded jokes and Christmas gifts for nearly twenty years.

Paid informants risk life and limb for leniency and cold cash. Film and television are rife with depictions of small-time *stool pigeons* pointing local police to nearby ne'er-do-wells for a few hundred dollars. Indeed, nationwide there are thousands of full- and part-time registered informants *ratting out* friends and neighbors to local lawmen. The big money, however, is in federal fieldwork. In fiscal 2004, the U.S. Asset Forfeiture Fund seized $455 million in allegedly illicit lucre, passing $12,643,000 to lucky snitches as "awards for information."

 ## COMPENSATION AND REWARDS   *EARNINGS:* **B+** *PERKS:* **B+**

The Drug Enforcement Administration usually caps lifetime payments to private informants at $200,000; however, superstar snitches, such as Andrew Chambers, can earn that much in a single case. Between 1984 and 1995, the DEA paid Chambers at least $1.6 million, ignoring his occasional arrests for assault, forgery, and theft, and convictions for impersonating a federal agent and soliciting a prostitute. Chambers is believed to have *dropped the dime* in over 150 federal drug cases with more than three hundred arrests—partnering with the FBI, the U.S. Customs Service, postal inspectors, the IRS, and the Secret Service. He normally worked on a percentage basis, collecting up to 25 percent of the value of drugs and cash seized from sting operations. His career earnings are thought to exceed

$4 million, though he reportedly has not filed a tax return for the last six years.

Advanced practitioners recruit surrogates and subcontractors to broaden their potential service offerings. Guillermo Francisco Jordan-Pollito, a former Mexican police officer, earned more than $400,000 ratting out Southern California coke and meth dealers over the last decade. To facilitate a high volume of "deal-flow," Jordan-Pollito employed a shadowy network of undisclosed subinformants, who were paid only on completion of successful *buys*. They, in turn, used high-pressure telemarketing techniques to enlist former school friends and other largely law-abiding acquaintances to broker introductions to low-level local dealers.

One retired U.S. customs officer, with a long-established network of in-the-know snitches, has inked a deal with a south Florida antidrug task force for a 25 percent commission on all assets he helps seize. He netted $625,000 in the first year of the task force's operation and then negotiated side contracts with his subinformants for an additional 15 percent of *their* earnings.

ENFORCEMENT AND PENALTIES   *ARRESTS:* **B+**   *SENTENCING:* **B+**

Since the 1980s, snitches have successfully evaded prosecution, secured leniency, and negotiated preferential treatment in thousands of major felonies. The House Government Reform Committee recently complained that the use of notorious criminals as informants constitutes "one of the greatest failures in the history of federal law enforcement." When the jealously guarded cop-snitch relationship does sour, however, retribution may quickly follow. When "Whitey" Bulger's longtime sponsor finally retired from the FBI, the agency sullied nearly two decades of cordiality with indictments for racketeering and extortion.

THOSE FICKLE FEDS . . .
James "Whitey" Bulger snitched for the FBI for nearly twenty years. The bureau disowned him in 1995, over a trifling eighteen counts of murder.
Source: FBI

Snitches are universally reviled in criminal cultures, and face all manner of direct and delayed retribution for their self-interested acts. Although judges customarily allow confidential informants to remain anonymous, tendering written or recorded testimony, successful motions for disclosure of confidential sources are becoming much more common. The Internet poses a more serious threat to the anonymity that informants require for serenity and survival. Whosarat.com ("who's a rat") boasts of maintaining the "largest online database of informants and agents." Leon Carmichael, an Alabama federal drug-trafficking and money-laundering defendant, put up a site resembling a "wanted" poster, to solicit information on anonymous informers in his case. Though prosecutors argued the site amounted to a threat against witnesses, a judge approved Carmichael's information-gathering gambit, noting, "The use of a Web site would be particularly useful for a defendant with few resources."

Some career snitches experience feelings of isolation, betrayal, and devaluation. Joe Clarke spent seventeen years as one of the top informants in the war on drugs, before he was put out to pasture by the FBI after a botched infiltration of the Mongols motorcycle club (see Outlaw Biker). "I've sacrificed a great part of my life, and become a nonperson, to accomplish my mission," he told a reporter in 2005. "People who know nothing about what I do are automatically repulsed by anybody in my field. I became an informant to balance my karma up."

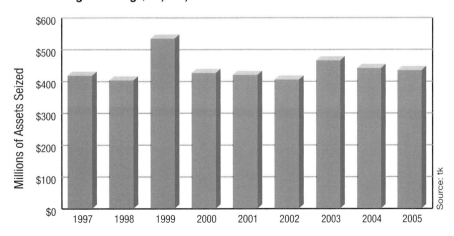

SEIZE THE DAY
The U.S. Asset Forfeiture Fund has swelled to $148 million, generating $12,643,000 in commissions fro snitches

The indoor and outdoor workplaces infiltrated by informants vary greatly in creature comforts, accoutrements, and levels of bodily risk. Although wearing a *wire* (a hidden recording or broadcasting device) can be physically and emotionally awkward, advances in miniaturization are improving this perennial annoyance.

Most successful snitches immerse themselves in the darker pools of criminal subculture, yet this diverse field offers special opportunities for mainstream newcomers. The IRS, for instance, pays up to 15 percent of monies recovered for tips on tax scofflaws. Interest penalties, however, are not included and awards are capped at $2 million. The Department of Homeland Security's Operation TIPS aimed to recruit *millions* of working Americans as amateur informants—though former secretary Tom Ridge avowed "the last thing we want is Americans spying on Americans."

Occasionally a snitch's assignment can be outright pleasant. Over three years, Nashville police paid confidential informants almost $120,000 to engage in sex with prostitutes as part of an undercover crackdown on massage parlors, adult bookstores, and escort services. "It may be distasteful to some people," explained police Captain Todd Henry, "but it's better that we have those places shut down."

SPAMMER

RANK: 13 out of 50   **AVERAGE GRADE:** B

DUTIES: Spammers transmit unsolicited bulk e-mail messages in contravention to U.S.S.877 (the "CAN-SPAM Act") or other widely recognized codes of Internet conduct (*netiquette*). The boundaries between illegal and merely unethical practice are rapidly evolving in this exciting field. Under 2004's CAN-SPAM, a bulk e-mail message is regarded as spam only if it contains false or misleading transmission information, includes a deceptive subject line, fails to offer an Internet-based method to prevent future mailings, and/or fails to identify itself as an advertisement. Nongovernmental antispam groups, in contrast, regard *any* unsolicited bulk e-mail as impermissible spam. Some of these independent groups have mushroomed to astounding size. The spam blocklist maintained by www.spamhaus.org helps more than 260 million global Internet

A SPAM GLOSSARY

HAM—Legitimate e-mail, that which recipients do not consider spam.

HONEYPOT—A system on the Internet set up to attract and trap spammers and hackers. Usually this is a mail server set up to appear to be unsecured.

JOE JOB—A spam campaign forged to appear as though it came from an innocent party, with the intention of incriminating or pinning blame onto that party.

RATWARE—Software used to automate spam campaigns and generate, send, and track spam messages.

SPOOFING—Spammers forge an e-mail address to hide the true origin of their messages. Scammers spoof address lines to fool people into thinking an e-mail has arrived from a legitimate source.

users maintain mailbox sanity.

Estimates of the prevalence of U.S. spam range from 38 percent to an astounding 83 percent of the 31 billion e-mails sent each day (2005). Most experts agree on a figure of at least 60 percent. In 2001, spam represented a mere 7 percent of all messages sent. Spammers must maintain phenomenal delivery volumes to ensure profits. Response rates have fallen steadily since 2000 and now average only .25 percent.

An elite group of roughly two hundred spammers is responsible for nearly 80 percent of all English-language spam. South Florida is a veritable e-garbage enterprise zone, housing nearly a quarter of the world's most insidious senders. Boca Raton, with eleven of Spamhaus's top two hundred, is at the epicenter of the hurricane. Boca's favorite son, Alan Ralsky, has been frequently lauded as the number-one spammer in the world. He maintains 190 e-mail servers in the United States, Canada, China, Russia, and India, capable of sending out more than one billion messages a day.

Many superstar spammers avoid ostracism from domestic connectivity vendors by partnering with less picky overseas providers. Others steal the requisite bandwidth and processing power. Building on the achievements of pioneering hackers, spammers use viruses, worms, and port scanning attacks to trans-form millions of servers and home PCs into *zombies* or *spambots*. Comcast's six-million-user network has proved an exceptionally fertile hatching ground for zombies. Of the nearly 800 million e-mails sent across Comcast's network each day, over 700 million are thought to arise from zombie PCs.

Another recent tactical innovation, *war spamming*, combines spamming with the increasingly popular pastime of locating and hacking into unencrypted wireless networks. War spammers drive around densely populated areas brandishing laptop-based attack systems. They identify and compromise small clusters of unprotected computers, broadcast high-intensity bursts of spam, then drive on.

Spammers employ a rich array of gambits to collect and validate active e-mail addresses. Many use automated *harvesting* or *scraping*

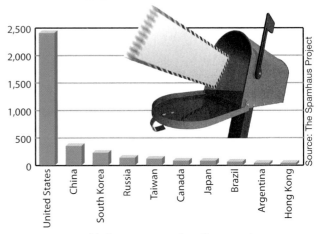

AMERICA LEADS THE SPAM-PRODUCING WORLD
The U.S. clogs more inboxes than the other nine leading spammer nations combined

Source: The Spamhaus Project

Nations generating the most major spamissues for 2005

programs to automatically *crawl* through millions of Web pages and newsgroup postings in search of words containing the telltale "@" symbol. Others engage hackers to steal lists from established sites or direct marketers, or purchase such stolen lists on the black market. Spammers with access to substantial networks of zombie PCs may prefer to mount brute force *dictionary attacks*, indiscriminately mailing millions of e-mails to addresses representing almost every possible short combination of letters and numbers.

COMPENSATION AND REWARDS   EARNINGS: B+   PERKS: C

Despite the enactment of CAN-SPAM, this New Economy superoccupation is still in its early gold-rush period; in fact, spam has actually accelerated since the passage of that legislation! Many merchants use spam as a modest supplement to traditional streams of revenue; however, a whole new breed of electronic entrepreneurs has achieved remarkable wealth at record speed. Take Jeremy Jaynes, a thirty-two-year-old from North Carolina, who parlayed e-mail lists stolen from AOL and eBay, and a hard drive full of zoophilia pornography and work-at-home advice, into a $24 million fortune. In the nineties, Jaynes earned a modest living fronting postage costs for a series of junk mail schemes. In the new millennium, a monthly investment of $50,000 for sixteen T1 Internet connections brought him earnings of up to $750,000 a month. Alan Ralsky, Spamhaus's longtime archnemesis, currently charges fees of up to $22,000 for a single mailing to his database.

YOU'VE GOT SPAM! 2004
AOL's top ten spam subject lines of 2004

1	"We carry the most popular medications" (Vioxx appeared often)
2	"You've been sent an Insta-Kiss!" (phishing/ID theft scam)
3	"You Have 17 New Pictures" (phishing/ID theft scam)
4	"STEAMY HOT LESBIAN ACTION LIVE ON CAMERA!"
5	"All orders are shipped from authorized locations" (re: online medications)
6	"2005 Digital Cable Filters"
7	"F R E E* 30 Second Pre-Qualification MORTGAGE Application"
8	"HURRY HURRY Hot Stock on the RISE"
9	"Sale PRICES ARE BEST ONLINE!"
10	"Breaking news on the Top Pick stock"

Source: America Online

Public, legislative, and judicial outrage at the practical and psychic costs of spam have resulted in a spate of recent actions against nationally known players. Although civil judgments and criminal convictions are still rare, penalties can be severe. In December 2004, a federal judge ordered three spam groups to pay a total of more than $1 billion to an Iowa Internet service provider whose servers were deluged with up to 10 million unsolicited spam e-mails a day in 2000. CAN-SPAM carries fines of up to $2.5 million and jail terms of up to five years. Spammers are also eligible for a potpourri of racketeering, fraud, and deceptive-practices charges. In a bid to legitimize the bulk e-mailing of its members, the Direct Marketing Association has funded "Operation Slam Spam," a cross-disciplinary task force developing cases against the nation's most active spammers. Jeremy Jaynes, once a poster boy for nonchalant defiance, was sentenced to nine years in prison in November 2004.

WORLD'S TOP 10 SPAMMERS (2005)

Rank	Name	Country
1	Alan Ralsky	United States
2	Michael Lindsay/iMedia Networks	United States
3	Leo Kuvayev/BadCow	Russia
4	Jeffrey Peters/JTel/CPU Solutions	United States
5	Andrew Westmoreland	United States
6	Alexey Panov/ckync.com	Russia
7	Ivo Ottavio Reali Camargo	Brazil
8	Ruslan Ibragimov/send-safe.com	Russia
9	Robert Soloway/Newport Internet Marketing	United States
10	Levon Gillespie/spamforum.biz	United States

Source: The Spamhaus Project

STRESSES AND HAZARDS

Much of the developed world is united in a commitment to stamp out unsolicited e-mails and deprive spammers of their sustenance. Such universal scorn can be very hurtful and isolating. Spammers must maintain a positive mindset while overcoming constantly evolving technical, logistical, and legal challenges. Superspammers such as Alan Ralsky are lightning rods for public hostility. "There were threats against him, cars driving by and people checking out his house," reports Ralsky's attorney. "Someone even left a package of what appeared to be dog feces."

While spammers live under the constant threat of being effectively blocked, they may take solace in knowing that one of the world's largest ISPs suffers from the same concerns. In 2004, Mail Abuse Prevention Systems placed a large percentage of AOL's mail servers on its Real-time Blackhole List, which is used by many of the top ISPs on the planet . . . including AOL itself!

WORK ENVIRONMENT

Though interactions with vendors and offshore affiliates afford occasional opportunities for foreign travel, spamming tends to be a solitary home-based activity.

Pioneers in this field made their mark by working eighteen-hour days in improvised basement "war rooms." Indeed, this occupation seems to favor work- and greed-obsessed individuals who require little separation between home life and job responsibilities. Spammers compete for wallet- and mindshare on a 24/7/365 basis. The richest among them can usually be found tending floor-to-ceiling racks of home-based PCs, tirelessly crafting new messages and optimizing returns.

TELEMARKETING SCAMMER

RANK: 5 out of 50 **AVERAGE GRADE:** B

DUTIES: Telemarketing Scammers defraud individuals and organizations through an ever-evolving variety of phone-based gambits. Fraudulent telemarketers craft, improvise, and deliver false and misleading statements, offers, and promises. They identify, contact, and cajole prospective customers to prompt them to tender funds via wire transfers (30 percent of funds transferred), bank debits (26 percent), checks (14 percent), credit cards (10 percent), or money orders (9 percent).

Many telephone schemes center on the sale of fictitious goods and services, or delivery of items of substantially inflated value. Scammers employ cheapo *gimme gifts* to legitimize prize and charity schemes or they deliver run-of-the-mill products at exorbitantly high markups. In all cases, the central objective is to secure payment before consumers can assess the actual value of the consideration they receive. Often such advance payments are initiated without a customer's full knowledge or consent.

PITCHES THAT PAY
Four classic scams account for more than half of all phone fraud

Prizes and sweepstakes	Advance processing fees are demanded to redeem large fictitious prizes or virtually worthless gimme gifts. Alternatively, a caller poses as a federal official and informs the "lucky winners" that taxes or customs fees must be paid before the caller can release their valuable prizes.	Market share: 31%	Average gain: $3,135
Credit card offers	Cards are promised to the questionably credit-worthy for large upfront fees, or worthless fraud protection insurance is peddled to overly cautious holders of existing cards. No cards are tendered and no service is rendered.	Market share: 15%	Average gain: $256
Scholarships and grants	Fees are charged for bogus assistance in securing real or imaginary scholarships or grants.	Market share: 7%	Average gain: $504

Statistical Source: National Fraud Information Center

Phone fraudsters thrive by cultivating and monetizing consumer trust. Often they imply or claim association with prestigious commercial or governmental entities. Since 2004, callers posing as representatives of the Better Business Bureau have been contacting companies across the country. They've deceived scores of businesses into surrendering exploitable credit information under the pretext of updating their records. Their return contact, 1-800-CALL-BBB, is not affiliated with the bureau and is constantly busy. In West Virginia, scammers posing as Federal Emergency Management Agency staffers contacted flood victims with promises of relief funds. To receive their benefits, the grateful West Virginians were told, they need only provide detailed information on their bank accounts.

U.S. seniors compose a key demographic for perpetrators of telephonic fraud. Though our elders account for just one-third of the U.S. population, half of all scam victims are over fifty. Seniors' numbers are purchased from *lead brokers* (at $10 to $100 per lead) or traded among brother telemarketers. Some elder victims are contacted *many* times with new false promises—a practice known as *reloading*. To bolster credibility, far-thinking firms employ *touts* or *singers*—paid references who sing their cohorts' praises.

Recovery-room scams are value-added extensions of existing victimizations. Many victims of phone fraud are desperate

PROFESSIONALLY SPEAKING

Tape transcripts from Department of Justice phone fraud prosecutions.

"I just lawnmower over these people. I know exactly what buttons to hit and if I hit 'em right, they're not gonna say [expletive] except, you know, [yes] the whole time."

"We targeted to people who were homebound. It was kind of like entertainment for the homebound. Um, there's no dispute about that."

Source: U.S. Department of Justice

to recoup their losses but are initially too chagrined to reveal their gullibility to law enforcers. A recovery-room scammer contacts the victim, claiming affiliation with an official entity poised to offer immediate, shame-free assistance. Most frequently, phone-fibbers impersonate FBI, IRS, FTC, or Immigration and Customs Enforcement agents. Some more nebulously state that they "are working with the court." The impostor informs the mark that he or she is involved in a legal action against the phone fraud perpetrator. For a small "court fee" the caller can return the bulk of the departed funds. The impostor authenticates him/herself by disclosing details of the past fraud that only an official—or an offender—would know.

Congress estimates that Americans share $40 billion a year with fraudulent phonesters—or more than $4 million per hour. One out of six consumers has contributed to this vibrant sector of the underground economy. The largest ruse on record involved almost 800,000 marks. The average successful phony pitch yields $1,987.

RINGING SUCCESSES
A few outstanding recent achievements in communications fraud

YEAR: 2005

HAUL: $45 million–plus

PITCH: Advance fee loans, credit card offers

SCOOP: A twenty-eight-man, Montreal-based cold calling operation vended phony preapproved loans and credit cards to about 100,000 Americans. The group asked for advance fees of $300 to process fictional credit card applications, and $249 to initiate low-interest loans. The equal-opportunity group targeted seniors but employed callers ranging from eighteen to seventy-one years old.

YEAR: 2003

HAUL: $74 million

PITCH: High-yield investment

SCOOP: A Seattle phone brokerage group induced 3,200 American and Canadian marks to make long-term investments in two fictitious funds. Investors were "guaranteed" a too-good-to-be-true return of 120 percent per year. The six-man group was actually operating a classic Ponzi scheme, in which early investors were paid by later participants. The sophisticated scammers laundered the bulk of their bounty through offshore accounts in Samoa, the Bahamas, and Costa Rica. Only $20 million dollars has been recouped from their domestic accounts.

YEAR: 2003

HAUL: $150 million

PITCH: High-yield investment

SCOOP: Four high-level scammers recruited independent insurance agents to vend worthless promissory notes to their existing phone-based clients. Investors—whose average age was sixty-eight—were promised nine-month yields at 21 percent. The money, however, went straight into the pockets of the ring's leaders and commissioned salesmen. To date, less than $90 million has been recovered.

Competition for gullible phone prospects can be intense. The Federal Trade Commission estimates that at least fourteen thousand fraudulent telemarketing organizations currently are competing in the North America market.

ENFORCEMENT AND PENALTIES   *ARRESTS:* **B+**   *SENTENCING:* **C-**

The Department of Justice tenaciously pursues telecom offenders with criminal and civil proceedings. Potential criminal charges include wire fraud, mail fraud, or conspiracy to engage in these acts. Each of these counts carries a maximum penalty of five years off the hook. Lately, prosecutors have also tended to invoke federal money-laundering statutes, carrying penalties of up to twenty years. Key executives in recent multimillion-dollar phone deceptions have suffered real-world sentencing of up to seventeen and a half years in prison. On the plus side, AARP estimates that 73 percent of telemarketing marks never report their losses, and clearance rates for all flavors of fraud remain consistently low.

STRESSES AND HAZARDS   *DANGERS:* **A-**   *PRESSURES:* **B-**

Telemarketing is a labor-intensive activity, and low-response *cold calling* can be especially tedious and demoralizing. Frequent rejection and immutable sales quotas may contribute to an atmosphere of tension, and prolonged use of headsets can precipitate neck discomfort. Entry-level phone reps are often expected to place as many as 250 ingratiating calls a day.

Recently, foreign telemarketers have made troublesome inroads into the American fraud sector. In 2005 they claimed a 28 percent market share. The growing popularity of the national Do Not Call registry is also a serious threat. Stings like the FBI's Operation Senior Sentinel—in which retired law officers and civilian volunteers posed as vulnerable seniors—have also created unwelcome levels of work-time anxiety and distrust.

Legitimate and illicit telemarketers have traditionally worked out of *boiler rooms:* spartan rental spaces jammed with phone-covered tables. Twenty-first-century practitioners are increasingly adopting *rip-and-tear* business models, minimizing their paper trails and emphasizing rapid mobility. They make calls from pay phones or prepaid cell phones, obscure payments via use of commercial mailbox services (rented under aliases), electronic wire transfers, and middlemen. They also exploit jurisdictional intricacies by targeting victims in different states or countries. Following a morning or afternoon sales meeting, phone reps spend their shifts rapidly dialing leads and delivering high-pressure pitches. Advances in call room technology generally spell higher expectations for frontline sales reps. After a less experienced caller makes an initial, qualifying contact, a seasoned *closer* is often brought in for the *kill. Reloaders* are proven supersalesmen, trusted to service and revictimize established marks.

A 2002 survey of interdicted illicit telemarketers revealed that the average phone felon is male, is 42.4 years of age, has worked in the industry for 8.25 years, is married with children, and has little or no previous criminal history. Most respondents praised the casual atmosphere in their workplaces and took pride in their own predatorily persuasive abilities. Many evolved relative value systems, which allowed them to view their work as largely benign.